An Inquiry into the Original, Nature, Institution, Power, Order, and Communion of Evangelical Churches

John Owen

Vintage Puritan Series
GLH Publishing
Louisville, KY

Sourced from *The Works of John Owen,* Vol. XV.
Edited by William Goold. Robert Carter & Brothers, New York, 1851.

Republished by GLH Publishing, 2020.

ISBN:
 Paperback 978-1-64863-010-1
 Epub 978-1-64863-011-8

CONTENTS

Prefatory Note. 1
To the Reader. 4
Preface. 10
I. Of the Original of Churches. 60
II. The Especial Original of the Evangelical Church-State. 69
III. The Continuation of a Church-State and of Churches unto the end of the World — what are the causes of it, and whereon it depends. 89
IV. The Especial Nature of the Gospel Church-State appointed by Christ. 105
V. The State of the First Churches after the Apostles, to the end of the Second Century. 125
VI. Congregational Churches alone suited unto the ends of Christ in the Institution of His Church. 154
VII. No other Church-State of Divine Institution. 167
VIII. The Duty of Believers to join themselves in Church-Order. 175
IX. The Continuation of a Church-State and of the Administration of Evangelical Ordinances of Worship briefly Vindicated. 184
X. What sort of Churches the Disciples of Christ may and ought to join themselves unto as unto entire Communion. 193
XI. Of Conformity and Communion in Parochial Assemblies. 205
XII. Of Schism. 229

An Answer to Dr Stillingfleet's Book of the Unreasonableness of Separation; in defence of the vindication of nonconformists from the guilt of schism. 240
    Section I. 240
    Section II. 262
    Section III. 299

PREFATORY NOTE.

A GENERAL account of the controversy occasioned by Stillingfleet's sermon "On the Mischief of Separation," will be found prefixed to Owen's pamphlet, entitled "A Brief Vindication of the Nonconformists," etc., vol. xiii. of his works. Stillingfleet in reply published a large work, with the title, "The Unreasonableness of Separation; or, an Impartial account of the history, nature, and pleas of the present separation from the communion of the Church of England. To which several late letters are annexed of eminent protestant divines abroad, concerning the nature of our differences, and the way to compose them." The first part of this elaborate work consists of a long preface, in which the author first retorts upon the Nonconformists the charge of encouraging Popery from the schism and divisions they had fomented, from their opposition to episcopal polity, which was a main bulwark against Popery, and from certain curious facts, according to which the Jesuits, it would seem, had insinuated themselves among the early Puritans, in order to excite them against the Church of England. He next mentions that he had been led to preach the sermon which had given rise to the controversy by a perusal of two works of Mr Baxter, in which the Church of England was assailed, and to which he had a right to offer a reply. He alludes, finally, to the five antagonists, Owen, Baxter, Howe, Alsop, and Barret, whom his present work was intended to answer. Of Owen, whom he mentions first, he says, "He treated me with that civility and decent language, that I cannot but return him thanks for it." The work itself is divided into three parts, — an historical account of the rise and progress of separation, the nature of the present separation, and an examination of the pleas for separation. The praise of great tact and ability must be accorded to this production of Stillingfleet. He takes up the weapons of the Presbyterians against the Independents, during the discussions of the Westminster Assembly, and wields them against the Presbyterians themselves in defence of his own church. With both, his main argument is simply, that separation from a church which they admitted to be a true church of Christ was of necessity schism, and that no grounds could justify separation where there was agreement "in regard to doctrine and the substantials of religion." In the appendix to the work there are three letters, expressing concurrence with his views, from foreign divines, — Le Moyne, De l'Angle, and Claude. It is affirmed by Robinson, in his Life of Claude, that these letters were procured by Compton, bishop of London, on an unfair representation of the case at issue between Stillingfleet and his opponents, and published as the judgment of these foreign divines against English Nonconformity; and that, on a true statement of the case, they complained of the duplicity with which they had been treated, and gave forth an opinion adverse to the cause of the bishop and Stillingfleet. It is certain that in the letter by Le Moyne, he argues as if the question related to the possibility of salvation within the pale of the Church of England, accounting it "a very strange thing" that the Nonconformists should have "come to that extreme as to believe that a man cannot be saved in the Church of England." He might well have felt such surprise if there had been the least ground for imputing this uncharitable sentiment to Owen and his compeers in the defence of Nonconformity. Perhaps Stillingfleet himself had most reason to complain of the mistake, by whatever means it was occasioned, for it really deprived his chief argument against them of all its strength and relevancy.

In its first aspect, the following work of Owen, in reply to the Dean of St Paul's, seems irregular and confused. The dean is assailed, however, in a way most effective, and extremely characteristic of our author, who commonly refutes an antagonist not so much by exposing the weakness of his reasoning, as by establishing on solid grounds the positive truth to be embraced. He had been preparing a work on the nature of evangelical churches before "The Unreasonableness of Separation" appeared. He felt that the substance of his views on the main points involved in the controversy was contained in it, and, like another Scipio, he transfers the war to Africa, by putting the Church of England on its defence for innovations in its ecclesiastical polity, which had no sanction in Scripture or apostolic antiquity, the guilt of schism lying with the church that depart-

PREFATORY NOTE.

ed from the apostolic model, not with the church that adhered to it. Opinions, of course, will vary, as to the perfect success of the argument. Few will question the ability with which it is conducted; and his sagacity in selecting this point of attack may be gathered from the fact, that in the view which he presents of the constitution and working of the primitive churches, he has but anticipated the judgment of the learned Neander.

In a preliminary note to the reader, he disposes of the calumny that the Dissenters were abettors of the papal interest in Britain, classing it with stories still more ridiculous, as that they had been receiving large bribes to pursue this unprincipled course. Then follows a preface of some length, in which he meets the argument contained in the first part of Stillingfleet's work, and founded on the history of separation. He appends to the treatise on evangelical churches a long answer to the remaining parts of his opponent's work, in which the Nonconformists are charged with schism, and their pleas in vindication of themselves are met and considered. The main treatise — the Inquiry into Evangelical Churches — is but the first part of a work which was completed by the publication in 1689 of "The True Nature of a Gospel Church." See vol. xvi. of his works. —ED.

TO THE READER.

I THOUGHT to have wholly omitted the consideration of that part of the discourse of Dr Stillingfleet, in his preface, which concerneth *the furtherance and promotion of the designs of the Papists and interest of Popery by Nonconformists*, and accordingly I passed it by in the ensuing discourses; for I supposed that all unprejudiced persons would assign it unto the provocation which he seems to have received from those who answered his sermon, or otherwise, and so have passed it by among such other excursions as divines are incident unto in their controversial writings, for that no countenance was given unto it, either from truth or any useful end as unto the present state of the protestant religion amongst us, is evident unto all. But things are fallen out more according unto the humour of the times, or rather the supposed interest of some, than any just, rational projections. For what other success this book hath had I know not, nor am solicitous. Certain it is that many Of the same mind and persuasion with himself have been encouraged and emboldened by it confidently to report that "the Nonconformists are great promoters of the papal interest," yea, and do the work of the Papists to facilitate its introduction; for it is now made so evident in the preface of that book (I will not say on what topics, which seem not wakeful thoughts in such an important cause, and such a season as this is) that no man need doubt of the truth of it. Some, indeed, think that it were better at this time to consider how to get out Popery from amongst us than to contend about the ways whereby it came in, as unto our present danger of it. But if nothing will prevail against the resolutions of others, influenced by interest and the sweetness of present advantages, to desist from this inquiry, it will be necessary that such an account be given of the true reasons and means of the advance of Popery in this nation as shall give them occasion to consider themselves and their own ways; for we are to look for the causes of such effects in things and means that are suited and fitted to be productive of them, so as that they cannot but follow on their being and operation, and not in old stories, surmises, and far-fetched or feigned inferences. And if we do reckon that the real advancement of religion depends only on the secular advancement of some that do profess it, we may be mistaken in our measures, as others have been before us.

But, at present, the insinuations of that preface do seem to prevail much with those of the same party with its author, who want nothing at any time but the countenance of such a pen and story to vent their ill-will against Nonconformists "Report," say they, "and we will report it." But also as he said, "*Mendacium mendacio tegendum ne perpluat.*" First, evil inventions always tend unto, and stand in need of, new additions, to render them useful unto their end; without which they quickly evaporate. Wherefore, lest the insinuations of this worthy person should not be sufficiently subservient unto the uniting of all Protestants in one common interest against Popery, which was the original design of the Doctor's sermon, some have added unto it that which is homogeneal, as unto truth, and so easily with the other discourse, that "the Nonconformists, some of them at least, do receive, or have received, money from the Papists, to act their affairs and promote their interest." And although this be such a putid calumny, such a malicious falsehood, such a frontless lie, as impudence itself would blush at being made an instrument to vent it, and withal extremely ridiculous, yet because it seems useful unto the good end of uniting Protestants and opposing Popery, it hath not only been reported by sundry of the clergy, but embraced and divulged also by some of their weak and credulous followers, who seem to believe that other men's advantage is their religion. But when the utmost bounds of modesty are passed, nothing but an outrage in lying and calumny, out of hopes that something will stick at last, can give countenance to men in such false accusations. And those by whom they are first whispered probably understand better than the Nonconformists what influence money, or the things which they know how to turn into it, hath into their profession and actings in religion. It seems to me that some such men are afraid lest the present opposition unto Popery should issue in such an establishment of the protestant religion as that hereafter it should not be in the disposal of any, nor in their power to make a bargain of it, either for their advantage or in their necessity. For unless we should suppose such a defect in common prudence as is not chargeable on men of understanding in other affairs, it is hard to judge that these things can proceed from any other ground but a design to increase distrusts and jealousies amongst Protestants, to heighten their differences, to exasperate and provoke them to animosities, to weaken the hands of each party by a disbelief of the sincerity of each other in the same common cause; whence, whether it be designed or no, it will follow that we shall be all made a prey unto our restless adversaries. For what else but a strong inclination thereto can give the least credit or reputation to such vile insinuations, false surmises, and fables (I do not say in the preface, but in the reports that have been occasioned thereby), wherein folly and malice rival one another against that plain, open, uncontrollable evidence, which the Nonconformists always gave, and yet continue to give, of their faithful, cordial adherence unto the protestant religion and interest in the nation? And what now if, in way of retaliation, a charge should be laid and managed against those of the episcopal way, that they should contribute their assistance (whether knowingly or being deluded it is all one) to the introduction of Popery, would not all things be cast into an admirable posture amongst us for an opposition thereunto? But let none mistake nor deceive themselves; neither the past sufferings of the Nonconformists, nor their present hopes of liberty, nor the reproaches cast upon them, shall shake them in their resolutions for a conjunction with all sincere Protestants in the preservation of their religion, and opposition unto all popish designs whatever. And (to speak with modesty enough) as they have hitherto, in all instances of zeal and duty for the preservation of the protestant religion, been as ready and forward as any other sort of men, so whatever may befall them, however they may be traduced or falsely accused, they do and will continue in giving the highest security that conscience, profession, principles, interest, and actions can give, of their stability in the same cause. Only, they desire to be excused if they make not use of this notable engine for opposing of Popery, — namely, the stirring up at this present time of jealousies, fears, and animosities amongst Protestants, — which others judge serviceable unto that end. But that which animates all these insinuations, charges, and reports, is our thankful acceptance of the indulgence granted by his majesty by a public declaration some years ago; whereby it should seem the Papists thought to make some advantage, though they were deceived in their expectation. I must needs say, that whatever be the true case in reference thereto in point of law, in my judgment it scarcely answereth that loyalty and regard unto his majesty's honour which Some men profess, when all his actions are suited to their interests, to continue such outcries about that which was his own sole act, by the advice of his council. We did, indeed, thankfully accept and make use of this royal favour; and after that, for so many years, we had been exposed to all manner of sufferings and penalties, whereby multitudes were ruined in their estates, and some lost their lives, and that without hopes of any remission of severity from the parliament that then sat, by their mistake of the true interest of the kingdom, wherein alone they did not miss it, we were glad to take a little breathing space from our troubles under his majesty's royal protection, designed only as an expedient (as was usual in former times) for the peace and prosperity of the kingdom, until the whole matter might be settled in parliament. And if this were a crime, *"habetis confitentem reum"* as to my part. But because I know myself herein peculiarly reflected on, I do avow that never any one person in authority, dignity, or power in the nation, nor any one that had any relation unto public affairs, nor any from them, Papist or Protestant, did once speak one word to me or advise with me about any indulgence or toleration to be granted unto Papists. I challenge all the world who are otherwise minded to intermit their service for a season unto the great false accuser, and prove the contrary if they can. The persons are sufficiently known of whom they may make their inquiry.

But I can cast this also into the same heap or bundle of other false surmises and reports concerning me, almost without number; which it would be a wonder that some men should pretend to believe and divulge, as they have done, if we were bound to judge that their charity and prudence were proportionable unto their dignities and promotions. These things must be, whilst interest, with hopes and fears, vain love, and hatred thence arising, do steer the minds of men.

But what if we have not designed the prevalence or introduction of Popery, yet, being a company of silly fellows, we have suffered ourselves to be wheedled by the Jesuits to be active for the cutting of our own throats? for we are full well satisfied that we should be the very first who should drink of the cup of their fury, could they ruin the protestant interest in England. And into such an unhappy posture of affairs are we fallen, that whereas it is evident we do nothing for the promotion of Popery, but only pray against it, preach against it, write against it, instruct the people in principles of truth whereon to avoid it, and cordially join with all true Protestants in the opposition of it, wherein we are charged with an excess that is like to spoil all, yet these crafty blades know how to turn it all unto their advantage. As it should seem, therefore, there remains nothing for Nonconformists to do in this matter, but to bind themselves hand and foot and give themselves up unto the power of the Papists; for all they do against them doth but promote their interest. But this, I am persuaded, they will be greatly unwilling unto, unless they are well assured that their episcopal friends will be more ready to expose themselves to hazard for their preservation and deliverance than yet they have reason to expect that they will. But, for my part, I was a long time since taught an expedient by an eminent personage for the freeing myself from any inclination to a compliance with Popery, and that in the instance of himself; for being in Ireland when there was, in former days, a great noise about reconciliation, a person of his own order and degree in the court of England wrote unto him, to inform him of a report that he was inclined to a reconciliation with Popery, or a compliance on good terms with the church of Rome, and withal desired him, that if it were so he would communicate Unto him the reason of his judgment. But that great and wise personage, understanding full well whereunto these things tended, returned no answer but this only, that he knew no reason for any such report; for he was sure that he believed the pope to be antichrist, which put an absolute period unto the intercourse. And I can insist on the same defensative against forty such arguments as are used to prove us compliant with the papal interest; and so I believe can all the Nonconformists. And if this be not enough, I can, for my part, subscribe unto the conclusion which that most eminent champion of the protestant religion in England, namely, Whitaker, gives unto his learned disputation about antichrist: "*Igitur,*" saith he, "*sequamur præeuntem Spiritum Sanctum, et libere dicamus, defenda-*

mus, clamemus, et per eum qui vivit in æternum juremus, pontificem Romanum esse antichristum."

If this will not suffice, we know better how to spend our remaining hours of life in peace than in contending about impertinent stories and surmises, exhaled by wit and invention out of the bog of secular interest; and shall, therefore, only assure those by whom we are charged, in the pulpit, or coffee-houses, or from the press, to countenance the promotion of the papal interest in the nation, that as they deal unjustly with us herein, and weaken the protestant interest what lies in them, so let them and others do and say what they please, nothing shall ever shake us in our resolution, by the help of God, to abide in a firm conjunction with all sincere Protestants for the preservation of our religion, and in opposition to the Papists; yea, that we would do so with our lives at the stake, if there were none left to abide in the same testimony but ourselves. But if they think that there is no way for us to be serviceable against Popery but by debauching our consciences with that conformity which they prescribe unto us, we beg their pardon, we are of another mind.

PREFACE.

An examination of the general principles of Dr Stillingfleet's book of the "Unreasonableness of Separation."

THE differences and contests among professed Christians about the nature, power, order, rule, and residence of the gospel church-state, with the interest of each dissenting party therein, have not only been great and of long continuance, but have also so despised [defied?] all ways and means of allaying or abatement, that they seem to be more and more inflamed every day, and to threaten more pernicious consequents than any they have already produced; which yet have been of the worst of evils that the world for some ages hath groaned under: for the communion so much talked of amongst churches is almost come only unto an agreement and oneness in design for the mutual and forcible extermination of one another; at least, this is the professed principle of them who lay the loudest claim to the name and title, with all the rights and privileges, of the church. Nor are others far remote from the same design, who adjudge all who dissent from themselves into such a condition as wherein they are much inclined to think it meet they should be destroyed. That which animates this contest, which gives it life and fierceness, is a supposed enclosure of certain privileges and advantages, spiritual and temporal, real or pretended, unto the church-state contended about. Hence, most men seem to think that the principal, if not their only concernment in religion, is of what church they are; so as that a dissent from them is so evil as that there is almost nothing else that hath any very considerable evil in it. When this is once well rivetted in their minds by them whose secular advantages lie in the enclosure, they are in a readiness to bear a share in all the evils that unavoidably ensue on such divisions. By this means, among others, is the state or condition of Christian religion, as unto its public profession, become at this day so deplorable as cannot well be expressed.

What with the bloody and desolating wars of princes and potentates, and what with the degeneracy of the community of the people from the rule of the gospel, in love, meekness, self-denial, holiness, zeal, the universal mortification of sin, and fruitfulness in good works, the profession of Christianity is become but a sad representation of the virtues of Him who calls out of darkness into his marvellous light. Neither doth there seem at present to be any design or expectation in the most for the ending of controversies about the church but force and the sword; which God forbid.

It is, therefore, high time that a sober inquiry be made, *whether there be any such church-state of divine institution as those contended about*; for if it should appear upon trial that indeed there is not, but that all the fierce digladiations of the parties at variance, with the doleful effects that attend them, have proceeded on a false supposition, in an adherence whereunto they are confirmed by their interests, some advances may be made towards their abatement. However, if this may not be attained, yet directions may be taken from the discovery of the truth, for the use of them who are willing to be delivered from all concernment in these fruitless, endless contests, and to reduce their whole practice in religion unto the institutions, rules, and commands of our Lord Jesus Christ. And where all hopes of a general reformation seem to fail, it savours somewhat of an unwarrantable severity to forbid them to reform themselves who are willing so to do; provided they admit of no other rule in what they so do but the declaration of the mind of Christ in the gospel, carrying it peaceably towards all men, and firmly adhering unto the faith once delivered unto the saints.

To make an entrance into this inquiry the ensuing discourse is designed. And there can be no way of the management of it but by a diligent, impartial search into the nature, order, power, and rule of the gospel church-state, as instituted, determined, and limited by our Lord Jesus Christ and his apostles. When we depart from this rule, so as not to be regulated by it in all instances of fact or pleas of right that afterward fall out, we fall into the confusion of various presumptions, suited unto the apprehensions and interests of men, imposed on them from the circumstances of the ages wherein they lived. Yet is it not to be denied but that much light into the nature of apostolical institutions may be received from the declared principles and practices of the first churches, for the space of two hundred years or thereabouts. But that, after this, the churches did insensibly depart in various degrees from the state, rule, and order of the apostolical churches, must, I suppose, be acknowledged by all those who groan under the final issue of that gradual degeneracy in the papal antichristian tyranny; for Rome was not built in a day, nor was this change introduced at once or in one age. Nor were the lesser alterations which began this declension so prejudicial unto the being, order, and purity of the churches, as they proved afterward, through a continual additional increase in succeeding ages.

Having affirmed something of this nature in my brief "Vindication of the Nonconformists from the Guilt of Schism," the Rev. Dr Stillingfleet, in his late treatise, entitled "The Unreasonableness of Separation," doth not only deny it, but reflects with some severity upon the mention of it, part 2 sect. 3, pp. 225, 226, etc. I shall, therefore, on this occasion, resume the consideration of it, although it will be spoken unto also afterwards.

The words he opposeth are these:— "It is possible that an impartial account may, ere long, be given of the state and ways of the first churches after the decease of the apostles; wherein it will be made to appear how they did insensibly deviate in many things from the rule of their first institution; so as that though their mistakes were of small moment, and not prejudicial unto their faith and order, yet occasion was administered unto succeeding ages to increase those deviations until they issued in a fatal apostasy." I yet suppose these words inoffensive, and agreeable unto the sentiments of the generality of Protestants; for, —

1. Unto *the first churches* after the apostles I ascribe nothing but such *small mistakes* as did no way prejudice their faith or order; and that they did preserve the latter as well as the former, as unto all the substantial parts of it, shall be afterwards declared. Nor do I reflect any more upon them than did Hegesippus in Eusebius, who confines the virgin purity of the church unto the days of the apostles, lib. iii. cap. 29. The greater deviations, which I intend, began not until after the end of the second century. But, —

2. To evince the improbability of any alteration in church rule and order upon my own principles, he intimates, both here and afterward, that "my judgment is that the government of

the church was democratical, and the power of it in the people, in distinction from its officers:" which is a great mistake; I never thought, I never wrote any such thing. I do believe that the authoritative rule or government of the church was, is, and ought to be, in the elders and rulers of it, being an act of the office-power committed unto them by Christ himself. Howbeit, my judgment is, that they ought not to rule the church with force, tyranny, and corporal penalties, or without their own consent; whereof we shall treat afterward. There are also other mistakes in the same discourse, which I shall not insist upon.

3. This, therefore, is that which he opposeth, — namely, that *there was a deviation in various degrees, and falling off from the original institution, order, and rule of the church, until it issued in a fatal apostasy.* This is that which, on the present occasion, must be farther spoken unto; for if this be not true, I confess there is an end of this contest, and we must all acquiesce in the state, rule, and order that was in the church of Rome before the Reformation. But we may observe something yet farther in the vindication and confirmation of this truth, which I acknowledge to be the foundation of all that we plead for in point of church reformation; as, —

(1.) That the reasons and arguings of the Doctor in this matter, — the necessity of his cause compelling him thereunto, — are the same with those of the Papists about the apostasy of their church, in faith, order, and worship, wherewith they are charged, namely, when, where, how was this alteration made? who made opposition unto it? and the like. When these inquiries are multiplied by the Papists, as unto the whole causes between them and us, he knows well enough how to give satisfactory answers unto them, and so might do in this particular unto himself also; but I shall endeavour to ease him of that trouble at present. Only, I must say that it is fallen out somewhat unexpectedly that the ruins of the principal bulwark of the Papacy, which hath been effectually demolished by the writings of Protestants of all sorts, should be endeavoured to be repaired by a person justly made eminent by his defence of the protestant religion against those of the church of Rome.

(2.) But it may be pleaded, that although the churches following the first ages did insensibly degenerate from the purity and simplicity of gospel faith and worship, yet they neither did nor could do so from an adherence unto and abiding in their original constitution, or from the due observation of church order, rule, and discipline, least of all could this happen in the case of diocesan episcopacy. I answer, —

[1.] That as unto the *original* of any thing that looks like diocesan episcopacy, or the pastoral relation of one person of a distinct order from presbyters unto many particular complete churches with officers of their own, with power and jurisdiction in them and over them, unto the abridgment of the exercise of that right and power unto their own edification which every true church is intrusted withal by Jesus Christ, it is very uncertain, and was introduced by insensible degrees, according unto the effectual working of the mystery of iniquity. Some say that there were two distinct orders, — namely, those of bishops and presbyters, — instituted at first in all churches planted by the apostles; but as the contrary may be evidently proved, so a supposition of it would no way promote the cause of diocesan episcopacy, until those who plead for it have demonstrated the state of the churches wherein they were placed to be of the same nature with those now called diocesan. Wherefore, this hypothesis begins generally to be deserted as it seems to be by this author. Others suppose that immediately upon, or at, or after the decease of the apostles, this new order of bishops was appointed, to succeed the apostles in the government of the churches that were then gathered or planted; but how, when, or by whom, — by what authority, apostolical and divine, or ecclesiastical only and human, — none can declare, seeing there is not the least footstep of any such thing either in the Scripture or in the records that remain of the primitive churches. Others think this new order of officers took its occasional rise from the practice of the presbyters of the church at Alexandria, who chose out one among themselves constantly to preside in the rule of the church and in all matters of order, unto whom they ascribed some kind of pre-eminence and dignity, peculiarly appropriating unto him the name of bishop. And if this be true as unto matter of fact, I reckon it unto the beginnings of those less harmful deviations from their original constitution which I assigned unto primitive churches; but many additions must be made hereunto before it will help the cause of diocesan episcopacy. What other occasions hereof were given or taken, what advantages were made use of to promote this alteration, shall be touched upon afterwards.

[2.] Why may not the churches be supposed to have departed from their original constitution, order, and rule, as well as from their first faith and worship? which they did gradually, in many successive ages, until both were utterly corrupted. The causes, occasions, and temptations leading unto the former, are to the full as pregnant as those leading unto the latter; for, —

1st. There was no vicious, corrupt disposition of mind that began more early to work in church-officers, nor did more grow and thrive in the minds of many, than *ambition*, with desire of pre-eminence, dignity, and rule. It is not to be supposed that Diotrephes was alone in his desire of pre-eminence, nor in the irregular actings of his unduly assumed authority. However, we have one signal instance in him of the deviation that was in the church with him, from the rule of its original constitution; for he prevailed so far therein as, by his own single episcopal power, to reject the authority of the apostles, and to cast them out of the church who complied not with his humour. How effectually the same ambition wrought afterward, in many others possessing the same place in their churches with Diotrephes, is sufficiently evident in all ecclesiastical histories. It is far from being the only instance of the corruption of church order and rule by the influence of this ambition, yet it is one that is pregnant, which is given us by Ambrose; for, saith he, "*Ecclesia ut synagoga, seniores habuit, quorum sine consilio nihil agebatur in ecclesia; quod quÂ negligentiÂ obsoleverit nescio, nisi forte doctorum desidiÂ, aut magis superbiÂ, dum soli volunt aliquid videri,*" in 1 ad Timoth. cap. 5. It seems there was some alteration in church rule and order in his time, whose beginning and progress he could not well discover and trace, but knew well enough that so it was then come to pass. And if he, who lived so near the times wherein such alterations were made, could not yet discover their first insinuation nor their subtle progress, it is unreasonable to exact a strict account of us in things of the same nature, who live so many ages after their first introduction. But this he judgeth, that it was the pride or ambition of the doctors of the church which introduced that alteration in its order. Whereas, therefore, we see in the event that all deviations from the original constitution of churches, all alterations in their rule and order, did issue in a compliance with the ambition of church-rulers, as it did in the papal church, — and this ambition was signally noted as one of the first depraved inclinations of mind that wrought in ecclesiastical rulers, and which, in the fourth and fifth centuries, openly proclaimed itself, unto the scandal of Christian religion, — there was a greater disposition in them unto a deviation from the original institution, rule, and order of the church, no way suited unto the satisfaction of that ambition, than unto a defection from the purity of faith and worship; which yet also followed.

2*dly*. As the inclination of many lay towards such a deviation, so their interests led them unto it, and their temptations cast them upon it. For, to acknowledge the truth unto our author and others, the rule and conduct of the church, the preservation of its order and discipline according unto its first institution, and the directions given in the Scripture about it, are, according unto our apprehension of these things, a matter so weighty in itself, so dangerous as unto its issue, attended with so many difficulties, trials, and temptations, laid under such severe interdictions of lordly power, or seeking either of wealth or dignity, that no wise man will ever undertake it, but merely out of a sense of a call from Christ unto it, and in compliance with that duty which he owes unto him. It is no pleasant thing unto flesh and blood to be engaged in the conduct and oversight of Christ's volunteers; — to bear with their manners; to exercise all patience towards them in their infirmities and temptations; to watch continually over their walkings and conversation, and thereon personally to exhort and admonish them all; to search diligently and scrupulously into the rule of the Scripture for their warranty in every act of their power and duty; under all their weaknesses and miscarriages, continuing a high valuation of them, as of the flock of God, "which he hath purchased with his own blood;" with sundry other things of the like kind; all under an abiding sense of the near approach of that great account which they must give of the whole trust and charge committed unto them before the judgment-seat of Christ: for the most part peculiarly exposed unto all manner of dangers, troubles, and persecutions, without the least encouragement from wealth, power, or honour. It is no wonder, therefore, if many in the primitive times were willing gradually to extricate themselves out of this uneasy condition, and to embrace all occasions and opportunities of introducing insensibly another rule and order into the churches, that might tend more unto the exaltation of their own power, authority, and dignity, and free them in some measure from the weight of that important charge, and continual care with labour, which a diligent and strict adherence unto the first institution of churches, and rules given for their order and government in the Scripture, would have obliged them unto. And this was done accordingly, until, in the fourth and fifth centuries, and so onward, the bishops, under various titles, began by their arbitrary rules and canons to dispose of the flock of Christ, to part and divide them among themselves, without their own knowledge or consent, as if they had conquered them by the sword. "This bishop shall have such a share and number of them under his power, and that other so many; so far shall the jurisdiction of one extend, and so far that of another," was the subject of many of their decrees and laws for the rule of the church. But yet neither did they long keep within those bounds and limits which their more modest ambition had at first prescribed unto them, but took occasion from these beginnings to contend among themselves about pre-eminence, dignity, and power; in which the bishop of Rome at length remained master of the field, thereby obtaining a second conquest of the world.

3*dly*. That there was such a gradual deviation from the original institution of churches, their order and rule, is manifest in the *event*; for the change became at length as great as the distance is between the gospel and the rule of Christ over his church on the one hand, and the canon law with the pope or antichrist set over the Church on the other. This change was not wrought at once, not in one age, but by an insensible progress, even from the days of the apostles unto those dark and evil times wherein the popes of Rome were exalted into an absolute tyranny over all churches, unto the satiety of their ambition; for, —

4*thly*. This mystery of iniquity began to work in the days of the apostles themselves, in the suggestions of Satan and the lusts of men, though in a manner latent and imperceptible unto the wisest and best of men; for that this mystery of iniquity consisted in the effectual workings of the pride, ambition, and other vices of the minds of men, excited, enticed, and guided by the craft of Satan, until it issued in the idolatrous, persecuting state of the church of Rome, wherein all church rule, order, and worship of divine institution was utterly destroyed or corrupted, we shall believe, until we see an answer given unto the learned writings of all sorts of Protestants, whereby it hath been proved.

These things are sufficient to vindicate the truth of the assertion which the Doctor opposeth, and to free it from his exceptions; but because, as was observed before, the supposition hereof is the foundation of all our present contests about church order and rule, I shall yet proceed a little farther in the declaration of the way and manner whereby the apostasy asserted was begun and carried on. And I shall not herein insist on particular instances, nor make a transcription of stories out of ancient writers giving evidence unto the truth, because it hath been abundantly done by others, especially those of Magdeburg in the sixth and seventh chapters of their Centuries, unto whose observations many other learned men have made considerable additions; but I shall only treat in general of the causes, ways, and manner of the beginning and progress of the apostasy or declension of churches from their first institution, which fell out in the successive ages after the apostles, especially after the end of the second century, until when divine institutions, as unto the substance of them, were preserved entire.

Decays in any kind, even in things natural and political, are hardly discernible but in and by their effects. When an hectic distemper befalls the body of any man, it is ofttimes not to be discerned until it is impossible to be cured. The Roman historian gives this advice unto his readers, after he hath considered the ways and means whereby the empire came to its greatness: "*Labente deinde disciplinâ velut dissidentes primo mores sequatur animo; deinde ut magis magisque lapsi sint, tum ire cæperint præcipites, donec ad hæc tempora, quibus nec vitia nostra, nec remedia pati possumus, periculum est,*" Liv. Præfat. His words do not give us a more graphical description of the rise and decay, as unto virtue and vice, of the Roman empire, than of the Roman church, as unto its rise by holiness and devotion, and its ruin by sensuality, ambition, the utter neglect of the discipline of Christ, and superstition. But yet let any man peruse that historian, who wrote with this express design, he shall hardly fix upon many of those instances whereby the empire came into that deplorable condition whereto it was not able to bear its distempers nor its cure, such as was the state of the church before the Reformation. But besides the common difficulty of discovering the beginnings and gradual progression of decays, declensions, and apostasy, those which we treat of were begun and carried on in a mysterious manner; that is, by the effectual working of "the mystery of iniquity." As this almost hid totally the work of it from the ages wherein it was wrought, so it renders the discovery of it now accomplished the more difficult. Passengers in a ship setting out to sea ofttimes discern not the progressive motion of the ship, yea, for a while the land rather seems to move from them than the vessel wherein they are from it; but after a season, the consideration of what distance they are at from their port gives them sufficient assurance of the progress that hath been made: so this declension of the churches from their primitive order and institution is discoverable rather by measuring the distance between what it left and what it arrived unto, than by express instances of it. But yet is it not altogether like unto that of a ship at sea, but rather unto "the way of a serpent on a rock," which leaves some slime in all its turnings and windings, whereby it may be traced. Such marks are left on record of the serpentine works of this mystery of iniquity as whereby it may be traced, with more or less evidence, from its original interests unto its accomplishment.

The principal promoting causes of this defection on the part of men were those assigned by St Ambrose, in one instance of it, — namely, the negligence of the people, and the ambition of the clergy. I speak as unto the state, rule, discipline, and order of the church; for as unto the doctrine and worship of it, there were many other causes and means of their corruption, which belong not unto our present purpose. But as unto the alterations that were begun and carried on in the state, order, and rule of the church, they arose from those springs of negligence on the one hand, and ambition on the other, with want of skill and wisdom to manage outward occurrences and incidences, or what alteration fell out in the outward state and condition of the church in this world. For hence it came to pass, that in the accession of the nations in general unto the profession of the gospel, church-order was suited and framed unto their secular state, when they ought to have been brought into the spiritual state and order of the church, leaving their political state entire unto themselves. Herein, I say, did the guides of the church certainly miss their rule and depart from it, in the days of Constantine the emperor, and afterward under other Christian emperors, when whole towns, cities, yea, and nations, offered at once to join themselves unto it. Evident it is that they were not wrought hereunto by the same power, nor induced unto it on the same motives, or led by the same means, with those who formerly under persecution were converted unto the faith of our Lord Jesus Christ. And this quickly manifested itself in the lives and conversations of many, yea, of the most of them. Hence those which were wise quickly understood that what the church had got in multitude and number it had lost in the beauty and glory of its holy profession. Chrysostom in particular complains of it frequently, and in many places cries out, "What have I to do with this multitude? A few serious believers are more worth than them all." However, the guides of the church thought meet to receive them, with all their multitudes, into their communion, at least so far as to place them under the jurisdiction of such and such episcopal sees; for hereby their own power, authority, dignity, revenues, were enlarged and mightily increased. On this occasion, the ancient, primitive, way of admitting members into the church being relinquished, the consideration of their personal qualifications and real conversion unto God omitted, such multitudes being received as could not partake in all acts and duties of communion with those particular churches whereunto they were disposed, and being the most of them unfit to be ruled by the power and influence of the commands of Christ on their minds and consciences, it was impossible but that a great alteration must ensue in the state, order, and rule of the churches, and a great deviation from their original institution. Men may say that this alteration was necessary, that it was good and useful, that it was but the accommodation of general rules unto especial occasions and circumstances; but that there was an alteration hereon in all these things none can with modesty deny. And this is enough unto my present design, being only to prove that such alterations and deviations did of old fall out. Neither ought we to cover the provoking degeneracy of the generality of Christians in the fourth and fifth centuries, with those that followed. The consideration of it is necessary unto the vindication of the holy providence of God in the government of the world, and of the faithfulness Of Christ in his dealing with his church; for there hath been no nation in the world which publicly received Christian religion, but it hath been wasted and destroyed by the sword of pagan idolaters, or such as are no better than they. At first, all the provinces of the western empire were, one after another, made desolate by the Pagan nations of the northern countries; who themselves did afterward so turn Christians as to lay among them the foundation of Antichristianism, Rev. xvii. 12, 13. The eastern empire, comprehending the residue of the provinces that had embraced the Christian religion, was first desolated in the chief branches of it by the Saracens, and at length utterly destroyed by the Turks. And I pray God that the like fate doth not at this day hang over the reformed nations, as from their profession they are called. Do we think that all this was without cause? Did God give up his inheritance to the spoil of barbarous infidels without such provocations as the passing by whereof was inconsistent with the holiness and righteousness of his rule? It was not the wisdom, nor the courage, nor the multitude of their enemies, but their own sins, wickedness, superstition, and apostasy from the rule of gospel order, worship, and obedience, which ruined all Christian nations.

But to give farther evidence hereunto, I shall consider the causes aforementioned distinctly and apart. And the first of them is *the negligence of the people themselves*. But in this negligence I comprise both the ignorance, sloth, worldliness, decay in gifts and graces, with superstition in sundry instances, that in many of them were the causes of it. Dr Stillingfleet pleads that "it is very unlikely that the people would forego their interest in the government of the churches, if ever they had any such thing, without great noise and trouble. For," saith he, "government is so nice and tender a thing, and every one is so much concerned for his share in it, that men are not easily induced to part with it. Let us suppose the judgment of the church to have been democratical at first, as Dr Owen seems to do; is it probable that the people would have been wheedled out of the sweetness of government so soon and made no noise about it?" p. 226. His mistake about my judgment herein hath been marked before. No other interest or share in the government is ascribed by us unto the people, but that they may be ruled by their own consent, and that they may be allowed to yield obedience in the church unto the commands of Christ and his apostles, given unto them for that end. This interest they neither did nor could forego without their own sin and guilt, in neglecting the exercise of the gifts and graces which they ought to have had, and the performance of the duties whereunto they were obliged. But for any engagement on their minds from the "sweetness of government," wherein their concern principally consists, in an understanding, voluntary obedience unto the commands of

Christ, they had nothing of it. Take also, in general, government to be, as the government of the church is, merely a duty, labour, and service, without those advantages of power, ease, dignity, and wealth, which have been annexed unto it, and it will be hard to discover such "a nicety" or "sweetness" in it as to oblige unto pertinacy in an adherence unto it. If the government of the church were apprehended to consist in men's giving themselves wholly to the word and prayer; in watching continually over the flock; in accurate carefulness to do and act nothing in the church but in the name and authority of Christ, by the warranty of his commands; with a constant exercise of all gifts and graces of the Holy Spirit, which they have received, in these and all other duties of their office; and that without the least appearance of domination, or the procuring of dignity, secular honours, and revenues thereby, — it may be, a share and interest in it would not be so earnestly coveted and sought after as at present it is. Nor is there any more pertinency in his ensuing supposal of a "change in the government of the congregational churches in London, in setting up one man to rule over them all and to appoint their several teachers," etc., p. 227, "which could not be done without noise." It is in vain to fear it, —

— "Non isto vivimus illicQuo tu rere, modo,"

and impertinent in this case to suppose it; for it speaks of a sudden total alteration in the state, order, and rule of churches, to be made at once, whereas our discourse is of that which was gradual in many ages, by degrees almost imperceptible. But yet I can give no security that the churches of our way shall not, in process of time, decline from their primitive constitution and order, either in their power and spirit, in faith and love, or in the outward practice of them, unless they continually watch against all beginnings and occasions of such declensions, and frequently renew their reformation; or if it be otherwise, they will have better success man any churches in the world ever yet had, even those that were of the planting of the apostles themselves, as is manifested in the judgment that our Lord Jesus Christ passed on them, Rev. ii., iii. The negligence of the people, which issued in their unfitness to be disposed of and ruled according to the principles of the first constitution of church-order, may be considered either as it gave occasion unto those lesser deviations from the rule, which did not much prejudice the faith and order of the churches, or as it occasioned greater alterations in the ensuing ages. And, —

1. The great, and perhaps in some things excessive, veneration which they had of their bishops or pastors, did probably occasion in them some neglect of their own duty; for they were easily induced hereon, not only implicitly to leave the management of all church affairs unto them, but also zealously to comply with their mistakes. The church of Smyrna, giving an account of the martyrdom of holy Polycarpus, tells us that when he ascended the pile wherein he was to be burned, "he pulled off his own clothes, and endeavoured to pull off his shoes, which he had not done before, because the faithful strove among themselves who should soonest touch his body," Eusebius lib. iv. cap. 15. I think there can be no veneration due to a man which was not so unto that great and holy person. But those who did so express it might easily be induced to place too much of their religion in an implicit compliance with them unto whom they were so devoted. Hence a negligence in themselves as unto their particular duties did ensue. They were quickly far if rein esteeming it their duty to say unto their pastor or bishop that he should "take heed to the ministry which he had received in the Lord, to fulfil it," as the apostle enjoins the Colossians to say to Archippus their pastor, chap. iv. 17, but began to think that the glory of obsequious obedience was all that was left unto them. And hence did some of the clergy begin to assume to themselves, and to ascribe unto one another, great swelling titles of honour and names of dignity (amongst which the blasphemous title of "His Holiness" was at length appropriated unto the bishop of Rome); wherein they openly departed from the apostolical simplicity and gravity. But these things fell out after the writing of the epistle of Clemens, and of those of the churches of Vienne and Smyrna, wherein no such titles do appear.

2. Many of the particular churches of the first plantations increasing greatly in the number of their members, it was neither convenient nor safe that the whole multitude should on all occasions come together, as they did at first, to consult about their common concerns, and discharge the duties of their communion; for by reason of danger from their numerous conventions, they met in several parcels as they had opportunity. Herewith they were contented, unless it were upon the greater occasions

of choosing their officers and the like, whereon the whole church met together. This made them leave the ordinary administration of all things in the church unto the elders of it, not concerning themselves farther therein; but still continuing members of the same particular church. It is altogether improbable what Platina from Damasus affirms, in the Life of Euarestus, about the end of the first century, that he distributed the faithful at Rome into distinct titles or parishes, with distinct presbyters of their own; for it is apparent that in those days, wherein persecution was at its height, the meetings of believers were occasional, with respect unto their security, ofttimes by night, sometimes in caves under the earth, or in deserted burial-places, at best in private houses. And they had for what they did the example of the apostolical churches, Acts i. 13, 14, ii. 46, iv. 23–31, xii. 12, xviii. 7, xx. 8, xxi. 8. Instances of such meetings may be multiplied, especially in the church of Rome. And to manifest that they took this course upon necessity, when peace began to be restored at any time unto them, they designed temples that might receive the whole multitude of the church together. The distribution mentioned into titles and parishes began a long time after, and in very few places within three hundred years. In this state it is easy to conceive what alterations might fall out in some churches from their primitive order, especially how the people might desert their diligence and duty in attending unto all the concerns of the church. And if those things which the apostles wrote unto them in their epistles, the instructions, directions, and commands how in all things they should act and deport themselves in the church, be esteemed to be obligatory in all ages, I cannot see how, after the second century, they were much complied withal, unless it were in the single instance of *choosing their own officers* or rulers.

But, secondly, After these there ensued greater occasions of greater variations from the primitive institution and order of the churches on the part of the people; for, —

1. Such *numbers* of them were received into a relation unto particular churches as was inconsistent with the ends of their institution and the observance of the communion required in them; as will afterward appear. And the reliefs that were invented for this inconveniency in distinct conventions, supplied with the administration of the word and sacraments from the first church, or by stated titles, did alter the state of the church.

Among those multitudes which were added unto the churches, especially in the fourth century, many, if not the most, did come short inexpressibly in knowledge, gifts, grace, holiness, and uprightness of conversation of the primitive Christians, as the writers of that age complain. And being hereby incapable of walking according unto the order, rule, and discipline of the apostolical churches, there seemed to be a necessity of another rule, of other ways and means for their government, without their own concurrence or consent, than what was at first appointed, which were gradually introduced; whence the original of a multitude of those canons, which were arbitrarily invented afterward for their rule and government, is to be derived. And it may be made to appear that the accommodation of the rule, yea, and of the worship of the church, in the several ages of it, unto the ignorance, manners, and inclinations of the people, who were then easily won unto the outward profession of Christian religion, was one means of the ruin of them both, until they issued in downright tyranny and idolatry.

But much more of the cause of the deviation of the churches from their primitive rule and order is to be ascribed unto the ambition and love of pre-eminence in many of the clergy, or rulers of the churches; but this is no place nor season to manifest this by instances, besides it hath been done by others. I shall therefore inquire only into one or two things in particular, which are of principal consideration in the declension of the churches from their primitive institution, order, and rule; and, —

(1.) It is evident that there was an *alteration* made in the state of the church as *to its officers*; for it issued at last in popes, patriarchs, cardinals, metropolitan and diocesan bishops, who were utterly foreign unto the state and order of the primitive churches, and that for some ages. Nor were these officers introduced into the church at once, or in one age, nor with the powers which they afterward claimed and assumed unto themselves. It was done gradually, in many succeeding ages, working by design to accommodate the state of the church unto the political state of the empire in the distribution of its government.

(2.) The *beginnings* of this great alteration were *small*, nor at all perceived in the days wherein they were first acted. Nor is it agreed, nor, as far as I see, will it ever be agreed among learned men, when first a disparity among the ordinary officers of the church, in order, degree, or power, did first begin, nor by what means it was brought about. The apostles were all equal among themselves; no one had either office or office-power above others. So were all the ordinary bishops and presbyters mentioned in the Scripture, as shall be proved afterward. No intimation is given of any pre-eminence or superiority amongst them of one over others. Yet afterward, in the third and fourth centuries, much of that nature appears. It begins to be granted that the bishops and elders mentioned in the Scripture were the same, and that there was no difference in name, office, or power, during the apostles' times; which was the judgment of Jerome, and our author seems to me to be of the same mind, p. 267. But they say that after the decease of the apostles, there were some appointed to succeed them in that part of their office which concerned the rule of many churches. And this, they say, was done for the prevention of schism, but with ill success; for as Clemens affirms that the apostles foresaw that there would be strife and contention about episcopacy, even when it was confined unto its original order, because of the ambition of Diotrephes and others like him, so it became much more the cause of all sorts of disorders, in schisms and heresies, when it began to exalt itself in dignity and reputation. The first express attempt to corrupt and divide a church, made from within itself, was that in the church of Jerusalem, made by Thebuthis, because Simon Cleophas was chosen bishop, and he was refused, Eusebius, lib. iv. cap. 22. The same rise had the schisms of the Novatians and Donatists, the heresies of Arius, and others. Neither is there any thing certain in this pretended succession of some persons unto the apostles in that part of their office which concerns the rule of many churches by one overseer. No intimation of any such appointment by the apostles, or any of them, — no record of the concurrence of the churches themselves in and unto this alteration, — can be produced. Nor is there any analogy between the extraordinary power of every apostle over all churches and care for them, and the ordinary power of a bishop over a small number, which lot or accident disposeth unto him. Besides, it cannot be proved, no instance can be given, or hath been, for the space of two hundred years, or until the end of the second century, of any one person who had the care of more churches than one committed unto him, or did take the charge of them on himself. But whereas this change did fall out, and appears evidently so to have done, in the fourth century, we may briefly inquire into the causes and occasions of it.

Churches were originally planted in cities and towns for the most part; not absolutely, for the word was preached and churches gathered by the apostles κατὰ πόλεις καὶ χώρας, as Clemens testifieth. In such cities there was but one church, whereunto all believers did belong. I mention this the rather because our present author, who is pleased frequently to mistake my words and principles, affirms "that the thing which I should have proved is, that there were more churches at first planted in one city than one." I know not why I should be obliged to do so, because I never said so. I do believe, indeed, that there may be more particular churches than one in one city; and that sometimes it is better that it should be so than that all believers in the same city should be kept up unto one congregation, to the obstruction of their edification. But that there were originally, or in the days of the apostles, more churches than one, in any one city or town, I do wholly deny; though I grant, at the same time, there were churches in villages also, as will appear afterward. But though there was one church only in one town or city, yet all the believers that belonged unto that church did not live in that city, but sundry of them in the fields and villages about. So Justin Martyr tells us, that on the first day of the week, when the church had its solemn assemblies, all the members of it, in the city and out of the country, the fields and villages about, met together in the same place. In process of time these believers in the country did greatly increase, by the means of the ministry of the city church, which diligently attended unto the conversion of all sorts of men, with some extraordinary helps besides. But hereon the example of the apostles was overseen; for on this account of the conversion of many unto the faith in the towns and villages of any province, they erected and planted new churches among them, not obliging them all unto that first church from whence the word went forth for their conversion. But those who succeeded them, being hindered by many reasons, which may be easily recounted, from thoughts of the multiplication of churches, chose rather to give the believers scattered up and down in the country occasional assistance by presbyters of their own, than to dispose them into a church-state and order. But after a while, their number greatly increasing, they were necessitated to supply them with a constant ministry, in several parcels or divisions. The ministers or elders thus disposed amongst them for their edification, in the administration of the ordinances of the gospel, did still relate unto and depend upon that *city first church* from whence they came. But the numbers of believers daily increasing, and a succession of presbyters in their distinct assemblies being found necessary, they came to be called churches, though continuing in dependence, both for a supply of officers and for rule, on the first or city church, whereunto they esteemed themselves to belong. This was the way and manner of the multiplication of Christian assemblies throughout the Roman empire; and hereby all the bishops of the first churches became, by common consent, to have a distinction from and pre-eminence above the presbyters that were fixed in the country, and a rule over those assemblies or churches themselves. And, therefore, when they met together in the council of Nice, among the first things they decreed, one was to confirm unto the bishops of the great cities that power over the neighbouring churches which they had enjoyed from this occasional rise and constitution of them. Hereby was a difference and distinction between bishops and presbyters, between mother and dependent churches, introduced, equally almost in all places, without taking any notice of the departure which was therein from the primitive pattern and institution. But these things fell out long after the days of the apostles, — namely, in the third and fourth centuries, there being no mention of them before.

2. But, secondly, There was another occasion of this alteration, which took place before that insisted on; for in many of those city churches, especially when the number of believers much increased, there were *many bishops or elders, who had the rule of them in common*. This is plain in the Scripture, and in the ensuing records of church affairs; and they had all the same office, the same power, and were of the same order. But after a while, to preserve order and decency among themselves and in all their proceedings, they chose one from among them who should preside in all church affairs for order's sake, unto whom, after a season, the name of bishop began to be appropriated. Whether the rule they proceeded by herein was to choose them unto this dignity who had been first converted unto the faith, or first called and ordained to be presbyters, or had respect unto the gifts and graces of those whom they chose, is not certain; but this way began in those churches wherein some extraordi-

nary officer, apostle or evangelist, had long resided. It cannot, therefore, be doubted but they had some design to represent hereby somewhat of the dignity of such an officer, and a resemblance of the continuance of his presence among them; and this, I suppose, fell out early in the churches, though without ground or warrant. And the principal pastors of other churches, which had not any great number of elders in them, yet quickly assumed unto themselves the dignity which the others had attained.

Justin Martyr, in the account he gives of the church, its order, rule, worship, and discipline in his days, mentions one singular person in one church, whom he calls Προεστώς, who presided in all the affairs of the church, and himself administered all the sacred ordinances, every Lord's day, unto the whole body of the church gathered and met out of the city and the villages about. This was the bishop; and if any one desired this office, he desired a "good work," as the apostle speaks. Whatever accessions were made unto the church, these προεστῶτες, — which were either the first converted to the faith, or the first ordained presbyters, or obtained their pre-eminence, *"non pretio, sed testimonio,"* as Tertullian speaks, upon the account of their eminency in gifts and holiness, — were yet quickly sensible of their own dignity and prelation, and by all means sought the enlargement of it; supposing that it belonged unto the honour and order of the church itself.

Under this state of things, the churches increasing every day in number and wealth, growing insensibly more and more (*"indies magis magisque decrescente disciplina"*) into a form and state exceeding the bounds of their original institution, and becoming unwieldy as unto the pursuit of their ends, unto mutual edification, it is not hard to conjecture how a stated distinction between bishops and presbyters did afterward ensue; for as the first elder, bishop, or pastor, had obtained this small pre-eminence in the church wherein he did preside and the assemblies of the villages about, so the management of those affairs of the church which they had in communion with others was committed unto him, or assumed by him. This gave them the advantage of meeting in synods and councils afterward; wherein they did their own business unto the purpose. Hereon, in a short time, the people were deprived of all their interest in the state of the church, so as to be governed by their own consent;

which, indeed, they also had rendered themselves unmeet to enjoy and exercise; — other elders were deprived of that power and authority which is committed unto them by Christ, and thrust down into an order or degree inferior unto that wherein they were originally placed; — new officers in the rule of the church, utterly unknown to the Scripture and primitive antiquity, were introduced; — all charitable donations unto the church, for the maintenance of the ministry, the poor, and the redemption of captives, were for the most part abused, to advance the revenues of the bishops; — such secular advantages, in honour, dignity, and wealth, were annexed unto episcopal sees, as that ambitious men shamefully contested for the attaining of them; which, in the instance of the bloody conflict between the parties of Damasus and Ursacius at Rome, Ammianus Marcellinus, a heathen, doth greatly and wisely reflect upon. But yet all these evils were as nothing in comparison of that dead sea of the Roman tyranny and idolatry whereinto at last these bitter waters ran, and were therein totally corrupted.

I thought, also, to have proceeded with an account of the declension of the churches from their first institution, in their matter, form, and rule; but because this would draw forth my discourse beyond my present intention, I shall forbear, having sufficiently vindicated my assertion in this one instance.

It is no part of my design to give an answer at large unto the great volume that Dr Stillingfleet hath written on this occasion, much less to contend about particular sayings, opinions, the practices of this or that man, which it is filled withal. But whereas his treatise, so far as the merit of the cause is concerned in it, doth consist of two parts, the first whereof contains such stories, things, and sayings as may load the Cause and persons whom he opposeth with prejudices in the minds of others, — in which endeavour he exceeds all expectation, — and [the second] what doth more directly concern the argument in hand; I shall, at the end of the ensuing discourse, speak distinctly unto all that is material of the second sort, especially so far as is needful unto the defence of my former "Vindication of the Nonconformists from the Guilt of Schism."

For the things of the first sort, — wherein the Doctor doth so abound, both in his preface and in the first part of his book, as to manifest himself, I fear, to be a little too sensible of provocation (for the actings of interest in wise men are usually more sedate),

— I shall only oppose some general considerations unto them, without arguing or contending about particulars; which would be endless and useless. And whereas he hath gathered up almost every thing that hath been done, written, or spoken to the prejudice of the cause and persons whom he opposeth (though frequently charged before), adding the advantage of his style and method unto their reinforcement, I shall reduce the whole unto a few heads, which seem to be of the greatest importance.

I shall leave him without disturbance unto the satisfaction he hath in his own love, moderation, and condescension, expressed in his preface. Others may possibly call some things in it unto a farther account. But the first part of his book is cast under two heads:— 1. A *commendation of the first reformers and their reformation*, with some reflections upon all that acquiesce not therein, as though they esteemed themselves wiser and better than they. From this topic proceed many severe reflections and some reproaches. 2. The other consists in a story of the rise and progress of separation from the church of England, with the great miscarriages among them who first attempted it, and the opposition made unto them by those who were themselves Nonconformists. The whole is closed with the difference and debate between the divines of the assembly of the presbyterian way, and the "dissenting brethren," as they were then called. Concerning these things the discourse is so prolix, and so swelled with long quotations, that I scarce believe any man would have the patience to read over a particular examination of it; especially considering how little the cause in hand is concerned in the whole story, whether it be told right or wrong, candidly or with a design to make an advantage unto the prejudice of others. I shall, therefore, only mark something with respect unto both these heads of the first part of the book, which, if I mistake not, will lay it aside from being of any use to our present cause:—

1. As unto the first reformers and reformation in the days of King Edward, the plea from them and it, which we have been long accustomed unto, is, that they were persons great, wise, learned, holy; that some of them died martyrs; that the work of the reformation was greatly owned and blessed of God: and, therefore, our non-acquiescency therein, but desiring a farther reformation of the church than what they saw and judged nec-

essary, is unreasonable; and that what we endeavour therein, though never so peaceably, is schismatical. But, —

(1.) None do more bless God for the first reformers, and the work they did, than we do; none have a higher esteem of their persons, abilities, graces, add sufferings, than we have; none cleave more firmly to their doctrine, which was the life and soul of the reformation, than we, nor desire more to follow them in their godly design. They are not of us who have declared that the death of King Edward was a happiness or no unhappiness to the church of England, nor who have reflected on the Reformation as needless, and given assurance that if it had not been undertaken, salvation might have been obtained safely enough in the church of Rome. Nor were they of us who have questioned the zeal and prudence of the martyrs in those days of suffering. We have other thoughts concerning them, — another kind of remembrance of them.

(2.) The titles assigned unto them, of wise, learned, holy, zealous, are fully answered by that reformation of the church in its doctrine and worship which God wrought by their ministry; so that none without the highest ingratitude can derogate any thing from them in these things. But it is no disparagement unto any of the sons of men, any officers of the church since the days of the apostles, the first reformers, or those that followed them, to judge that they were not infallible, that their work was not absolutely perfect, like the work of God, whereunto nothing can be added nor aught taken away. Wherefore, —

(3.) We are not obliged to make what they did, and what they attained unto, and what they judged meet as unto the government and worship of the church, to be our absolute rule, from which it should be our sin to dissent or depart. They never desired or designed that it should be so; for to do so would have been to have cast out one Papacy and to have brought in another. And the arguments of the Papists for their absolute adherence unto the men of their veneration, those who have been formerly of great reputation in their church, for learning, holiness, and devotion, are as forcible unto them as any can be unto us for an adherence unto the first reformers in all things; but yet are they not excused in their errors thereby. Had we received a command from heaven to hear them in all things, it had altered the case: but this we have received only with respect unto Jesus Christ; and shall, therefore, in these things, ultimately attend only unto what he speaks. And we have sundry considerations which confirm us in the use and exercise of that liberty wherewith Christ hath made us free, to inquire ourselves into our duty in these things, and to regulate our duty in them by his word, notwithstanding what was done by our first reformers; for, —

[1.] They did not think themselves obliged, they did not think meet, to abide within the bounds and limits of that reformation of the church which had been attempted before them, by men wise, learned, and holy, even in this nation. Such was that which was endeavoured by Wickliffe and his followers; in giving testimony whereunto many suffered martyrdom, and prepared the way unto those that were to come after. They approved of what was then done, or attempted to be done, for the substance of it, yet esteemed themselves at liberty to make a farther progress in the same work; which they did accordingly. Surely such persons never designed their own judgment and practice to give boundaries unto all reformation for evermore, or pretended that they had made so perfect a discovery of the mind of Christ, in all things belonging unto the rule and worship of the church, as that it should not only be vain but sinful to make any farther inquiries about it. Some thought they were come unto the utmost limits of navigation and discovery of the parts of the world before the West Indies were found out; and some men, when in any kind they know as much as they can, are apt to think there is no more to be known. It was not so with our reformers.

[2.] They did not at once make what they had done themselves to be a *fixed rule* in these things, for themselves made many alterations in the service-book which they first composed; and if they judged not their first endeavour to be satisfactory to themselves they had no reason to expect their second should be a standing rule unto all future ages. Nor did they so, but frequently acknowledged the imperfection of what they had done.

[3.] The first reformers, both bishops and others, both those who underwent martyrdom at home and those who lived in exile abroad, *differed* among themselves in their judgments and apprehensions about those things which are now under contest, whereas they perfectly agreed in all doctrines of faith and gospel obedience. The public records of these differences do so remain as that they cannot modestly be denied nor handsomely covered. And this must needs weaken the influence of their authority in the settlement of the church, which was an act only of the prevalent party among them.

[4.] They *differed in these things from all other reformed churches*, with whom they did absolutely agree in doctrine, and had the strictest communion in faith and love; for it is known that their doctrine, which they owned and established, was the same with that of the churches abroad called particularly Reformed, in distinction from the Lutherans. But as unto the state, rule, and order of the church, they differed from them all. I press not this consideration unto the disadvantage of what they attained unto and established in the way of reformation, or in a way of preferring other churches above them, but only to evidence that we have reason enough not to esteem ourselves absolutely obliged unto what they did and determined as unto all endeavours after any farther reformation.

[5.] In their reformation they avowedly proposed *a rule and measure* unto themselves Which was both uncertain and in many things apparently various from the original rule of these things given by Christ and his apostles, with the practice of the first churches; and this was the state and example of the church under the first Christian emperors, as our author confesseth. This rule is uncertain; for no man living is able to give a just and full account of what was the state and rule of all the churches in the world in the reign of any one emperor, much less during the succession of many of them, continual alterations in the state or order of the church following one upon another. And that in those days there was a prevalent deviation from the original rule of church-order hath been before declared. We dare not, therefore, make them and what they did to be our rule absolutely, who missed it so much in the choice of their own.

[6.] We may add hereunto the consideration of *the horrid darkness* which they newly were delivered from; the close adherence of some traditional prejudices unto the best of men in such a condition; the difficulties and oppositions they met withal as unto their whole work; their prudence, as they judged it, in an endeavour to accommodate all things unto the inclinations and desires of the body of the people (extremely immersed in their old traditions), which might not be destructive unto their salvation, in heresy or idolatry; — all which could not but leave some marks of imperfection on their whole work of reformation.

Upon these and the like considerations it is that we are enforced to assert the use of our own liberty, light, and understanding, in the inquiring after and compliance with the true original state and order of the evangelical churches, with our duty in reference thereunto, and not to be absolutely confined unto what was judged meet and practised in these things by the first reformers. And the truth is, if present interest and advantage did not prevail with men to fix the bounds of all church-reformation in what was by them attained and established, they would think it themselves a papal bondage, to be bound up absolutely unto their apprehensions; from a confinement whereunto in sundry other things they declare themselves to be at an absolute liberty. Wherefore, neither we nor our cause are at all concerned in the rhetorical discourse of Dr Stillingfleet concerning the first reformers and their reformation; neither do we at all delight in reflecting on any of the defects of it, desiring only the liberty avowed on protestant principles, in the discharge of our own duty.

2. Nor, secondly, are we any more concerned in the long story that ensues about *the rise and progress of separation from the church of England*, with the mistakes of some in principles, and miscarriages in practice, who judged it their duty to be separate; for as, in our refraining from total communion with the parochial assemblies of the church of England, we proceed not on the same principles, so we hope that we are free from the same miscarriages with them, or any of an alike nature. But it is also certain, that after the great confusion that was brought on the whole state and order of the church under the Roman apostasy, many of those who attempted a reformation fell into different opinions and practices in sundry things; which the Papists have made many a long story about. We undertake the defence only of our own principles and practices according unto them; nor do we esteem ourselves obliged to justify or reflect on others.

And it were no difficult task to compose a story of the proceedings of some in the church of England, with reference unto these differences, that would have as ill an aspect as that which is here reported. Should an account be given of their unaccountable rigour and severity, in that through so many years, yea ages, they would never think of the least abatement of their impositions, in any one instance, though acknowledged by themselves indifferent and esteemed by others unlawful, although they saw what woful detriment arose to the churches thereby; yea, how, instead thereof, they did to the last of their power make a progress in the same course, by attempting new canons, to inflame the difference, and increased in severities towards all dissenters; — should an account be given of the silencings, deprivings, imprisonings, by the High Commission Court, and in most of the dioceses of the kingdom, of so great numbers of godly, learned, faithful, painful ministers, to the unspeakable disadvantage of the church and nation, with the ruin of the most Of them and their families; — the representation of their names, qualifications, evident usefulness in the ministry, with the causes of their sufferings, wherein the Observance of some ceremonies was openly preferred before the edification of the church and a great means of the conversion of souls, would give as ill a demonstration of Christian wisdom, love, moderation, condescension, zeal for the propagation of the gospel, as any thing doth, on the other hand, in the history before us. It would not be omitted, on such an occasion, to declare what multitudes of pious, peaceable Protestants were driven by their severities to leave their native country, to seek a refuge for their lives and liberties, with freedom for the worship of God, in a wilderness in the ends of the earth; and if it be said that what some did herein they did in the discharge of the duties of their office, I must say I shall hardly acknowledge that office to be of the institution of Christ, whereunto it belongs, in a way of duty, to ruin and destroy so many of his disciples, for no other cause but a desire and endeavour to serve and worship him according unto what they apprehend to be his mind revealed in the gospel. Should there be added hereunto an account of the administration of ecclesiastical discipline in the courts of chancellors, commissaries, officials, and the like, as unto the authority and causes, with the way and manner of their proceedings in the exercise of their jurisdiction, with the woful scandals that have been given thereby, with an addition of sundry other things which I will not so much as mention, I suppose it would as much conduce unto peace and reconciliation among Protestants as the story here given us by our author.

But setting aside the aggravations of things gathered out of controversial writings (wherein few men do observe the due rules of moderation, but indulge unto themselves the liberty of severe censures and sharp reflections on them they do oppose), the sum and truth of the story concerning these things may be reduced into a narrow compass; for, —

(1.) It is certain that, from the first dawning of the Reformation in this nation, there were different apprehensions, among them that jointly forsook the Papacy, as unto its doctrine and worship, about the state, rule, order, and discipline of the church, with sundry things belonging unto its worship also. I suppose this will not be denied.

(2.) There doth not remain any record of a due attempt and endeavour for the composing these differences before one certain way was established by those in power. And Whereas, [from] the state and condition wherein they were at that time, from the confusions about religion that were then abroad, and the pertinaciousness of the generality of the people in an adherence unto their old ways and observances in religion, with a great scarcity in able ministers, the greatest part of the bishops and clergy disliking the whole Reformation, they found themselves, as they judged, necessitated to make as little alteration in the present state of things as was possible, so as to keep up an appearance of the same things in the church which had been in former use, — on these grounds the state and rule of the church was continued in the same form and posture that it was before under the Papacy, the authority of the pope only being excluded, and the power of disposal of ecclesiastical affairs, usurped by him, declared to be in the king; so also, in imitation of that book of worship and service which the people had been accustomed unto, another was established, with the ceremonies most obvious unto popular observation.

(3.) This Order was unsatisfactory unto great numbers of ministers and others; who yet, considering what the necessity of the times did call for, did outwardly acquiesce in it in several degrees, in hopes of a farther reformation in a more convenient season. Nor did they cease to plead and press for it by all quiet and peaceable means, abstaining, in the meantime, from the use of the ceremonies, and full compliance with episcopal jurisdiction.

(4.) Hereon those who were for the establishment, having secured their interests therein and obtained power, began after a while to oppress, excommunicate, silence, deprive, and imprison those who dissented from them, and could not come up unto a full practical compliance with their institutions and rules. Yet the generality of those so silenced and deprived abode in privacy under their sufferings, hoping for a reformation at one time or another, without betaking themselves unto any other course for the edification of themselves or their people.

(5.) After sundry years, some men, partly silenced and deprived as unto their ministry, and partly pursued with other censures and penalties, began to give place unto severe thoughts of the church of England and its communion, and, withdrawing themselves into foreign parts, openly avowed a separation from it. And if the extremities which many had been put unto for their mere dissent and nonconformity unto the established rule, — which, with a good conscience, they could not comply with, — were represented, it might, if not excuse, yet alleviate the evil of that severity in separation which they fell into.

(6.) But hereon a double inconvenience, yea, evil, did ensue, whence all the advantages made use of in this story to load the present cause of the Nonconformists did arise. For, —

[1.] Many of those who refused to conform unto the church in all its constitutions yet thought it their duty to wait quietly for a *national reformation*, thinking no other possible, began to oppose and write against them who utterly separated from the church, condemning its assemblies as unlawful. And herein, as the manner of men is on such occasions, they fell into sharp invectives against them, with severe censures and sentences concerning them and their practice. And, —

[2.] Those who did so separate, being not agreed among themselves as unto all principles of church-order, nor as unto the measure of their separation from the church of England, there fell out differences and disorders among them, accompanied with personal imprudences and miscarriages in not a few. Neither was it scarcely ever otherwise among them who first attempted any reformation; unless, like the apostles, they were infallibly guided. These mutual contests which they had among themselves, and with the Nonconformists who abode in their private stations in England, with their miscarriages also, were published unto the world, in their own writings and those of their enemies.

"*Hinc omnis pendet Lucilius.*" These were the things that gave advantage unto, and are the substance of, the history of our author concerning separation; wherein all I can find unto our present instruction is, that

"Iliacos intra muros peccatur et extra;"

There are and ever were sins, faults, follies, and miscarriages among all sorts of men; which might be farther evidenced by recounting, on the other hand, what were the ways, acts, and deeds, at the same time, of those by whom the others were cast out and rejected. And whereas it was the design of the reverend author to load the cause and persons of the present Nonconformists with prejudice and contempt, it is well fallen out, in the merciful disposal of things towards and amongst us, by the providence and grace of God, that he is forced to derive the principal matter of his charge from what was done by a few private persons, three or four score years ago and more, in whose principles and practices we are not concerned. And as for the difference that fell out more lately among the divines in the assembly at Westminster, about the ways, means, and measures of reformation and mutual forbearance, which he gives us a large account of in a long transcription out of their writings, I must have more health, and strength, and leisure than now I have (which I look not for in this world), before I esteem myself concerned to engage in that contest, or to apologize for the one side or other The things in agitation between them had no relation unto our present dissent from the church of England, being here insisted on merely to fill up the story, with reference unto the general end designed.

Neither, to my knowledge, did I ever read a book wherein there was a greater appearance of diligence in the collection of things, words, sayings, expressions, discourses unto other ends, which might only cast odium on the cause opposed, or give advantage for arguings unto a seeming success, very little or no way at all belonging unto the cause in hand, than there is in this of our reverend author; though much in the same way and kind hath been before attempted.

But separation it is and schism which we are all charged withal; and the evil thereof is aggravated in the words of the author himself, and in large transcriptions out of the writings of others. Schism, indeed, we acknowledge to be an evil, a great evil, but are sorry that with some a pretended, unproved schism is become almost all that is evil in the churches or their members; so that let men be what they will, drenched, yea, overwhelmed in ignorance, vice, and sin, so they do not separate (which, to be sure, in that state they will not do, for why should he who hath plague-sores upon him depart from the society of them that are infected?) they seem to he esteemed, as unto all the concerns of the church, very unblamable.

The truth is, considering the present state and condition of the inhabitants of this nation, who are generally members of the church of England, — how "the land is filled with sin against the Holy One of Israel," God giving us every day renewed tokens and indications of his displeasure, no compliance with his calls, no public reformation being yet attempted, — it seems a more necessary duty, and of more importance unto them upon whom the care of such things is incumbent, to endeavour in themselves, and to engage a faithful ministry throughout the nation, both to give a due example in their conversations, and to preach the word with all diligence, for the turning of the people from the evil of their ways, than to spend their time and strength in the management of such charges against those who would willingly comply with them as unto all the great ends of religion amongst men.

But this must be farther spoken unto. I say, therefore, first, in general, that whereas the whole design of this book is to charge all sorts of Nonconformists with schism, and to denounce them schismatics, yet the author of it doth not once endeavour to state the true notion and nature of schism, wherein the consciences of men may be concerned. He satisfies himself in the invectives of some of the ancients against schism, applicable unto those which were in their days, wherein we are not concerned. Only, he seems to proceed on the general notion of it, that it is a causeless separation from a true church; which departs from that of the Romanists, who will allow no separation from the church but what is causeless. To make application hereof unto us, it is supposed, —

(1.) That *the church of England* is a true church in its *national constitution*, and so are all the parochial churches in it; which can be no way justified but by a large, extensive interpretation of the word "true," for there is but one sort of churches instituted by Christ and his apostles, but national and parochial churches differ in their whole kind, and therefore cannot both of them be of a divine original.

(2.) That we are members of this church *by our own consent*. How we should come to be so otherwise, I know not. If we are so by being born and baptized in England, then those who are born beyond sea and baptized there are made members of this church by an act of Parliament for their naturalization, and no otherwise.

(3.) That we *separate* from this church in things wherein we are obliged by the *authority of Christ* to hold communion with it; which neither is nor will ever be proved, nor is it endeavoured so to be by any instances in this treatise.

(4.) That to withhold communion from *parochial assemblies* in the worship of God, as unto things confessedly not of divine institution, is schism, — that kind of schism which is condemned by the ancient writers of the church. Upon these and the like suppositions it is no uneasy thing to make vehement declamations against us and severe reflections on us; all is schism and schismatic, and all of the same kind with what was written against by Cyprian, and Austin, and others a great many.

But the true state of the controversy between him and us is this, and no other, — namely, *Whether a dissent in, and forbearance from, the communion of churches, in their state and kind not of divine institution, or so far as they are not of divine institution, and from things in other churches that have no such divine institution, nor any scriptural authority to oblige us unto their observance, be to be esteemed schism in them who maintains and professedly avow communion in faith and love with all the true churches of Christ in the world*? This is the whole of what we are concerned in; which, where it is spoken unto, it shall be considered. But because there were in the primitive churches certain persons who, on arbitrary principles of their own, consisting for the most part in gross and palpable errors, which they would have imposed on all others, did separate from the catholic church, — that is, all other Christians in the world, and all the churches of Christ, condemning them as no churches, allowing not the administration of sacraments unto them nor salvation unto their members, — whom the ancient church condemned with great severity, and that justly, as guilty of schism, their judgment, their words and expressions, are applied unto us, who are no way concerned in what they speak of or unto. We are not, therefore, in the least terrified with what is alleged out of the ancients about schism; no more than he is when the same instances, the same authorities, the same quotations, are made use of by the Papists against the church of England, as they are continually: for, as was said, we know that we are no way concerned in them. And suppose that all that the

Doctor allegeth against us be true, and that we are in the wrong in all that is charged on us, yet I dare refer it to the Doctor himself to determine whether it be of the same nature with what was charged on them who made schisms in the church of old. I suppose I guess well enough what he will say to secure his charge; and it shall be considered when it is spoken.

But, as was said, the great and only design of the author of this book is to prove all Nonconformists to be schismatics, or guilty of the sin of schism. How he hath succeeded in this attempt shall be afterward considered. And something I have spoken in the ensuing discourse concerning the nature of schism, which will manifest how little we are concerned in this charge. But yet it may not be amiss in this place to mind both him and others of some of those principles whereon we ground our justification in this matter, that it may be known what they must farther overthrow, and what they must establish, who shall persist in the management of this charge; that is, indeed, through want of love, in a design to heighten and perpetuate our divisions. And, —

The first of these principles is, That *there is a rule prescribed by our Lord Jesus Christ unto all churches and believers, in a due attendance whereunto all the unity and peace which he requireth amongst his disciples do consist.*

We acknowledge this to be our fundamental principle. Nor can the rhetoric or arguments of any man affect our consciences with a sense of the guilt of schism until one of these things be proved; namely, either, first, That the Lord Christ hath *given no such rule* as in the observance whereof peace and unity may be preserved in his church; or, secondly, That we *refuse a compliance* with that rule in some one instance or other of what therein he hath himself appointed. Unless one or the other be proved, and that strictly and directly, not pretended so to be by perpetual diversions from the things in question, no vehement assertions of any of us to be schismatics nor aggravations of the guilt of schism will signify any thing in this cause.

But that our principle herein is according unto truth we are fully persuaded. There is a rule of Christ's given, which whosoever walk according unto, "peace shall be on them, and mercy, and upon the whole Israel of God," Gal. vi. 16. And we desire no more, no more is needful unto the peace and unity of the church; and this rule, whatever it be, is of his giving and appointment. No rule of men's invention or imposition can, by its observance, secure us of an interest in that peace and mercy which is peculiar unto the Israel of God. God forbid we should entertain any such imagination! We know well enough men may be thorough conformists to such rules, unto whom, as unto their present state and condition, neither peace nor mercy do belong; for "there is no peace to the wicked." He who hath directed and commanded the end of church unity and peace hath also appointed the means and measures of them. Nothing is more disagreeable unto, nothing more inconsistent with, the wisdom, care and love of Christ unto his church, than an imagination that whereas he strictly enjoins peace and unity in his church, he hath not himself appointed the rules, bounds, and measures of them, but left it unto the will and discretion of men. As if his command unto his disciples had been, "Keep peace and unity in the church, by doing and observing whatever some men, under a pretence of being the guides of the church, shall make necessary unto that end;" whereas it is plainly otherwise, — namely, that we should so keep the peace and unity of the church by doing and observing all whatever that he commands us. And, besides, we strictly require that some one instance be given us of a defect in the rule given by Christ himself, which must be supplied by human additions, to render it complete for the end of church peace and unity. In vain have we desired, in vain may we for ever expect, any instance of that kind.

This principle we shall not be easily dispossessed of; and whilst we are under the protection of it, we have a safe retreat and shelter from the most vehement accusations of schism for a non-compliance with a rule, none of his, different from his, and in some things contrary unto his, for the preservation of church peace and unity. All the dispute is, whether we keep unto this rule of Christ or no; wherein we are ready at any time to put ourselves upon the trial, being willing to teach or learn, as God shall help us.

Secondly, we say, That *this rule in general is the rule of faith, love, and obedience contained and revealed in the Scripture; and in particular, the commands that the Lord Christ hath given for the order and worship that he requires in his churches.* It may seem strange to some that we should suppose the due observance of the rule of faith, love, and obedience, — that is, of faith real and unfeigned, love fervent and without dissimulation, and of universal, gracious, evangelical obedience, — to be necessary unto the preservation of church peace and unity; but we do affirm, with some confidence, that the only real foundation of them doth lie herein, nor do we value that ecclesiastical peace which may be without it or is neglective of it. Let all the Christian world, or those therein who concern themselves in us, know that this is our principle and our judgment — that no church peace or unity is valued by or accepted with Jesus Christ that is not founded in, that doth not arise from, and is the effect of, a diligent attendance unto and observance of the entire gospel rule of faith and obedience. In the neglect hereof, peace is but carnal security, and unity is nothing but a conspiracy against the rule of Christ. Add hereunto the particular, the due observation of what the Lord Christ hath appointed to be done and observed in his churches, as unto their order, rule, and worship; and they who walk according unto this rule need not fear the charge of schism from the fiercest of their adversaries. Wherefore we say, —

Thirdly, Those who recede *from this rule, in any material branch of it, are guilty of the breach of church-unity, according to the measure of their exorbitancy;* — as suppose that any preach, teach, or profess doctrines that are contrary to the form of wholesome words, especially with reference unto the person, offices, and grace of Christ, which are the subject of doctrines purely evangelical, they break the peace of the church, and we are bound to separate or withdraw communion from them; which is a means of preserving the true peace and unity of the church. "*Speciosum quidem est nomen pacis, et pulchra opinio unitatis, sed quis ambigat eam solam, unicam, ecclesiæ pacem esse, quæ Christi est,*" saith Hilary. Suppose that men retain a form of godliness in the profession of the truth, but deny the power of it, acting their habitual lusts and corruptions in a vicious conversation; they overthrow the foundation of the church's unity, and we are obliged from such to turn away. The like may be said of those who live in a constant neglect of any of the commands of Christ with respect unto the order, rule, and worship of the church, with a contempt of the means appointed by him for their edification. All these, according unto the measures of their deviations from the rule of Christ, do disturb the foundation of all church peace and unity. And therefore we say, —

Fourthly, That *conscience is immediately and directly concerned in no other church unity, as such, but what is an effect of the rule of*

Christ given unto that end. We know what is spoken concerning obedience unto the guides and rulers of the Church; which is a part of the rule of Christ. But we know withal, that this obedience is required of us only as they teach us to observe and do all that he hath commanded; for other commission from him they have none. When this rule is forsaken, and another substituted in the room of it, as it quickly diverts the minds of men from a conscientious attendance unto that rule of Christ as the only means of church-unity, so that other doth either proceed from men's secular interests or may easily be accommodated thereunto. And whereas the lines of it must be drawn in the fields of pretended *indifferences and real arbitrariness*, it will be the cause of endless contentions, whilst whatever some think themselves to *have* power to appoint, others will judge themselves to have liberty to refuse.

Fifthly, *It is unity of Christ's appointment that schism respects as a sin against it, and not uniformity in things of men's appointment.* And, —

Lastly, Those who charge schism on others for a dissent from themselves, or the refraining of total communion with them, must, —

1. *Discharge themselves* of the charge of it, in a consistence with their charge on them; for we find as yet no arrows shot against us but such as are gathered up in the fields, shot at them that use them out of the Roman quiver. Neither will it avail them to say that they have other manner of reason for their separation from the church of Rome than any we have for our withdrawing communion from them; for the question is not, what reasons they have for what they do? but, what right and power they have to do it? — namely, to separate from the church Whereof they were, constituting a new church-state of their own, without the consent of that church, and against the order and authority of the same.

2. *Require no communion* but by virtue of the rule before declared. In no other are we concerned, with respect unto the peace and unity of the church.

3. Give a farther confirmation than what we have yet seen unto the principles or presumptions they proceed upon in the management of the charge of schism; as that, — (1.) *Diocesan bishops*, with their *metropolitans, are* of divine institution; (2.) That the *power of rule* in and over all churches is committed unto

them alone; (3.) That the church hath power to *ordain* religious rites and ceremonies nowhere prescribed in the Scripture, and impose the observation of them on all members of the church; (4.) That *this church* they are; (5.) That no man's *voluntary consent* is required to constitute him a member of any church, but that every one is surprised into that state whether he will or no; (6.) That there is *nothing of force* in the arguments pleaded for non-compliance with arbitrary, unnecessary impositions; (7.) That the church standeth in no need of *reformation*, neither in doctrine, discipline, nor conversation; with sundry other things of an alike nature that they need unto their justification.

But yet, When all is done, it will appear that mutual forbearance, first removing animosities, then administering occasion of inoffensive converse, unto the revival of decayed affections, leading unto sedate conferences and considerations of a more entire conjunction in the things whereunto we have attained, will more conduce unto universal peace and gospel unity than the most fierce contentions about things in difference, or the most vehement charges of schism against dissenters.

But I must return to the argument, and shall add something giving light into the nature of schism, from an instance in the primitive churches.

That which is first in any kind gives the measure of what follows in the same kind, and light into the nature of them. Whereas, therefore, the schism that was among the churches about the observation of Easter was the first that fell out unto the disturbance of their communion, I shall give a brief account of it, as far as the question in hand is concerned in it.

It is evident that the apostles did with care and diligence teach the doctrine of Christian liberty, warning the disciples to "stand fast" in it, and not submit their necks unto any "yoke of bondage" in the things of the worship of God; especially the apostle Paul had frequent occasions to treat of this subject. And what they taught in doctrine, they established and confirmed in their practice; for they enjoined nothing to be observed in the church but what was necessary, and what they had the command of Christ for, leaving the observation of things indifferent unto their original indifference. But whereas they had decreed, by the direction of the Holy Ghost, some necessary condescensions in the Gentile believers towards the Jews, in case of offence or scandal, they did themselves make use of their liberty to comply with the same Jews in some of their observances not yet unlawful. Hereon there ensued in several churches different observations of some rites and customs, which they apprehended were countenanced by the practice of the apostles, at least as it had been reported unto them: for, immediately after the decease of the apostles, very many mistakes and untruths were reported concerning what they said, did, and practised; which some diligently collected from old men (it may be almost delirant), as Eusebius gives an instance in Papias, lib. iii. cap 36; and even the great Irenæus himself was imposed upon, in a matter directly contrary to the Scripture, under a pretence of apostolical tradition. Among those reports was that of the observation of Easter. And for a while the churches continued in these different observances, without the least disturbance of their communion, each One following that which it thought the most probable tradition; for rule of Scripture they pretended not unto. But after a while they began to fall into a contest about these things, which began at Laodicea; which church was as likely to strive about such things as any other: for Eusebius tells us that Melito, the bishop of Sardis, wrote two books about Easter, beginning the first with an account that he wrote them when Servilius Paulus was proconsul, there being then a great stir about it at Laodicea, Eusebius, lib. iv. cap. 26. But, as it falls out on such occasions, much talk and disputing ensuing thereon, the differences were increased, until one side or party at variance would make their opinion and practice the rule and terms of communion unto all other churches. But this was quickly condemned by those who were wise and sober; for, as Sozomen affirms, they accounted it "a frivolous or foolish thing to differ about a custom, whereas they agreed in all the principal heads of religion." And thereon he gives a large account of different rites and observances in many churches, without any breach of communion among them; adding, that besides those enumerated by him, there were many others in cities and villages which they did in a different manner adhere unto, Hist., lib. vii. cap. 19.

At length this matter fell into the handling of Victor, bishop of Rome; and his judgment was, that the observation of Easter on the Lord's day, and not on the fourteenth day of the first month precisely, according to the computation of the Jews in the observation of the passover, was to be imposed on all the churches of Christ everywhere. It had all along, until his time, been judged a thing indifferent, wherein the churches and all believers were left unto the use of their own liberty. He had no pretence of any divine institution making it necessary, the writers of those days constantly affirming that the apostles made no canons, rules, or laws about such things. He had persons of as great worth as any in the world, as Melito, Polycrates, Polycarpus, that opposed him, not only as unto the imposition of his practice on others, but as unto his error, as they judged, in the matter of fact and right; yet all this could not hinder but that he would needs have the reputation of the father of schisms among the churches of Christ by his impositions, and he cut off all the Asian churches from communion, declaring them and their members excommunicate, Eusebius, lib. v. cap. 23.

The noise hereof coming abroad unto other churches, great offence was taken at it by many of them, and Victor was roundly dealt withal by sundry of them who agreed with him in practice, but abhorred his imposition of it, and making it a condition of church-communion.

Among those who so opposed and rebuked him, Irenæus was the most eminent. And I shall observe some few things out of the fragment of his epistle, as it is recorded by Eusebius, lib. v. cap. 23.

And, — (1.) He tells us that "he wrote unto Victor in the name of those brethren in France whom he did preside amongst." The custom of considering things of this nature with all the brethren of the church, and writing their determination in their name, was not yet grown out of use, though the practice of it now would be esteemed novel and schismatical.

(2.) He tells Victor that "there were great varieties in this thing, as also in the times and seasons of fasting; which did not," saith he, "begin or arise in our days, but long before was introduced by such who, being in places of rule, rejected and changed the common and simple customs which the church had before." The Doctor, therefore, need not think it so strange that an alteration in church order and rule should fall out in after ages, when long before Irenæus' time such changes were begun.

(3.) He gives hereon that excellent rule: Ἡ διαφωνία τῆς νηστείας τὴν ὁμόνοιαν τῆς πίστεως συνίστησιν· — "The difference of fastings" (and consequently things of an alike nature) "commends the concord or agreement of faith."

This was the first effect of a departure from the only rule of unity and communion among the churches which was given by Christ himself and his apostles. As hereby great confusion and disorder was brought upon the churches, so it was the first public inroad that was made on the doctrine of the Scripture concerning Christian liberty. And as it was also the first instance of rejecting men otherwise sound in the faith from communion for nonconformity, or the non-observance of human restitutions or traditions, — which had therein an unhappy consecration unto the use of future ages, — so it was the first notorious entrance into that usurpation of power in the Roman bishops, which they carried on by degrees unto an absolute tyranny. Neither was there ever a more pernicious maxim broached in the primitive times, nor which had a more effectual influence into the ruin of the first institution and liberty of the churches of Christ; for although the fact of Victor was condemned by many, yet the principle he proceeded on was afterward espoused and put in practice.

Our reverend author will hardly find an instance before this of schism among any churches that retained the substance of the doctrine of faith, unless it be in those divisions which fell out in some particular churches, among the members of them. And this we affirm to be in general the case of the Nonconformists at this day: for admitting such variations as time and other circumstances must necessarily infer, and they are rejected from communion on the same grounds that Victor proceeded on in the excommunication of the churches of Asia; neither will there be any end of differences whilst the same principle is retained. Before this, schism was only esteemed a defect in love and breach of the rule of Christ's appointment for the communion and walking together of believers in the same church.

But this notion of schism is, in the judgment of Dr Stillingfleet, preface, p. 46, "so mean, so jejune, so narrow a notion of it, that I cannot," saith he, "but wonder that men of understanding should be satisfied with it." But, in my judgment, the author of it was a man of good understanding. Indeed, I have heard him spoken of as one of abstruse speculations, that did not advantage Christian religion; and one hath published in print that "he is one of the obscurest writers that ever he read;" but I never heard him before charged with mean and jejune notions. Now, this was St Paul, who expressly chargeth schism on the church of Corinth because of the divisions that were among them, — namely, the members of the same particular church, — so as they could not "come together in one place" in a due manner; nor, in all his writings, doth he anywhere give us any other notion of schism. "But," saith he, "this is short of that care of the church's peace which Christ hath made so great a duty of his followers." But if there be no other rule, no other duty for the preservation of the church's peace, but only that no separation be made from it, which is called schism, we might have been all quiet in the church of Rome. Let no man think to persuade us but that, for the preservation of the church's peace, it is required of us that we do and observe all things that Christ requireth of us, and that we enjoin not the observation of what he hath not commanded on Victor's penalty, of being excluded from communion: that faith, and love, and holiness be kept and promoted in the church, by all the ways of his appointment; and when these things are attended unto, St Paul's mean and jejune notion of schism will be of good use also.

Nor was there the least appearance of any other kind of schism among the churches of Christ until that which was occasioned by Victor; of which we have spoken. The schisms that followed afterward were, six to one, from the contentions of bishops, or those who had an ambition so to be: which the apostle foresaw, as Clemens witnesseth, and made provision against it; but that no banks are strong enough to confine the overflowing ambition of some sort of persons. But saith the Doctor, preface, p. 47, "The obligation to preserve the peace of the church extends to all lawful constitutions in order to it: therefore, to break the peace of the church we live in, for the sake of any lawful orders and constitutions made to preserve it, is directly the sin of schism."

1. Now, schism, he tell us, is "as great and dangerous a sin as murder," p. 45; and we know that "no murderer hath eternal life abiding in him," John iii. 15. So that all men here seem to be adjudged unto hell who comply not with, who submit not unto, our ecclesiastical constitutions or canons. God forbid that ever such doctrine should be looked on as to have the least affinity unto the gospel, or such censures to have any savour of the Spirit of Christ in them! The Lord Jesus Christ hath not cast the eter-

nal condition of those whom he purchased with his own most precious blood into the arbitrary disposal of any that shall take upon them to make ecclesiastical constitutions and orders, for conformity in rites and ceremonies, etc. Shall we think that he who, upon the best use of means for his instruction which he is capable of, with fervent prayers to God for light and direction, cannot comply with and submit unto some ecclesiastical constitutions and orders, however pretended to be made for the preservation of peace and unity in the church, on this ground principally, because they are not of the appointment nor have the approbation of Jesus Christ, though he should mistake herein, and miss of his duty, is guilty of no less sin than that of murder, — suppose of Cain in killing his brother? for all murder is from hatred and malice. This is that which inflames the differences amongst us; for it is a scandal of the highest nature, when men do see that persons who in any thing dissent from our ecclesiastical constitutions, though otherwise sober, honest, pious, and peaceable, are looked on as bad, if not worse than thieves and murderers, and are dealt withal accordingly. Nor can any thing be more effectual to harden others in their immoralities than to find themselves approved by the guides of the church, in comparison with such dissenters.

2. But who is it that shall make these orders and constitutions, that must be observed for the preservation of the unity and peace of the church? It can be none but those who have power so to do by being uppermost in any place or time. Who shall judge them to be lawful? No doubt they that make them. And what shall these constitutions be about, what shall they extend unto? Any thing in the world, so there be no mention of it in the Scripture, one way or other. What if any one should now dissent from these constitutions, and not submit unto them? Why, then, he is guilty of schism! — as great and dangerous a sin as that of murder!! But when all is done, what if these constitutions and orders should be no ways needful or useful unto the preservation of the peace of the church? what if a supposition that they are so reflects dishonour on the wisdom and love of Christ? what if they are unlawful and unwarrantable, the Lord Christ not having given power and authority unto any sort of men to make any such constitutions? what if they are the great ways and means of breaking the unity and peace of the church? These, and other inquiries of the like nature, must be clearly re-

solved, not by the dictates of men's own minds and spirits, but from the word of truth, before this intimation can be complied withal.

But that which is fallen out most beyond expectation in this whole discourse is, that the reverend author, seeking, by all ways and means countenanced with the least resemblance or appearance of truth, to load the Nonconformists and their cause with the imputation of things invidious and burdensome, should fix upon their prayers, by virtue of the grace and gift of prayer which they have received, ascribing the original of its use unto the artifice and insinuation of the Jesuits, as he doth, preface, pp. 14, 15. But because I look on this as a thing of the greatest importance of all the differences between them and us, — as that wherein the life of religion, the exercise of faith, and the labour of divine love do much consist, — the nature and necessity of that kind of prayer which is here reflected on and opposed shall, God willing, be declared and vindicated in a peculiar discourse unto that purpose; for the differences that are between us cannot possibly have any more pernicious consequence than if we should be influenced by them to oppose or condemn any principles or exercise of the duties of practical holiness, as thinking them to yield matter of advantage to one party or another.

The great pains he hath taken, in this preface, to prove the Nonconformists to have been the means of furthering and promoting Popery in this nation might, as I suppose, have been omitted without any disadvantage unto himself or his cause; for the thing itself is not true. As it is utterly impossible to affect the minds or consciences of the Nonconformists with a sense of it, because they have a thousand witnesses in themselves against the truth of the charge, so it is impossible it should be believed by any who are in the least acquainted with their principles, or have their eyes open to see any thing that is doing at this day in religion. But as there are many palpable mistakes in the account he gives of things among ourselves to this purpose, so if, on the other hand, any should, out of reports, surmises, Jesuits' letters and politics, particularly those of Contzen; books written to that purpose against them; agreement of principles; notorious compliance of some bishops and others of the same way with the Papists, some dying avowedly such; stories of what hath been said at Rome and elsewhere, which are not few nor unprovable, concerning the inclinations of many unto a fair composition of things with the church of Rome; the deportment of some before and since the discovery of the plot; with such other topics as the discourse of our author with respect unto the Nonconformists will furnish them withal; as also from the woful neglect there hath been of instructing the people in the principles of religion, so as to implant a sense of the life and power of it on their souls; with all things that may be spoken on that head with reference unto the clergy under their various distributions, with the casting out of so great a number of ministers, whom they knew in their own conscience to be firmly fixed against Popery and its interest in this nation, and could not deny but they might be useful to instruct the people in the knowledge of the truth, and encourage them by their example unto the practice of it; — if any, I say, should, on these and the like grounds, not in a way of recrimination, nor as a requital of the Doctor's story, but merely as a necessary part of the defence of their own innocency, charge the same guilt, of giving occasion unto the growth, increase, and danger of Popery in this nation, on the episcopal party, I know not now how they could be well blamed for it, nor what will be done of that kind; for they who will take liberty to speak what they please must be content sometimes to hear what will displease. For my part, I had rather, if it were possible, that these things at present might be omitted, and that all those who are really united in opposition unto Popery, — as I am assured in particular that this reverend author and I are, — would rather consider how we might come out of the danger of it wherein we are, than at present contest how we came into it. This I speak seriously, and that under the consideration of this discourse; which, upon the account of sundry mistakes in matter of fact, of great defects in point of charity, with a design to expose others unto reproach for their *great crime* of being willing to be a little freed from being beaten, fined, punished, and imprisoned, by their means and on their account, is as apt to excite new exasperations, and to provoke the spirits of them concerned, as any I have read of late. However, the defence of our own innocency must not be forsaken. But, —

"*Cumque superba foret Babylon spolianda trophæis,*"

it is not praiseworthy to abide in these contests beyond necessity.

This discourse, indeed, of the reverend author is increased into so large a volume as might justly discourage any from undertaking the examination of it who hath any other necessary duties to attend unto. But if there be separated from it the consideration of stories of things and persons long since past, wherein we are not concerned, with the undue application of what was written by some of the ancients against the schisms in their days unto our present differences; as also the repetition of a charge that we do not refrain communion from the parochial churches on the grounds and reasons which we know to the contrary that we do; with the report and quotation of the words and sayings of men by whose judgment we are not determined; with frequent diversions from the question, by attempting advantages from this or that passage or expression in one or another; and the rhetorical aggravations of things that might be plainly expressed and quickly issued, — the controversy may be reduced into a narrower compass.

It is acknowledged that the differences which are amongst Protestants in this nation are to be bewailed, because of the advantages which the common enemy of the protestant interest doth endeavour to make thereby. Howbeit the evil consequences of them do not arise from the nature of the things themselves, but from the interest, prejudices, and biassed affections of them amongst whom they are. Nor shall any man ever be able to prove but that, on the doctrinal agreement which we all profess (provided it be real), we may, notwithstanding the differences that remain, enjoy all that peace and union which are prescribed unto the churches and disciples of Christ, provided that we live in the exercise of that love which he enjoineth us; which whilst it continues, in the profession of the same faith, it is impossible there should be any schism among us. Wherefore, whereas some are very desirous to state the controversy on this supposition, that there is a schism among us, and issue it in an inquiry on which side the blame of it is to be laid, — wherein they suppose they need no farther justification but the possession of that church-state which is established by law, — I shall willingly forego the charging of them with the whole occasion of the schism pretended, until they can prove there is such a schism, which I utterly deny; for the refraining of communion with parochial assemblies, on the grounds whereon we do refrain, hath nothing of the nature of schism in it, neither as it is stated in the Scripture nor as it was esteemed of in the primitive churches, amongst whom there were differences of as great importance, without any mutual charges of schism. Wherefore, although we cannot forego utterly the defence of our own innocency against such charges as import no less than a heinous guilt of sin against God, and imminent danger of ruin from men, yet we shall constantly unite ourselves with and unto all who sincerely endeavour the promotion of the great ends of Christian religion, and the preservation of the interest of protestant religion in this nation.

Something I judge necessary to add concerning my engagement, or rather surprisal, into this controversy, against my inclination and resolution.

The Doctor tells us, preface, p. 51, "That when his sermon came first out, it went down quietly enough, and many of the people began to read and consider it, being pleased to find so weighty and necessary a point debated with so much calmness and freedom from passion; which being discovered by the leaders and managers of the party, it was soon resolved that the sermon must be cried down, and the people dissuaded from reading of it. If any of them were talked withal about it, they shrunk up their shoulders, and looked sternly, and shook their heads, and hardly forbore some bitter words, both of the author and the sermon," (which it seems he knows, though they did forbear to do so!) and much more to the same purpose. And, p. 53, "As if they had been the Papists' instruments to execute the fury of their wrath and displeasure against me, they summon in the power of their party, and resolve with their force and might to fall upon me;" with more to the same purpose. And p. 59, "After a while they thought fit to draw their strength into the open field; and the first who appeared was," etc.

I confess I was somewhat surprised, that, coming into this coast, all things should appear so new and strange unto me as that I could fix on no one mark to discover that I had ever been there before; for I am as utter a stranger unto all these things as unto the counsels of the Pope or Turk. The Doctor seems to apprehend that, at the coming forth of his sermon, at least after its worth and weight were observed, there was a consternation and disorder among the Nonconformists, as if Hannibal had been at the gates; for hereby he supposeth they were cast into those ugly postures of shrinking, and staring, and shaking, and swelling with what they could hardly forbear to utter. But these things, with those that follow, seem to me to be romantic, and somewhat tragically expressed, sufficiently evidencing that other stories told by the same author in this case stand in need of some grains of allowance to reduce them to the royal standard; for whereas I am the first person instanced in that should have a hand in the management of these contrivances, I know nothing at all of them, nor, upon the utmost inquiry I have made, can I hear of any such things among the parties, or the "managers" of them, as they are called. It is true, the preaching and publishing of the Doctor's sermon at that time was by many judged unseasonable, and they were somewhat troubled at it; more upon the account that it was done by him than that it was done. But otherwise, as to the charge of schism managed therein against them, they were neither surprised with it nor discomposed at it. And, so far as I know, it was the season alone, and the present posture of affairs in the nation, calling for an agreement among! all Protestants, that occasioned any answer unto it.

It is, therefore, no small mistake, that we "dissuaded" any from reading his sermon; which hath been commonly objected by some other writers of the same way. But if we were enemies unto these worthy persons, we could not desire they should have more false intelligence from our tents than they seem to have. This is not our way. Those who are joined with us are so upon their own free choice and judgment; nor do we dissuade them from reading the discourses of any on the subject of our differences. The rule holds herein, "Prove all things, and hold fast that which is good."

Nor do I know any thing in the least of advices or agreements to cry down and oppose, confute or answer, the Doctor's sermon; nor do I believe that there were ever any such among those who are charged with them. And what shall be said unto those military expressions of "summoning in the power of the party, resolved to fall on, think fit to draw their strength into the field?" etc. I say, what shall we say to these things? I am not a little troubled that I am forced to have any concernment in the debate of these differences, wherein men's sense of their interest, or of provocations they have received, cast them on such irregular ways of defence and retaliation; for all these things are but fruits of imagination, that have nothing of truth or substance to give countenance unto them.

PREFACE.

The way whereby I became to be at all engaged in this contest, and the reasons whereon I undertook a harmless defence of our innocency, as to the charge of schism at this time, I shall give a brief account of:—

Some days after the Doctor's sermon was printed and published, one of those whom he supposeth we persuaded not to read it brought it unto me, and gave it me, with such a character of it as I shall not repeat. Upon the perusal of it (which I did on his desire, being uncertain to this day whether, without that occasion, I had ever read it at all), I confess I was both surprised and troubled, and quickly found that many others were so also; for as there was then a great hope and expectation that all Protestants would cement and unite in one common cause and interest for the defence and preservation of religion against the endeavours of the Papists for its subversion, so it was thought by wise men of all sorts that the only medium and expedient for this end was the deposing of the consideration of the lesser differences among ourselves, and burying all animosities that had arisen from them. And I yet suppose myself at least excusable, that I judged the tendency of that discourse to lie utterly another way. Nor is it in my power to believe that a peremptory charge of schism upon any dissenters, — considering what is the apprehension and judgment of those who make that charge concerning it with respect unto God and men, — is a means to unite us in one common religious interest. And on this account, not knowing in the least that any other person had undertaken, — or would undertake, the consideration of the Doctor's sermon, I thought that my endeavour for the removal of the obstacle cast in the way unto a sincere coalition in the unity of faith among all sorts of Protestants, might not be unacceptable. Neither did I see any other way whereby this might be done but only by a vindication of the dissenters from the guilt of that state, which, if it be truly charged on them, must render our divisions irreconcilable. And continuing still of the same mind, I have once more renewed the same defensative, with no other design but to maintain hopes that peace and love may yet be preserved among us during the continuation of these differences. And whereas it is a work of almighty power to reduce Christian religion unto its first purity and simplicity, which will not be effected but by various providential dispensations in the world, and renewed effusions of the Holy Spirit from above, which are to be waited for; and seeing that all endeavours for national reformation are attended with insuperable difficulties, few churches being either able or willing to extricate themselves from the dust of traditions and time, with the rust of secular interests; I would hope that they shall not be always the object of public severities who, keeping the unity of the Spirit in the bond of truth and peace, with all sincere disciples of Christ everywhere, do design nothing but a reformation of themselves and their ways, by a universal compliance with the will and word of Christ alone, whom God hath commanded them in all things to hear and obey.

The reduction, I say, of the profession of Christianity in general unto its primitive purity, simplicity, separation from the world, and all implication with secular interests, so as that it should comprise nothing but the guidance of the souls of men in the life of God towards the enjoyment of him, is a work more to be prayed for to come in its proper season than to be expected in this age. Nor do any yet appear fitted in the least measure for the undertaking or attempting such a work, any farther than by their own personal profession and example. And whilst things continue amongst protestant churches in the state wherein they are, — under the influence of divided secular interests, and advantageous mixtures with them, with the relics of the old general apostasy, by differences in points of doctrine in rules of discipline, in orders of divine worship, — it is in vain to look for any union or communion among them, in a compliance with any certain rule of uniformity, either in the profession of faith or in the practice of worship and discipline. Nor would such an agreement among them, could it be attained, be of any great advantage unto the important ends of religion, unless a revival of the power of it in the souls of men do accompany it. In the meantime, the glory of our Christian profession, in righteousness, holiness, and a visible dedication of its professors unto God, is much lost in the world, innumerable souls perishing through the want of effectual means for their conversion and edification. To attempt public national reformation whilst things ecclesiastic and civil are so involved as they are, the one being rivetted into the legal constitution of the other, is neither the duty nor work of private men: nor will, as I suppose, wise men be over forward in attempting any such thing, unless they had better evidence of means to make it effectual than any that do as yet appear; for the religion of a nation, in every form, will answer the ministry of it. What is the present duty, in this state of things, of those private Christians or ministers who cannot satisfy their consciences, as unto their duty towards God, without endeavouring a conformity unto the will of Christ, in the observance of all his institutions and commands, confining all their concerns in religion unto things spiritual and heavenly? is the inquiry before us.

CHAPTER I.

Of the original of churches.

WHEN any thing which is pleaded to belong unto religion or the worship of God is proposed unto us, our first consideration of it ought to be in that inquiry which our Lord Jesus Christ made of the Pharisees concerning the baptism of John, "Whence is it? from heaven, or of men?" He distributes all things which come under that plea or pretence into two heads, as unto their original and efficient cause, — namely, "heaven" and "men." And these are not only different and distinct, but so contradictory one unto another, that, as unto any thing wherein religion or the worship of God is concerned, they cannot concur as partial causes of the same effect. What is of men is not from heaven; and what is from heaven is not of men. And hence is his determination concerning both sorts of these things: "Every plant, which my heavenly Father hath not planted, shall be rooted up," Matt. xv. 13.

Designing, therefore, to treat of churches, their *original, nature,* use, and *end,* my first inquiry must be whether they are from heaven or of men, — that is, whether they are of a divine original, having a divine institution, or whether they are an ordinance or creation of men; for their pedigree must be derived from one of these singly. They never concurred in the constitution of any part of divine worship, or any thing that belongs thereunto.

This would seem a case and inquiry of an exceeding easy determination; for the Scripture everywhere makes mention of the church or churches as the ordinances and institutions of God. But such things have fallen out in the world in latter ages as may make men justly question whether we understand the mind of God aright or no in what is spoken of them; at least, if they should allow that the churches so mentioned in the Scripture were of divine appointment, yet it might be highly ques-

Chapter I.

tionable whether those which have since been in the world be not a mere product of the invention and power of men.

1. For many ages, such things alone were proposed unto the world, and imposed on it for *the only church*, as were from hell rather than from heaven; at least from men, and thou none of the best: for all men in these western parts of the world were obliged to believe and profess, on the penalties of eternal and temporal destruction, that the pope of Rome and those depending on him were the only church in the world. If this should be granted, — as it was almost universally in some ages, and in this is earnestly contended for, — there would be a thousand evidences to prove that the institution of churches is not from heaven, but from men. Whether the inventions of men in the mystery of iniquity be to be received again or no, men of secular wisdom and interest may do well to consider; but he must be blind and mad, and accursed in his mind and understanding, who can think of receiving it as from heaven, as a divine institution. But I have treated of this subject in other discourses.

2. The name, pretence, and *presumed power of the church* or churches, have been made and used as the greatest engine for the promoting and satisfying the avarice, sensuality, ambition, and cruelty of men that ever was in the world. Never any thing was found out by men, or Satan himself, so fitted, suited, and framed to fill and satisfy the lusts of multitudes of men, as this of the church hath been, and yet continues to be: for it is so ordered, is of that make, constitution, and use, that corrupt men need desire no more for the attainment of wealth, honour, grandeur, pleasure, all the ends of their lusts, spiritual or carnal, but a share in the government and power of the church; nor hath an interest therein been generally used unto any other ends. All the pride and ambition, all the flagitious lives, in luxury, sensuality, uncleanness, incests, etc., of popes, cardinals, prelates, and their companions, with their hatred unto and oppression of good men, arose from the advantage of their being reputed "the church." To this very day, "the church" here and there, as it is esteemed, is the greatest means of keeping Christian religion in its power and purity out of the world, and a temptation to multitudes of men to prefer the church before religion, and to be obstinate in their oppositions unto it. These things being plain and evident unto wise men who had no share in the conspiracy

nor the benefit of it, how could they think that this church-state was from heaven, and not of men?

3. By "the church" (so esteemed), and in pursuit of its interests, by its authority and power, innumerable multitudes of Christians have been slain or murdered, and the earth soaked with their blood. Two emperors of Germany alone fought above *eighty battles* for and against the pretended power and authority of the church. It hath laid whole countries desolate with fire and sword, turning cities into ashes and villages into a wilderness, by the destruction of their inhabitants. It was the Church which killed, murdered, and burnt innumerable holy persons, for no other reason in the world but because they would not submit their souls, consciences, and practices unto her commands, and be subject unto her in all things. Nor was there any other church conspicuously visible in all these parts of the world; nor was it esteemed lawful once to think that this was not the true church, or that there was or could be any other. For men to believe that this church-state was from heaven, is for them to believe that cruelty, bloodshed, murder, the destruction of mankind, especially of the best, the wisest, and the most holy among them, is the only way to heaven.

4. The *secular, worldly interest* of multitudes lying in this presumptive church and the state of it, they preferred and exalted it above all that is called God, and made the greatest idol of it that ever was in the world; for it was the faith and profession of it, that its authority over the souls and consciences of men is above the authority of the Scriptures, so that they have no authority towards us unless it be given unto them by this church, and that we neither can nor need believe them to be the word of God unless they inform us and command us so to do. This usurpation of divine honour, in putting itself and its authority above that of the Scripture or word of God, discovers full well whence it was. In like manner, those who assumed it unto themselves to be the church, without any other right, title, or pretence unto it, have exalted one amongst them, and with him themselves in their several capacities, above all emperors, kings, and princes, nations and people, trampling on them at their pleasure. Is this church-state from heaven? Is it of divine institution? Is it the heart and centre of Christian religion? Is it that which all men must be subject to on pain of eternal damnation? Who that

knows any thing of Christ or the gospel can entertain such a thought without detestation and abhorrency?

5. This *pretence of the church* is at this day one of the greatest causes of the atheism that the world is filled withal. Men find themselves, they know not how, to belong unto this or that church; they suppose that all the religion that is required of them is no more but what this church suggests unto them; and abhorring, through innumerable prejudices, to inquire whether there be any other ministerial church-state or no, understanding at length the church to be a political combination, for the wealth, power, and dignity of some persons, they cast away all regard of religion, and become professed atheists.

6. Unto this very day, the woful *divisions*, distractions, and endless controversies that are among Christians, with the dangerous consequences and effects of them, do all spring and arise from the churches that are in the world. Some are for the church of Rome, some for the church of England, some for the Greek church, and so of the rest; which, upon an acknowledgment of such a state of them as is usually allowed, cannot but produce wars and tumults among nations, with the oppression of particular persons in all sorts of calamities. In one place men are killed for not owning of one church, and in another for approving of it. Amongst ourselves prisons are filled, and men's goods spoiled, divisions multiplied, and the whole nation endangered, in a severe attempt to cause all Christians to acknowledge that church-state which is set up among us. In brief, these Churches, in the great instance of that of Rome, have been, and are, the scandal of Christian religion, and the greatest cause of most of the evils and villanies which the world hath been replenished withal. And is it any wonder if men question whether they are from heaven or of men.

For my part, I look upon it as one of the greatest mercies that God hath bestowed on any professed Christians in these latter ages, that he hath, by the light and knowledge of his word, disentangled the souls and consciences of any that do believe from all respect and trust unto such churches, discovering the vanity of their pretences and wickedness of their practices; whereby they openly proclaim themselves to be of men, and not from heaven. Not that he hath led them off from a church-state thereby; but by the same word revealed that to them which is pure, simple, humble, holy, and so far from giving occasion unto any of the evils mentioned as that the admittance of it will put an immediate end unto them all. Such shall we find the true and gospel church-state to be in the following description of it. He that comes out of the confusion and disorder of these human (and, as unto some of them, hellish) churches, who is delivered from this "mystery of iniquity," in darkness and confusion, policies and secular contrivances, coming thereon to obtain a view of the true native beauty, glory, and use of evangelical churches, will be thankful for the greatness of his deliverance.

Whereas, therefore, for many ages, the church of Rome, with those claiming under it and depending on it, was esteemed to be the only true church in the world, and nothing was esteemed so highly criminal, — not murder, treason, nor incest, — as to think of or to assert any other church-state, it was impossible that any wise man not utterly infatuated could apprehend a church, any church whatever, to be of divine institution or appointment; for all the evils mentioned, and others innumerable, were not only occasioned by it, but they were effects of it, and inseparable from its state and being. And if any other churches also, which, although the people whereof they consist are of another faith than those of the Roman church, are like unto it in their make and constitution, exercising the right, power, and authority which they claim unto themselves by such ways and means as are plainly of this world and of their own invention, they do leave it highly questionable from whence they are, as such; for it may be made to appear that such Churches, so far as they are such, are obstructive of the sole end of all churches, — which is the edification of them that do believe, — however any that are of them or belong unto them may promote that end by their personal endeavours.

But, notwithstanding all these things, it is most certain that churches are of a divine original, — that they are the ordinance and institution of Christ. I am not yet arrived, in the order of this discourse, to a convenient season of declaring what is the especial nature, use, and end of such churches as are so the institution of God, and so to give a definition of them, which shall be done afterward; but treat only as unto the general notion of a church, and what is signified thereby. These are of God. And in those churches before described, under a corrupt, degenerate estate, three things may be considered:— 1. *What is of man*, without the least pretence unto the appointment or command of God. Such is the very form, fabric, and constitution of the church of Rome, and those that depend thereon or are conformed thereunto. That which it is, that whereby it is what it is, in its kind, government, rule, and end, is all of man, without the least countenance given unto it from any thing of God's institution. This is that which, through a long effectual working of men and Satan, in a mystery of iniquity, it arrived unto. Herewith the saints of God ought to have no compliance, but bear witness against it with their lives, if called thereunto. This in due time the Lord Christ will utterly destroy. 2. Such things as pretend unto a countenance to be given them by *divine institution*, but horribly corrupted. Such are the name of a church and its power, a worship pretended to be religious and divine, an order as to officers and rulers different from the people, with sundry things of the like nature. These things are good in themselves, but as engrossed into a false church-state and worship, corrupt in themselves, they are of men, and to be abhorred of all that seek after the true church of Christ. 3. There is that which is the essence of a true church, — namely, that it be a society of men united for the celebration of divine worship. This, so far as it may be found among them, is to be approved.

But churches, as was said, are of a divine original, and have the warrant of divine authority. The whole Scripture is an account of God's institution of churches, and of his dealing with them.

God laid the foundation of church societies and the necessity of them in the law of nature, by the creation and constitution of it. I speak of churches in general, as they are societies of the human race, one way or other joined and united together for the worship of God. Now, the sole end of the creation of the nature of man was the glory of God, in that worship and obedience which it was fitted and enabled to perform. For that end, and no other, was our nature created, in all its capacities, abilities, and perfections. Neither was man so made merely that every individual should singly and by himself perform this worship, though that also every individual person is obliged unto. Every man alone, and by himself, will not only find himself indigent and wanting supplies of sundry kinds, but also that he is utterly disabled to act sundry faculties and powers of his soul, which by nature he is endued withal. Hence the Lord God said, "It is not good that man should be alone," Gen. ii. 18.

These things, therefore, are evident in themselves: — 1. That God created our nature, or made man, for his *own worship* and service, and fitted the powers and faculties of his soul thereunto. 2. That this nature is so fitted for *society*, so framed for it as its next end, that without it, it cannot act itself according unto what it is empowered unto; and this is the foundation of all order and government in the world among mankind. 3. That by the light of nature this *acting in society* is principally designed unto the worship of God. The power, I say, and necessity of acting in society is given unto our nature for this end principally, that we may thus glorify God in and by the worship which he requires of us. 4. That without the *worship of God in societies* there would be an absolute failure of one principal end of the creation of man; nor would any glory arise unto God from the constitution of his nature, so fitted for society as that it cannot act its own powers without it. 5. All societies are to be regulated, in the light of nature, by such circumstances as whereby they are suited onto their end, for which they may be either too large or too much restrained.

Hence have we the original of churches in the light of nature. Men associating themselves together, or uniting in such societies for the worship of God, which he requires of them, as may enable them unto an orderly performance of it, are a church. And hereunto it is required, — 1. That the persons so uniting are sensible of their duty, and have not lost the knowledge of the end of their creation and being. 2. That they are acquainted with that divine religious worship which God requires of them. The former light and persuasion being lost issues in atheism; and by the loss of this, instead of churches, the generality of mankind have coalesced into idolatrous combinations. 3. That they do retain such innate principles of the light of nature as will guide them in the discharge of their duties in these societies. As, — (1.) That the societies themselves be such as are meet for their end, fit to exercise and express the worship of God in them, not such as whose constitution makes them unfit for any such end; and this gives the natural bounds of churches in all ages, which it is in vain for any man to endeavour an alteration of, as we shall see afterward. (2.) That all things be done decently and in order, in and by these societies. This is a prime dictate of the law of nature, arising from the knowledge of God and ourselves, which hath been wrested into I know not what religious ceremonies of men's invention. (3.) That they be ready to receive all divine revelations with faith and obedience, which shall either appoint the ways of God's worship and prescribe the duties of it, or guide and direct them in its performance, and to regulate their obedience therein. This also is a clear, unquestionable dictate of the light and law of nature, nor can be denied but on the principles of downright atheism.

Farther we need not seek for the divine original of churches, or societies of men fearing God, for the discharge of his public worship, unto his glory and their own eternal benefit, according unto the light and knowledge of his mind and will which he is pleased to communicate unto them.

What concerns the framing and fashioning of churches by arbitrary and artificial combinations, in provinces, nations, and the like, we shall afterward inquire into. This is the assured foundation and general warranty of particular societies and churches, whilst men are continued on the earth; the especial regulation of them by divine revelation will in the next place be considered. And he who is not united with others in some such society, lives in open contradiction unto the law of nature and its light, in the principal instances of it.

1. Whereas the directions given by the light of nature in and unto things concerning the outward worship of God are general only, so as that by them alone it would be very difficult to erect a church-state in good and holy order, God did always from the beginning, by especial revelations and institution, ordain such things as might perfect the conduct of that light unto such a complete order as was accepted with himself. So, first, he appointed a *church-state* for man in innocency, and completed its order by the *sacramental* addition of the two trees, — the one of life, the other of the knowledge of good and evil.

2. That before the coming of Christ, — who was to perfect and complete all divine revelations, and state all things belonging unto the house and worship of God, so as never to admit of the least change or alteration, — this church-state, as unto outward order, rites of worship, ways and manner of the administration of things sacred, with its bounds and limits, was changeable, and variously changed. The most eminent change it received was in the giving of the law, which fixed its state unalterably unto the coming of Christ, Mal. iv. 4–6.

3. That it was *God himself alone* who made all these alterations and changes; nor would he, nor did he, ever allow that the wills, wisdom, or authority of men should prescribe rules or measures unto his worship in any thing, Heb. iii. 1–6.

4. That the foundation of every church-state that is accepted with God is in an express covenant with him, that they receive and enter into who are to be admitted into that state. A church not founded in a covenant with God is not from heaven, but of men. Hereof we shall treat more at large, as I suppose, afterward. See it exemplified, Exod. xxiv.

5. There is no good in, there is no benefit to be obtained by, any church-state whatever, unless we enter into it and observe it by *an act of obedience*, with immediate respect unto the authority of Christ, by whom it is appointed and the observation of it prescribed unto us, Matt. xxviii. 18–20. Hence, —

6. Unless men, by their voluntary choice and consent, out of a sense of their duty unto the authority of Christ in his institutions, do enter into a church-state, they cannot, by any other ways or means, be so framed into it as to find acceptance with God therein, 2 Cor. viii. 5. And the interpositions that are made by custom, tradition, the institutions and ordinances of men, between the consciences of them who belong or would belong unto such a state, and the immediate authority of God, are highly obstructive of this divine order and all the benefits of it;[1] for hence it is come to pass that most men know neither how nor whereby they come to be members of this or that church, but only on this ground, that they were born where it did prevail and was accepted.

---

[1] See "Discourse concerning Evangelical Love," p. 88 of this volume.

CHAPTER II.

The especial original of the evangelical church-state.

OUR principal concernment at present is in the evangelical church-state, or the state of churches under the New Testament; for this is that about which there are many great and fierce contests among Christians, and those attended with pernicious consequents and effects. What is the original, what is the nature, what is the use and power, what is the end of the churches, or any church, what is the duty of men in it and towards it, is the subject of various contests, and the principal occasion of all the distractions that are at this day in the Christian world; for the greatest part of those who judge themselves obliged to take care and order about these things having interwoven their own secular interests and advantages into such a church-state as is meet and suited to preserve and promote them, supposing πορισμὸν εἶναι τὴν εὐσέβειαν, or that religion may be made a trade for outward advantage, they do openly seek the destruction of all those who will not comply with that church form and order that they have framed unto themselves. Moreover, from men's various conceptions and suitable practices about this church-state is advantage and occasion taken to charge each other with schism, and all sorts of evils which are supposed to ensue thereon. Wherefore, although I design all possible brevity, and only to declare those principles of truth wherein we may safely repose our faith and practice, avoiding as much as possibly I can, and the subject will allow, the handling of those things in a way of controversy with others, yet somewhat more than ordinary diligence is required unto the true stating of this important concernment of our religion. And that which we shall first inquire into is the special original and authoritative constitution of this church-state. Wherefore, —

1. The church-state of the New Testament doth not less relate unto, and receive force from, *the light or law of nature*, than

any other state of the church whatever. Herein, as unto its general nature, its foundation is laid. What that directs unto may receive new enforcements by revelation, but changed, or altered, or abolished, it cannot be. Wherefore, there is no need of any new express institution of what is required by that light and law in all churches and societies for the worship of God, but only an application of it unto present occasions and the present state of the church, which hath been various. And it is merely from a spirit of contention that some call on us or others to produce express testimony or institution for every circumstance in the practice of religious duties in the church, and on a supposed failure herein, do conclude that they have power themselves to institute and ordain such ceremonies as they think meet, under a pretence of their being circumstances of worship; for as the directive light of nature is sufficient to guide us in these things, so the obligation of the church unto it makes all stated additions to be useless, as on other accounts they are noxious. Such things as these are:— the times and seasons of church assemblies; the order and decency wherein all things are to be transacted in them; the bounding of them as unto the number of their members, and places of habitation, so as to answer the ends of their institution; the multiplication of churches when the number of believers exceeds the proportion capable of edification in such societies; what especial advantages are to be made use of in the order and worship of the church, such as are methods in preaching, translations and tunes of psalms in singing, continuance in public duties, and the like. The things themselves being divinely instituted, are capable of such general directions in and by the light of nature as may, with ordinary Christian prudence, be on all occasions applied unto the use and practice of the church. To forsake these directions, and instead of them to invent ways, modes, forms, and ceremonies of our own, which the things whereunto they are applied and made use of in do no way call for, require, or own (as it is with all humanly-invented stated ceremonies); and thereon, by laws and canons, to determine their precise observation at all times and seasons to be one and the same, which is contrary to the very nature of the circumstances of such acts and duties as they are applied unto, — their use, in the meantime, unto the general end of edification, being as indemonstrable as their necessity unto the duties whereunto they are annexed is also, — is that which hath no warranty either from divine authority or Christian prudence.

This respect of the gospel church-state unto the light of nature the apostle demonstrates, in his frequent appeals unto it in things that belong unto church-order, 1 Cor. vii. 29, 33, 37, ix. 7, xi. 14–16, xiv. 8–11, 32, 33, 40; and the like is done in sundry other places. And the reasons of it are evident.

2. But such is the especial nature and condition of the evangelical church-state; such the relation of it unto the person and mediation of Jesus Christ, with all things thereon depending; such the nature of that especial honour and glory which God designs unto himself therein (things that the light of nature can give no guidance unto nor direction about); and, moreover, so different and distant from all that was before ordained in any other church-state are the ways, means, and duties of divine worship prescribed in it, — that it must have a *peculiar, divine institution* of its own, to evidence that it is from heaven, and not from men. The present state of the church under the New Testament the apostle calls τελείωσις, Heb. vii. 11, — its perfection, its consummation, that perfect state which God designed unto it in this world. And he denies that it could be brought into that state by the law, or any of the divine institutions that belonged thereunto, chap. vii. 19, ix. 9, x. 1. And we need go no farther, we need no other argument to prove that the gospel church-state, as unto its especial nature, is founded in a peculiar divine institution; for it hath a τελείωσις, a perfect consummate state, which the law could not bring it unto, though itself, its ordinances of worship, its rule and policy, were all of divine institution. And herein doth its excellency and preference above the legal church-state consist, as the apostle proves at large. To suppose that this should be given unto it any other way but by divine authority in its institution, is to advance the wisdom and authority of men above those of God, and to render the gospel church-state a machine to be moved up and down at pleasure, to be new moulded or shaped according unto occasions, or to be turned unto any interest, like the wings of a mill unto the wind.

All the dignity, honour, and perfection of the state of the church under the Old Testament depended solely hereon, that it was, in the whole and all the particulars of it, of divine institution. Hence it was "glorious," that is, very excellent, as the apostle declares, 2 Cor. iii. And if the church-state of the New

Testament have not the same original, it must be esteemed to have a greater glory given unto it by the hand of men than the other had, in that it was instituted by God himself; for a greater glory it hath, as the apostle testifieth. Neither can any man, nor dareth any man alive, to give any instance in particular wherein there is the least defect in the being, constitution, rule, and government of the gospel church-state, for want of divine institution, so as that it should be necessary to make a supply thereof by the wisdom and authority of men. But these things will be more fully spoken unto, after we have declared who it is who hath divinely instituted this church-state.

3. The name of the church under the New Testament is capable of a threefold application, or it is taken in a threefold notion; as, — (1.) For the *catholic invisible church*, or society of elect believers in the whole world, really related by faith in him unto the Lord Jesus Christ as their mystical head; (2.) For the whole *number of visible professors* in the whole world, who, by baptism, and the outward profession of the gospel, and obedience unto Christ, are distinguished from the rest of the world; and, — (3.) For such a state as wherein *the worship of God is to be celebrated* in the way and manner by him appointed, and which is to be ruled by the power which he gives it, and according to the discipline which he hath ordained. Of the nature of the church under these distinct notions, with our relation unto either or all of them, and the duties required of us thereon, I have treated fully in my discourse of Evangelical Love, Church Peace, and Unity; and thither I must remit the reader. It is the church in the latter sense alone whose original we now inquire after; and I say, —

4. The original of this church-state is directly, immediately, and solely from *Jesus Christ*; he alone is the author, contriver, and institutor of it. When I say it is immediately and solely from him, I do not intend that in and by his own person, or in his personal ministry here in the earth, he did absolutely and completely finish this state, exclusively unto the ministry of any others that he was pleased to make use of therein; for as he took it on himself as his own work to build his church, and that upon himself as its foundation, so he employed his apostles to act under him and from him, in the carrying on that work unto perfection. But what was done by them is esteemed to be done all by himself. For, —

(1.) It was immediately from him that they received *revelations of* what did belong unto this church-state, and what was to be prescribed therein. They never did, neither jointly nor severally, once endeavour, in their own wisdom, or from their own invention, or by their own authority, to add or put into this church-state, as of perpetual use, and belonging unto it as such, either less or more, any one thing greater or less whatever. It is true, they gave their advice in sundry cases of present emergencies, in and about church-affairs; they gave direction for the due and orderly practice of what was revealed unto them, and exercised authority both as unto the ordination of officers, and the rejection of obstinate sinners from the society of all the churches; — but to invent, contrive, institute, or appoint any thing in the church and its state, which they had not by immediate revelation from Christ, they never attempted it nor went about it. And unto this rule of proceeding they were precisely obliged by the express words of their commission, Matt. xxviii. 19, 20. This, I say, is so plainly included in the tenor of their commission, and so evident from all that is divinely recorded of their practice, that it will admit of no sober contradiction. In what others think it meet to do in this kind, we are not concerned.

(2.) The *authority* whereby they acted in the institution of the church in its order, whereon the consciences of all believers were obliged to submit thereunto, and to comply with it in a way of obedience, was the authority of Christ himself, acted in them and by them, 2 Cor. i. 24, iv. 5. They everywhere disclaim any such power and authority in themselves. They pleaded that they were only stewards and ministers; not lords of the faith or obedience of the church, but helpers of its joy; yea, the servants of all the churches for Christ's sake. And hereon it follows, that what is recorded of their practice, in their institution, ordering, or disposing of any thing in the church that was to be of an abiding continuance, hath in it the obliging power of the authority of Christ himself. Wherefore, if the distinction that some make concerning the apostles, — namely, that they are to be considered as apostles, or as church-governors, — should be allowed, as it is liable to just exceptions, yet would no advantage accrue thereby unto what is pretended from it; for as what they did, appointed, and ordered in the church for its constant observation, as apostles, they did it by immediate revelation from Christ, and in his name and authority, so what, in distinction from hence, as church-governors, they did or ordered, they did it only by a due application unto present occasions of what they had received by revelation. But as they were apostles, Christ sent them, as his Father sent him; and he was so sent of the Father as that he did "stand and feed in the strength of the LORD, in the majesty of the name of the LORD his God," Mic. v. 4. So did they feed the sheep of Christ in his strength, and in the authority or majesty of his name.

5. Christ, therefore, alone is *the author of the gospel church-state*. And because this is the only foundation of our faith and obedience, as unto all that we are to believe, do, and practice, by virtue of that church-state, or in order thereunto, the Scripture doth not only plainly affirm it, but also declares the grounds of it, why it must be so, and whence it is so, as also wherein his doing of it doth consist.

Three things, amongst others, are eminently necessary in and unto him who is to constitute this church-state, with all that belongs thereunto; and as the Scripture doth eminently and expressly ascribe them all unto Christ, so no man, nor all the men of the world, can have any such interest in them as to render them meet for this work, or any part of it:—

(1.) The first of these is *right* and *title*. He who institutes this church-state must have a right and title to dispose of all men, in all their spiritual and eternal concernments, as seemeth good unto him; for unto this church-state, namely, as it is purely evangelical, no man is obliged by the law of nature, nor hath any creature power to dispose of him into a condition whereon all his concernments, spiritual and eternal, shall depend. This right and title to the sovereign disposal of mankind, or of his church, Christ hath alone, and that upon a treble account:— [1.] Of *donation* from the Father: he appointed him the "heir of all things," Heb. i. 2, 3. He gave him "power over all flesh," John xvii. 2. Especially he hath given unto him and put into his absolute disposal all those who are to be his church, verse 6. [2.] By virtue of *purchase*: he hath by the price of his most precious blood purchased them unto his own power and disposal. He "purchased his church with his own blood," Acts xx. 28; which the apostle makes the ground of that care which ought to be had of it. And this is pleaded as a sufficient reason why we should be wholly at his disposal only, and be free from any imposition of men in things spiritual: 1 Cor. vii. 23, "Ye are bought with a price; be ye not the servants of men." The purchase of this right and title was one great end of the principal mediatory acts of Christ: Rom. xiv. 9, 10, "For to this end," etc. [3.] Of *conquest*: for all those who were thus to be disposed by him were both under the power of his enemies, and were themselves enemies unto him in their minds. He could not, therefore, have a sovereign right unto their disposal but by a double conquest; — namely, first of their enemies, by his power; and then of themselves by his word, his Spirit, and his grace. And this twofold conquest of his is fully described in the Scripture.

Whereas, therefore, there is a disposal of the persons that are to belong unto this church-state, as unto their souls, consciences, and all the eternal concernments of them, by an indispensable moral obligation to a compliance therewithal, until men can manifest that they have such a right and title over others, and that either by the especial grant and donation of God the Father, or a purchase that they have made of them unto themselves, or conquest, they are not to be esteemed to have either right or title to institute any thing that belongs unto this church-state. And it is in vain pretended (as we shall see more afterward) that Christ, indeed, hath appointed this church-state in general, but that he hath appointed no particular form of churches or their rule, but left that unto the discretion and authority of men as they think meet, when they have outward power for their warranty. But if by these particular appointments and framings of churches with their order, men are disposed of, as unto their spiritual concernments, beyond the obligation of the light of nature or the moral law, we must yet inquire who gave them this right and title to make this disposal of them.

(2.) *Authority*. As right and title respect the persons of men to be reduced into a new form of government so authority respects the rules, laws, orders, and statutes to be made, prescribed, and established, whereby the privileges of this new society are conveyed, and the duties of it enjoined, unto all that are taken into it. Earthly potentates, who will dispose of men into a state and government absolutely new unto them, as unto all their temporal concernments of life, liberty, inheritances, and possessions, so as that they shall hold all of ahem in dependence on and according unto the rules and laws of their new government and kingdom, must have these two things; — namely, right and title unto the persons of men, which they have by conquest, or an absolute resignation of all their interests and concerns into their disposal; and authority, thereon to constitute what order, what kind of state, rule, and government, they please. Without these they will quickly find their endeavours and undertakings frustrate. The gospel church-state in the nature of it, and in all the laws and constitution of it, is absolutely new, whereunto all the world are naturally foreigners and strangers. As they have no right unto it as it containeth privileges, so they have no obligation unto it as it prescribes duties; wherefore, there is need of both these; — right, as unto the persons of men; and authority, as unto the laws and constitution of the church, unto the framing of it. And until men can pretend unto these things, both unto this right and authority with respect unto all the spiritual and eternal concernments of the souls of others, they may do well to consider how dangerous it is to invade the right and inheritance of Christ, and leave hunting after an interest of power in the framing or forming evangelical churches, or making of laws for their rule and government.

This authority is not only ascribed unto Jesus Christ in the Scripture, but it is *enclosed* unto him, so as that no other can have any interest in it. See Matt. xxviii. 18; Rev. iii. 7; Isa. ix. 6, 7. By virtue hereof he is the only "lawgiver" of the church, James iv. 12; Isa. xxxiii. 22. There is, indeed, a derivation of power and authority from him unto others, but it extends itself no farther, save only that they shall direct, teach, and command those whom he sends them unto to do and observe what he hath commanded, Matt. xxviii. 20. "He builds his own house," and he is "over his own house," Heb. iii. 3–6. He both constitutes its state, and gives laws for its rule.

The disorder, the confusion, the turning of the kingdom of Christ upside down, which have ensued upon the usurpation of men, taking upon them a legislative power in and over the church, cannot easily be declared; for upon a slight pretence, no way suited or serviceable unto their ends, — of the advice given and determination made by the apostles with the elders and brethren of the church of Jerusalem, in a temporary constitution about the use of Christian liberty, — the bishops of the fourth and fifth centuries took upon themselves power to make laws, canons, and constitutions for the ordering of the government and the rule of the church, bringing in many new institutions on a pretence of the same authority. Neither did others who followed them cease to build on their sandy foundation, until the whole frame of the church-state was altered, a new law made for its government, and a new Christ or antichrist assumed in the head of its rule by that law; for all this pretended authority of making laws and constitutions for the government of the church issued in that sink of abominations which they call the canon-law. Let any man but of a tolerable understanding, and freed from infatuating prejudices, but read the representation that is made of the gospel church-state, its order, rule, and government, in the Scripture on the one hand, and what representation is made on the other of a church-state, its order, rule, and government, in the canon-law, — the only effect of men's assuming to themselves a legislative power with respect unto the church of Christ, — if he doth not pronounce them to be contrary as light and darkness, and that by the latter the former is utterly destroyed and taken away, I shall never trust to the use of men's reason or their honesty any more.

This authority was first usurped by *synods*, or *councils* of *bishops*. Of what use they were at any time to declare and give testimony unto any article of the faith which in their days was opposed by heretics, I shall not now inquire; but as unto the exercise of the authority claimed by them to make laws and canons for the rule and government of the church, it is to be bewailed there should be such a monument left of their weakness, ambition, self-interest, and folly, as there is in what remaineth of their Constitutions. Their whole endeavour in this kind was at best but the building of wood, hay, and stubble on the foundation, in whose consumption they shall suffer loss, although they be saved themselves. But in making of laws to bind the whole church, — in and about things useless and trivial, no way belonging to the religion taught us by Jesus Christ; in and for the establishment or increase of their own power, jurisdiction, authority, and rule, with the extent and bounds of their several dominions; in and for the constitution of new frames and states of churches, and new ways of the government of them; in the appointment of new modes, rites, and ceremonies of divine worship; with the confusions that ensued thereon, in mutual animosities, fightings, divisions, schisms, and anathematisms, to the horrible scandal of Christian religion, — they ceased not until they had utterly destroyed all the order, rule, and government of the church of Christ, yea, the very nature of it, and introduced into its room a carnal, worldly church-state and rule, suited unto the interests of covetous, ambitious, and tyrannical prelates. The most of them, indeed, knew not for whom they wrought in providing materials for that Babel, which, by a hidden skill in a mystery of iniquity, was raised out of their provisions; for after they were hewed and carved, shaped, formed, and gilded, the pope appeared in the head of it, as it were, with those words of his mouth: "Is not this great Babylon, that I have built for the house of the kingdom by the might of my power, and for the honour of my majesty," This was the fatal event of men's invading the right of Christ, and claiming an interest in authority to give laws to the church. This, therefore, is absolutely denied by us, — namely, that any men, under what pretence or name soever, have any right or authority to constitute any new frame or order of the church, to make any laws of their own for its rule or government that should oblige the disciples of Christ in point of conscience unto their observation. That there is nothing in this assertion that should in the least impeach the power of magistrates, with reference unto the outward, civil, and political concerns of the church, or the public profession of religion within their territories, — nothing that should take off from the just authority of the lawful guides of the church, in ordering, appointing, and commanding the observation of all things in them, according to the mind of Christ, shall be afterward declared. In these things "the LORD is our judge, the LORD is our statute-maker, the LORD is our king; he will save us."

It is, then, but weakly pleaded, "That seeing the magistrate can appoint or command nothing in religion that God hath forbidden, nor is there any need that he should appoint or command what God hath already appointed and commanded; if so be he may not by law command Such things in the church as before were neither commanded nor forbidden, but indifferent, which are the proper field of his ecclesiastical legislative power, then hath he no power nor authority about religion at all;" — that is, if he hath not the same and a co-ordinate power with God or Christ, he hath none at all! One of the best arguments that can be used for the power of the magistrate in things ecclesiastical is taken from the approved example of the good kings under the Old Testament. But they thought it honour enough unto them, and their duty, to see and take care that the things which God had appointed and ordained should be diligently observed by all those concerned therein, both priests and people, and to destroy what God had forbidden. To appoint any thing of themselves, to make that necessary in the church and the worship thereof which God had not made so, they never esteemed it to be in their power, or to belong unto their duty. When they did any thing of that nature, and thereby made any additions unto the outward warship of God not before commanded, they did it by immediate revelation from God, and so by divine authority, 1 Chron. xxviii. 19. And it is left as a brand on those that were wicked, not only that they commanded and made "statutes" for the observation of what God had forbidden, Mic. vi. 16, but also that they commanded and appointed *what God had not appointed*, 1 Kings xii. 32, 33. And it will be found at last to be honour enough to the greatest potentate under heaven to take care that what Christ hath appointed in his church and worship be observed, without claiming a power like unto that of the Most High, to give laws unto the church for the observation of things found out and invented by themselves or other men.

Of the same nature is the other part of their plea against this denial of a legislative power in men with respect unto the constitution of the evangelical church-state, or the ordaining of any thing to be observed in it that Christ hath not appointed: for it is said, "That if this be allowed, as all the dignity, power, and honour of the governors of the church will be rejected or despised, so all manner of confusion and disorder will be brought into the church itself; for how can it otherwise be, when all power of law-making, in the preservation of the dignity of the rulers and order of the church, is taken away? And therefore we see it was the wisdom of the church in former ages that all the principal laws and canons that they made, in their councils or otherwise, were designed unto the exaltation and preservation of the dignity of church-rulers; wherefore, take this power away, and you will bring in all confusion into the church."

Ans. 1. They do not, in my judgment, sufficiently think of whom and of what they speak who plead after this manner; for the substance of the plea is, that if the church have its whole frame, constitution, order, rule, and government from Christ alone, though men should faithfully discharge their duty in doing and observing all what he hath commanded, there would be nothing in it but disorder and confusion. Whether this becomes that reverence which we ought to have of him, or be suited unto that faithfulness and wisdom which is particularly ascribed unto him in the constitution and ordering of his church, is not hard to determine, and the truth of it shall be afterward demonstrated.

Ans. 2. As unto the dignity and honour of the rulers of the church, the subject of so many ecclesiastical laws, they are, in the first place, to be desired themselves to remember the example of Christ himself in his personal ministry here on earth: Matt. xx. 28, "Even as the Son of man came not to be ministered unto, but to minister, and to give his life a ransom for many;" — with the rule prescribed by him thereon, verses 25–27, "But Jesus called them unto him, and said, Ye know that the princes of the Gentiles exercise dominion over them, and they that are great exercise authority upon them. But it shall not be so among you: but whosoever shall be great among you, let him be your minister; and whosoever will be chief among you, let him be your servant;" — with the occasion of the instruction given therein unto his apostles, verse 24, "And when the ten heard it, they were moved with indignation against the two brethren;" — as also the injunction given them by the apostle Peter, on whom, for their own advantage, some would fasten a monarchy over the whole church, 1 Pet. v. 2, 3, "Feed the flock of God which is among you, taking the oversight thereof, not by constraint, but willingly; not for filthy lucre, but of a ready mind; neither as being lords over God's heritage, but being ensamples to the flock;" — and the blessed expressions of the apostolical state by Paul, 1 Cor. iv. 1, "Let a man so account of us, as of the ministers of Christ, and stewards of the mysteries of God;" 2 Cor. i. 24, "Not for that we have dominion over your faith, but are helpers of your joy;" chap. iv. 5, "For we preach not ourselves, but Christ Jesus the Lord, and ourselves your servants for Jesus' sake." It may prepare their minds for the right management of that honour which is their due. For, secondly, there is, in and by the constitution of Christ and his express laws, an honour and respect due unto those church-guides which he hath appointed, abiding in the duties which he requireth. If men had not been weary of apostolical simplicity and humility, if they could have contented themselves with the honour and dignity annexed unto their office and work by Christ himself, they had never entertained pleasing dreams of thrones, pre-eminencies, chief sees, secular grandeur and power, nor framed so many laws and canons about these things, turning the whole rule of the church into a worldly empire. For such it was, that as of all the popes which ever dwelt at Rome, there was never any pretended or acted a greater zeal for the rule and government of the church, by the laws and canons that it had made for that end, than Gregory VII., so if ever there were any antichrist in the world (as there are many antichrists) he was one. His Luciferian pride; his trampling on all Christian kings and potentates; his horrible tyranny over the consciences of all Christians; his abominable dictates asserting of his own god-like sovereignty; his requiring all men, on the pain of damnation, to be sinful subjects to God and Peter (that is, himself), which his own acts and epistles are filled withal, — do manifest both who and what he was. Unto that issue did this power of law or canon making, for the honour and dignity of church rulers, at length arrive.

Ans. 3. Let the constitution of the church by Jesus Christ abide and remain, — let the laws for its rule, government, and worship, which he hath recorded in the Scripture, be diligently observed by them whose duty it is to take care about them, both to observe them themselves and to teach others so to do, — and we know full well there will be no occasion given or left unto the least confusion or disorder in the church. But if men will be froward, and, because they may not make laws themselves or keep the statutes made by others, will neglect the due observation and execution of what Christ hath ordained; or will deny that we may and ought, in and for the due observation of his laws, to make use of the inbred light of nature and rules of common prudence (the use and exercise of both which are included and enjoined in the commands of Christ, in that he requires a compliance with them in the way of obedience, which we cannot perform without them), — I know of no relief against the perpetuity of our differences about these things. But after so much scorn and contempt hath been cast upon that principle, that it is not lawful to observe any thing in the rule of the church or divine worship, in a constant way, by virtue of any human canons or laws, that is not prescribed in the Scripture, if we could prevail with men to give us one single instance, which they would abide by, wherein the rules and institutions of Christ are so defective as that, without their canonical additions, order cannot be observed in the church, nor the worship of God be duly performed, it shall be diligently attended unto.

Allow the general rules given us in Scripture for church order and worship to be applied unto all proper occasions and circumstances, with particular, positive, divine precepts; allow, also, that the apostles, in what they did and acted in the constitution and ordering of the churches and their worship, did and acted it in the name and by the authority of Christ; as also that there needs no other means of affecting and obliging our consciences in these things, but only that the mind and will of Christ be intimated and made known unto us, though not in the form of a law given and promulgated, which, I suppose, no men of sober minds or principles can disallow; and then give an instance of such a deficiency as that mentioned in the institutions of Christ, and the whole difference in this matter will be rightly stated, and not else. But to return from this digression.

The Scripture doth not only ascribe this authority unto Christ alone, but it giveth instances of his use and exercise thereof; which comprise all that is necessary unto the constitution and ordering of his churches and the worship of them. (1.) He *buildeth* his own *house*, Heb. iii. 3. (2.) He *appointeth offices* for rule in his churches, and officers, 1 Cor. xii. 5; Rom. xii. 6–8. (3.) He gives *gifts* for the administrations of the church, Eph. iv. 8, 11–13; 1 Cor. xi. 12. (4.) He gives *power and authority* unto them that are to minister and rule in the church, etc.; which things must be afterward spoken unto.

(3.) As unto this constitution of the gospel church-state, the Scripture assigneth, in an especial manner, *faithfulness* unto the Lord Christ, Heb. iii. 2–6. This power is originally in God himself; it belongs unto him alone, as the great sovereign of all his creatures. Unto Christ, as mediator, it was given by the Father, and the whole of it intrusted with him. Hence it follows, that in the execution of it he hath respect unto the mind and wilt of God, as unto what he would have done and ordered, with respect whereunto this power was committed unto him. And here his faithfulness takes place, exerted in the revelation of the whole mind of God in this matter, instituting, appointing, and commanding all that God would have so ordained, and nothing else. And what can *any man do that cometh after the King*?

Hereunto there is added, on the same account, the consideration of his wisdom, his love, and care for the good of his church; which in him were ineffable and inimitable. By all these things was he fitted for his office and the work that was reserved for him, so as that he might in all things have the pre-eminence. And this was to make the last and only full, perfect, complete revelation of the mind and will of God, as unto the state, order, faith, obedience, and worship of the church. There was no perfection in any of these things until he took this work in hand; wherefore, it may justly be supposed that he hath so perfectly stated and established all things concerning his churches and worship therein, being the last divine hand that was to be put to this work, and this his hand, Heb. i. 2, 3, that whatever is capable of a law or a constitution for the use of the church at all times, or is needful for his disciples to observe, is revealed, declared, and established by him. And in this persuasion I shall abide, until I see better fruits and effects of the interposition of the wisdom and authority of men, unto the same ends which he designed, than as yet I have been able, in any age, to observe.

The substance of the things pleaded may, for the greater evidence of their truth, be reduced unto the ensuing heads or propositions:—

First. *Every church-state that hath an especial institution of its own, giving [it] its especial kind*, supposeth and hath respect unto the law and light of nature, requiring and directing in general those things which belong unto the being, order, and preservation of such societies as that is. That there ought to be societies wherein men voluntarily join together for the solemn performance of divine worship and joint walking in obedience before God; that these societies ought to use such means for their own peace and order as the light of nature directs unto; that where many have a common interest they ought to consult in common for the due management of it, with other things of the like importance, are evident dictates of this light and law. Now, whatever church-state may be superinduced by divine institution, yet this light and law, in all their evident dictates, continue their Obliging power in and over the minds of men, and must do so eternally. Wherefore, things that belong hereunto need no new institution in any church-state whatever. But yet, —

Secondly. Whatever is required by the *light of nature* in such societies as churches, as useful unto their order, and conducing unto their end, is *a divine institution*. The Lord Christ, in the institution of gospel churches, their state, order, rule, and worship, doth not require of his disciples that in their observance of his appointments they should cease to be men, or forego the use and exercise of their rational abilities, according to the rule of that exercise, which is the light of nature. Yea, because the rules and directions are in this case to be applied unto things spiritual and of mere revelation, he giveth wisdom, prudence, and understanding, to make that application in a due manner, unto those to whom the guidance and rule of the church is committed. Wherefore, as unto all things which the light of nature directs us unto, with respect unto the observation of the duties prescribed by Christ in and unto the church, we need no other institution but that of the use of the especial spiritual wisdom and prudence which the Lord Christ gives unto his church for that end.

Thirdly. There are in the Scripture *general rules* directing us, in the application of natural light, unto such a determination of all circumstances, in the acts of church rule and worship, as are sufficient for their performance "decently and in order." Wherefore, as was said before, it is utterly in vain and useless to demand express institution of all the circumstances belonging unto the government, order, rule, and worship of the church, or for the due improvement of things in themselves indifferent unto its edification, as occasion shall require; nor are they capable to be any otherwise stated, but as they lie in the light of nature and spiritual prudence, directed by general rules of Scripture.

These things being premised, our principal assertion is, — *That Christ alone is the author, institutor, and appointer, in a way of authority and legislation, of the gospel church-state, its order, rule, and worship, with all things constantly and perpetually belonging thereunto, or necessary to be observed therein.* What is not so is of men, and not from heaven. This is that which we have proved in general, and shall farther particularly confirm in our progress. Hence, —

6. There is no spiritual use nor benefit of any church-state, nor of anything therein performed, but what, on the part of men, consists in *acts of obedience unto the authority of Christ*. If, in any thing we do of this nature, we cannot answer that inquiry which God directs in this case to be made, namely, "Why we do this or that thing," Exod. xii. 25–27, with this, "That it is because Christ hath required it of us," we do not acknowledge him the Lord over his own house, nor hear him as the Son. Nor is there any act of power to be put forth in the rule of the church, but in

them by whom it is exerted it is an act of obedience unto Christ, or it is a mere usurpation. All church-power is nothing but a faculty or ability to obey the commands of Christ in such a way and manner as he hath appointed; for it is his constitution that the administration of his solemn worship in the church, and the rule of it, as unto the observance of his commands, should be committed unto some persons set apart unto that end, according unto his appointment. This is all their authority, all that they have of order or jurisdiction, or by any other ways whereby they are pleased to express it. And where there is any gospel administration, any act of rule or government in the church, which those that perform do not give an evidence that they do it in obedience unto Christ, it is null, as unto any obligation on the consciences of his disciples. The neglect hereof in the world, — wherein many, in the exercise of church-discipline or any acts that belong unto the rule of it, think of nothing but their own offices, whereunto such powers are annexed, by human laws and canons, as enable them to act in their own names, without designing obedience unto Christ in all that they do, or to make a just representation of his authority, wisdom, and love thereby, — is ruinous unto church order and rule.

7. There is no *legislative power in* and over the church, as unto its form, order, and worship, left unto any of the sons of men, under any qualification whatever; for, —

(1.) There are none of them who have an interest in those *rights*, qualifications, and endowments, which are necessary unto an investiture into such a legislative power; for what was given and granted unto Christ himself unto this end, that he might be the lawgiver of the church, must be found also in them who pretend unto any interest therein. Have they, any of them, a right and title unto a disposal of the persons of believers in what way they please, as unto their spiritual and eternal concernments? Have they sovereign authority over all things, to change their moral nature, to give them new uses and significations, to make things necessary that in themselves are indifferent, and to order all those things by sovereign authority in laws obliging the consciences of men? And the like may be said of his personal qualifications, of faithfulness, wisdom, love, and care, which are ascribed unto him in this work of giving laws unto his churches, as he was the Lord over his own house.

(2.) The *event* of the assumption of this legislative power, under the best pretence that can be given unto it, — namely, in councils or great assemblies of bishops and prelates, — sufficiently demonstrates how dangerous a thing it is for any man to be engaged in; for it issued at length in such a constitution of churches, and such laws for the government of them, as exalted the canon law into the room of the Scripture, and utterly destroyed the true nature of the church of Christ, and all the discipline required therein.

(3.) Such an *assumption is* derogatory unto the glory of Christ, especially as unto his faithfulness in and over the house of God, wherein he is compared unto and preferred above Moses, Heb. iii. 3–6. Now, the faithfulness of Moses consisted in this, that he did and appointed all things according to the pattern showed him in the mount; that is, all whatever it was the will of God to be revealed and appointed for the constitution, order, rule, and worship of his church, and nothing else. But it was the will of God that there should be all those things in the gospel church-state also, or else why do men contend about them? And if this were the will of God, if they were not all revealed, appointed, prescribed, legalized by Christ, where is his faithfulness in answer to that of Moses? But no instance can be given of any defect in his institutions, that needs any supplement to be made by the best of men, as unto the end of constituting a church-state, order, and rule, with rites of worship in particular.

(4.) How it is derogatory unto the glory of the Scripture, as unto its *perfection*, shall be elsewhere declared.

8. There is no more required to give authority, obliging the consciences of all that do believe, unto any institution, or observation of duty, or acts of rule in the church, but only that it is made evident in the Scripture to be *the mind and will of Christ*. It is not necessary that every thing of this nature should be given out unto us in form of a law or precise command, in express words. It is the mind and will of Christ that immediately affects the consciences of believers unto obedience, by what way or means soever the knowledge of it be communicated unto them in the Scripture, either by express words, or by just consequence from what is so expressed. Wherefore, —

9. The example and practice of the apostles in the erection of churches, in the appointment of officers and rulers in them,

in directions given for their walking, order, administration of censures, and all other holy things, are *a sufficient indication* of the mind and will of Christ about them. We do not say that in themselves they are institutions and appointments, but they infallibly declare what is so, or the mind of Christ concerning those things. Nor can this be questioned without a denial of their infallibility, faithfulness, and divine authority.

10. The assertion of some, that *the apostles took their pattern for the state and rule of the churches, and as unto divers rites of worship, from the synagogues of the Jews, their institutions, orders, and rules*, not those appointed by Moses, but such as themselves had found out and ordained, is both temerarious and untrue. In the pursuit of such bold conjectures, one[2] of late hath affirmed that Moses took most of his laws and ceremonies from the Egyptians, whereas it is much more likely that many of them were given on purpose to alienate the people by prohibitions from any compliance with the Egyptians, or any other nation; whereof Maimonides, in his "Moreh Nevochim," gives us sundry instances. This assertion, I say, is rash and false; for, — (1.) As unto the instances given for its confirmation, who shall assure

---

2   It was not till five years after the publication of this work that Dr Spencer's celebrated work, "De Legibus Hebræorum Ritualibus," appeared, in which he contends that the Hebrew ritual had been borrowed from the religious ceremonies of the Egyptians, and accommodated by Moses to the purposes of divine revelation. It is impossible, therefore, that Owen can allude to this work, although, from the wide-spread influence it exerted on theological literature in this country and abroad, it has been named as one of the causes that gave birth and impulse to neological speculation. Mr Orme ("Biblioth. Biblic.") affirms that the hypothesis had been already borrowed from Maimonides, and warmly urged by Sir John Marsham in his "Canon Chronicus Ægyptiacus," published in 1672; and perhaps Dr Owen refers to this author. In a learned treatise, however, on the "Urim and Thummim," published by Spencer in 1669, the same opinion is maintained, and the allusion of our author may after all be to Spencer. The views of the latter as to the Egyptian origin of the Urim and Thummim had been already propounded by Le Clerc; and Grotius had long before committed himself to the notion of Maimonides, that the Hebrew rites had been copied from Egypt. Witsius and Shuckford have distinguished themselves in the refutation of this hypothesis. — Ed.

us that they were then in use and practice in the synagogues when the apostles gave rules unto the churches of the New Testament? We have no record of theirs, not one word in all the world, of what was their way and practice, but what is at least two hundred and fifty years younger and later than the writings of the New Testament; and in the first of their writings, as in them that follow, we have innumerable things asserted to have been the traditions and practices of their forefathers from the days of Moses, which we know to be utterly false. At that time when they undertook to compose a new religion out of their pretended traditions, partly by the revolt of many apostates from Christianity unto them, especially of the Ebionites and Nazarenes, and partly by their own study and observation, coming to the knowledge of sundry things in the gospel churches, their order and worship, they took them in as their own. Undeniable instances may be given hereof. (2.) Wherein there is a real coincidence between what was ordained by the apostles and what was practised by the Jews, it is in things which the light of nature and the general rules of the Scripture do direct unto. And it is dishonourable unto the apostles, and the Spirit of Christ in them, to think or say that in such things they took their pattern from the Jews, or made them their example. Surely the apostles took not the pattern and example for the institution of excommunication from the Druids, among whom there was some things that did greatly resemble it, so far as it hath its foundation in the light of nature.

CHAPTER III.

The continuation of a church-state and of churches unto the end of the world — what are the causes of it, and whereon it depends.

THAT there was a peculiar church-state instituted and appointed by Christ, and his apostles acting in his name and authority, with the infallible guidance of his Spirit, hath been declared; but it may be yet farther inquired, whether this church-state be still continued by *divine authority*, or whether it ceased not together with the apostles by whom it was erected.

There was a church-state under the Old Testament solemnly erected by God himself; and although it was not to be absolutely perpetual or everlasting, but was to continue only unto the time of reformation, yet unto that time its continuation was secured in the causes and means of it.

1. The *causes* of the continuation of this church-state unto its appointed period were two:— (1.) The *promise of God* unto Abraham that he would keep and preserve his seed in covenant with him, until he should be the heir of the world and the father of many nations in the coming of Christ, whereunto this church-state was subservient (2.) The *law of God itself*, and the institutions thereof, which God appointed to be observed in all their generations, calling the covenant, the statutes and laws of it, "perpetual" and "everlasting;" that is, never to cease, to be abrogated or disannulled, until by his own sovereign authority he would utterly change and take away that whole church-state, with all that belonged unto its constitution and preservation.

2. The *means* of its continuance were three:— (1.) *Carnal generation*, and that on a twofold account; for there were two constituent parts of that church, the priests and the people. The continuation of each of them depended on the privilege of carnal generation; for the priests were to be all of the family of Aaron, and the people of the seed of Abraham by the other heads

of tribes, which gave them both their foundation in and right unto this church-state. And hereunto were annexed all the laws concerning the integrity, purity, and legitimacy of the priests, with the certainty of their pedigree. (2.) *Circumcision*, the want whereof was a bar against any advantage by the former privilege of generation from those two springs; and hereby others also might be added unto the church, though never with a capacity of the priesthood. (3.) The *separation* of the people from the rest of the world, by innumerable divine ordinances, making their coalition with them impossible.

From these causes and by these means it was that the church-state under the Old Testament was preserved unto its appointed season. Neither the outward calamities that befell the nation, nor the sins of the generality of the people, could destroy this church-state; but it continued its right and exercise unto the time of reformation. And if it be not so, if there be not causes and means of the infallible continuance of the gospel church-state unto the consummation of all things, the time expressly allotted unto their continuance, then was the work of Moses more honourable, more powerful and effectual, in the constitution of the church-state under the Old Testament, than that of Christ in the constitution of the New; for that work and those institutions which had an efficacy in them for their own infallible continuation, and of the church thereby, throughout all generations, must be more noble and honourable than those which cannot secure their own continuance, nor the being and state of the church thereon depending. Nothing can be more derogatory unto the glory of the wisdom and power of Christ, nor of his truth and faithfulness, than such an imagination. We shall, therefore, inquire into the causes and means of the continuation of this church-state, and therein show the certainty of it; as also disprove that which by some is pretended as the only means thereof, when, indeed, it is the principal argument against their perpetual continuation that can be made use of.

The *essence* and *nature* of the church instituted by the authority of Jesus Christ was always the same from the beginning that it continues still to be. But as unto its outward form and order it had a double state; and it was necessary that so it should have, from the nature of the thing itself. For, — 1. The church may be considered in its relation unto those *extraordinary officers* or rulers whose office and power was antecedent unto the church,

CHAPTER III.

as that by virtue whereof it was to be called and erected. 2. With respect unto *ordinary officers,* unto whose office and power the church essentially considered was antecedent; for their whole work and duty, as such, is conversant about the church, and the object is antecedent unto all acts about it.

The first state has ceased, nor can it be continued; for these officers were constituted, — 1. By an *immediate call* from Christ, as was Paul, Gal. i. 1, which none now are, nor have been since the decease of them who were so called at first; 2. By *extraordinary gifts* and power, which Christ doth not continue to communicate; 3. By *divine inspiration* and infallible guidance, both in preaching the word and appointing things necessary in the churches, which none now pretend unto; 4. By *extensive commission,* giving them power towards all the world for their conversion, and over all churches for their edification. Of these officers, in their distinction into apostles and evangelists, with their call, gifts, power, and work, I have treated at large in my "Discourse of Spiritual Gifts."[3] The state and condition of the church with respect unto them has utterly ceased; and nothing can be more vain than to pretend any succession unto them, in the whole or any part of their office, unless men can justify their claim unto it by any or all of those things which concurred unto it in the apostles, which they cannot do.

But it doth not hence follow that the church-state instituted by Christ did fail thereon, or doth now so fail, because it is impossible that these apostles should have any successors in

---

3   These words are printed in the original edition as if they were the title of a particular treatise by our author. His treatise under that title will be found in vol. iv. of his doctrinal works; but it seems to have been published in 1693, twelve years after the present work appeared. Such a discourse is promised in his preface to his treatise on "the Work of the Holy Spirit in Prayer," which was published in 1682, a year after the publication of the present work. There is some discussion on the subject of spiritual gifts in the first chapter of his great work on the Holy Spirit; but a special and separate treatise seems alluded to in the text above. To the "Discourse of Spiritual Gifts," as published in 1693, there is a preface by Nathaniel Mather; from which the reader is led to infer that it was then published for the first time. Perhaps the difficulty may be obviated by the supposition that Owen intended to publish it immediately, and refers to it in this work by anticipation. — ED.

their office or the discharge of it; for by the authority of the Lord Christ, the church was to be continued under ordinary officers, without the call, gifts, or power of the others that were to cease. Under these the church-state was no less divine than under the former; for there were two things in it:— 1. That the offices themselves were of the appointment of Christ; and if they were not so, we confess the *divine right* of the church-state would have ceased. The office of the apostles and evangelists was to cease, as hath been declared; and it did cease actually, in that Christ after them did call no more unto that orifice, nor provided any way or means whereby any one should be made partaker of it. And for any to pretend a succession in office, or any part of their office, without any of those things which did constitute it, is extreme presumption. It is therefore granted, that if there were not other offices appointed by the authority of Christ, it had not been in the power of man to make or appoint any unto that purpose, and the church-state itself must have ceased. But this he hath done, Eph. iv. 11, 12; 1 Cor. xii. 28. 2. That persons were to be interested in these offices according unto the way and means by him prescribed; which were not such as depended on his own immediate extraordinary actings, as it was with the former sort, but such as consisted in the church's acting according to his law and in obedience unto his commands.

This church-state was appointed by the *authority of Christ*. The direction which he gave in his own person for addresses unto the church in case of scandal, which is an obliging institution for all ages, Matt. xviii. 17–20, proves that he had appointed a church-state that should abide through them all. And when there was a church planted at Jerusalem, there were not only apostles in it, according to its first state, but elders also, which respected its second state that was approaching, Acts xv. 23; the apostles being in office *before* that church-state, the elders [being] ordained in it: so chap. xi. 30. And the apostles "ordained them elders in every church," Acts xiv. 23, Tit. i. 5, 1 Tim. v. 17; whom they affirmed to be made so by the Holy Ghost, Acts xx. 28. The churches to whom the apostle Paul wrote his epistles were such, all of them under the rule of ordinary officers, Phil. i. 1. Rules and laws are given for their ordination in all ages, Tit. i.; 1 Tim. iii.; and the Lord Christ treateth from heaven with his churches in this state and order, Rev. i., ii., iii. He hath promised his presence with them unto the consummation of all things,

Chapter III.

Matt. xviii. 20, xxviii. 20, and assigned them their duty until his second coming, 1 Cor. xi. 26; with other evidences of the same truth innumerable.

Our inquiry, therefore, is, whereon the continuation of this church-state unto the end of the world doth depend; what are the causes, what are the means of it; whence it becomes infallible and necessary. I must only premise that our present consideration is not so much "*de facto*," as unto what hath fallen out in the world unto our knowledge and observation, but "*de jure*," or of a right unto this continuation; and this is such as makes it not only lawful for such a church-state to be, but requires also from all the disciples of Christ, in a way of duty, that it be always in actual existence. Hereby there is a warrant given unto all believers, at all times, to gather themselves into such a church-state, and a duty imposed on them so to do.

The reasons and causes appointing and securing this continuation are of various sorts, the principal whereof are these that follow:—

1. The supreme cause hereof is, the Father's grant of a perpetual kingdom in this world unto Jesus Christ, the mediator and head of the church, Ps. lxxii. 5, 7, 15–17; Isa. ix. 7; Zech. vi. 13. This grant of the Father our Lord Jesus Christ pleaded as his warranty for the foundation and continuation of the church, Matt. xxviii. 18–20. This everlasting kingdom of Jesus Christ, given him by the irrevocable grant of the Father, may be considered three ways:—

(1.) As unto the *real subjects* of it, — true believers; which are the object of the internal spiritual power and rule of Christ. Of these it is necessary, by virtue of this grant and divine constitution of the kingdom of Christ, that in every age there should be some in the world, and those perhaps no small multitude, but such as the internal rule over them may be rightly and honourably termed a kingdom. For as that which formally makes them such subjects of Christ gives them no outward appearance or visibility, so if, in a time of the universal prevalency of idolatry, there were seven thousand of these in the small kingdom of Israel, undiscerned and invisible unto the most eagle-eyed prophet who lived in their days, what number may we justly suppose to have been within the limits of Christ's dominions, which is the whole world, in the worst, darkest, most profligate, and idolatrous times, that have passed over the earth since the first erection of this kingdom? This, therefore, is a fundamental article of our faith, — that by virtue of this grant of the Father, Christ ever had, hath, and will have, in all ages, some, yea, a multitude, that are the true, real, spiritual subjects of his kingdom. Neither the power of Satan, nor the rage or fury of the world, nor the accursed apostasy of many or of all visible churches from the purity and holiness of his laws, can hinder but that the church of Christ in this sense must have a perpetual continuation in this world, Matt. xvi. 18.

(2.) It may be considered with respect unto the *outward visible profession* of subjection and obedience unto him, and the observation of his laws. This also belongs unto the kingdom granted him of his Father. He was to have a kingdom in this world, though it be not of this world. He was to have it not only as unto its being, but as unto its glory. The world and the worst of men therein were to see and know that he hath still a kingdom and multitude of subjects depending on his rule. See the constitution of it, Dan. vii. 13, 14. Wherefore it is from hence indispensably and absolutely necessary that there should, at all times and in all ages, be ever an innumerable multitude of them who openly profess faith in Christ Jesus, and subjection of conscience unto his laws and commands. So it hath always been, so it is, and shall for ever be in this world. And those who would, on the one hand, confine the church of Christ, in this notion of it, unto any one church falling under a particular denomination, as the church of Rome, which may utterly fail; or are ready, on the other hand, upon the supposed or real errors or miscarriages of them or any of them who make this profession, to cast them out of their thoughts and affections, as those that belong not unto the kingdom or the church of Christ, are not only injurious unto them, but enemies unto the glory and honour of Christ.

(3.) This grant of the Father may be considered with respect unto *particular churches* or congregations; and the end of these churches may be twofold:— [1.] That believers, as they are internal, spiritual, real subjects of Christ's kingdom, may together act that faith and those graces whereby they are so, unto his glory. I say, it is that true believers may together and in society act all those graces of the Spirit of Christ wherein, both as unto faculty and exercise, their internal spiritual subjection unto Christ doth consist. And as this is that whereby the glory of Christ in this world doth most eminently consist, — namely, in the joint

Chapter III.

exercise of the faith and love of true believers, — so it is a principal means of the increase and augmentation of those graces in themselves, or their spiritual edification. And from this especial end of these churches it follows, that those who are members of them, or belong to them, ought to be saints by calling, or such as are endued with those spiritual principles and graces in whose exercise Christ is to be glorified; and where they are not so, the principal end of their constitution is lost. So are those churches to be made up, fundamentally and materially, of those who in their single capacity are members of the church catholic invisible. [2.] Their second end is, that those who belong unto the church and kingdom of Christ under the second consideration, as visibly professing subjection unto the rule of Christ and faith in him, may express that subjection in acts and duties of his worship, in the observance of his laws and commands, according unto his mind and will; for this alone can be done in particular churches, *be they of what sort they will*; whereof we shall speak afterward. Hence it follows, that it belongs unto the foundation of these particular churches that those who join in them do it on a public profession of faith in Christ and obedience unto him; without which this end of them also is lost. Those, I say, who make a visible profession of the name of Christ and their subjection unto him, have no way to express it regularly and according to his mind but in these particular churches wherein alone those commandments of his, in whose observance our profession consisteth, do take place, being such societies as wherein the solemn duties of his worship are performed, and his rule or discipline is exercised.

Wherefore, this state of the church also, without which both the others are imperfect, belongs unto the grant of the Father, whereby a perpetual continuation of it is secured. Nor is it of any weight to object that such hath been the alterations of the state of all churches in the world, such the visible apostasy of many of them unto false worship and idolatry, and of others into a worldly, carnal conversation, with vain traditions innumerable, that it cannot be apprehended where there were any true churches of this kind preserved and continued, but that there were an actual intercision of them all; for I answer, — First, No individual man, nay, no company of men that come together, can give a certain account of what is done in all the world, and every place of it where the name of Christ is professed; so as that what is affirmed of the state of all churches universally is mere conjecture and surmise. Secondly, There is so great a readiness in most to judge the church-state of others, because in some things they agree not in judgment or practice with what they conceive to belong thereunto, as obstructs a right judgment herein; and it hath risen of late unto such a degree of frenzy, that some deny peremptorily the church-state, and consequently the salvation, of all that have not diocesan bishops. Alas! that poor men, who are known to others, whether they are unto themselves or no, what is their office, and what is their discharge of it, should once think that the being and salvation of all churches should depend on them and such as they are; yea, some of the men of this persuasion, that Christians cannot be saved unless they comply with diocesan bishops, do yet grant that heathens may be saved without the knowledge of Christ! Thirdly, Whatever defect there hath been "*de facto*" in the constitution of these churches and the celebration of divine worship, in any places or ages whatever, it will not prove that there was a total failure of them, much less a discontinuation of the fight of believers to reform and erect them according unto the mind of Christ.

It is hence evident that the perpetual continuation of the church-state instituted by Christ under the gospel depends originally on the grant of the kingdom unto him by his Father, with his faithfulness in that grant, and his almighty power to make it good. And they do but deceive themselves and trouble others who think of suspending this continuation on mean and low conditions of their own framing.

2. The continuation of this church-state depends *on the promise of Christ himself* to preserve and continue it He hath assured us that he will so build his church on the rock, that "the gates of hell shall not prevail against it," Matt. xvi. 18. Under what consideration soever the church is here firstly intended, the whole state of it, as before described, is included in the promise. If the gates of hell do prevail either against the faith of sincere believers, or the catholic profession of that faith, or the expression of that profession in the duties and ordinances to be observed in particular churches, the promise fails and is of no effect.

3. It depends *on the word or law of Christ*, which gives right and title unto all believers to congregate themselves in such a church-state, with rules and commands for their so doing. Suppose, — (1.) That there are a number of believers, or the disciples

of Christ, in any such place as wherein they can assemble and unite themselves or join together in a society for the worship of God; (2.) That they are as yet in no church-state, nor do know or own any power of men that can put them into that state; — I say, the institution of this church-state by the authority of Christ, his commands unto his disciples to observe therein whatever he hath commanded, and the rules he hath given whereby such a church-state is to be erected, what officers are to preside therein, and what other duties belong thereunto, are warranty sufficient for them to join themselves in such a state. Who shall make it unlawful for the disciples of Christ to obey the commands of their Lord and Master? Who shall make it lawful for them to neglect what he requires at any time? Where-ever, therefore, men have the word of the Scripture to teach them their duty, it is lawful for them to comply with all the commands of Christ contained therein. And whereas there are many privileges and powers accompanying this church-state, and those who are interested therein are, as such, the especial object of many divine promises, this word and law of Christ doth make a conveyance of them all unto those who, in obedience unto his institutions and commands, do enter into that state by the way and means that he hath appointed. Whilst we hear him, according to the reiterated direction given us from heaven, whilst we do and observe all that he hath commanded us, we need not fear that promised presence of his with us, which brings along with it all church power and privileges also. Wherefore, this state can have no intercision but on a supposition that there are none in the world who are willing to obey the commands of Christ; which utterly overthrows the very being of the church catholic.

4. It depends on *the communication of spiritual gifts* for the work of the ministry in this church-state, as is expressly declared, Eph. iv. 8, 11–15. The continuation of the church, as unto the essence of it, depends on the communication of saving grace. If Christ should no more give of his grace and Spirit unto men, there would be no more a church in the world, as unto its internal form and essence. But the continuation of the church as it is organical, — that is, a society incorporated according unto the mind of Christ, with rulers and officers for the authoritative administration of all its concerns, especially for the preaching of the word and administration of the sacraments, — depends on the communication of spiritual gifts and abilities; and if the

Lord Jesus Christ should withhold the communication of spiritual gifts, this church-state must cease. An image of it may be erected, but the true church-state will fail; for that will hold no longer, but whilst the "whole body fitly joined together and compacted by that which every joint supplieth, according to the effectual working in the measure of every part, maketh increase of the body unto the edifying of itself in love," Eph. iv. 16; whilst it "holds the Head," etc., Col. ii. 19. Such dead, lifeless images are many churches in the world. But this communication of spiritual gifts unto the use of his disciples, to the end of the world, the Lord Christ hath taken the charge of on himself, as he is faithful in the administration of his kingly power, Eph. iv. 8, 11–15.

Whereas, therefore, the Lord Christ, in the exercise of his right and power, on the grant of the Father of a perpetual visible kingdom in this world, and the discharge of his own promise, hath, — (1.) Appointed the ordinary offices, which he will have continue in his church by an unalterable institution; (2.) Ordained that persons shall be called and set apart unto those offices, and for the discharge of that work and those duties which he hath declared to belong thereunto; (3.) Furnished them with gifts and abilities for this work, and declared what their spiritual qualifications and moral endowments ought to be; (4.) Made it the duty of believers to observe all his institutions and commands, whereof those which concern the erection and continuance of this church-state are the principal; and, (5.) Hath, in their so doing, or their observance of all his commands, promised his presence with them, by which, as by a charter of right, he hath conveyed unto them an interest in all the power, privileges, and promises that belong unto this state; — it is evident that its perpetual continuation depends hereon and is secured hereby. He hath not left this great concernment of his glory unto the wills of men, or any order they shall think meet to appoint.

Lastly: As a means of it, it depends on three things in believers themselves:— (1.) *A due sense of their duty,* to be found in obedience unto all the commands of Christ. Hereby they find themselves indispensably obliged unto all those things which are necessary unto the continuation of this state; and that all believers should absolutely at any time live in a total neglect of their duty, though they may greatly mistake in the manner of its performance, is not to be supposed. (2.) *The instinct of the new creature* and those in whom it is to associate themselves in holy communion, for the joint and mutual exercise of those graces of the Spirit, which are the same, as unto the essence of them, in them all. The laws of Christ in and unto his church, as unto all outward obedience, are suited unto those inward principles and inclinations which, by his Spirit and grace, he hath implanted in the hearts of them that believe. Hence his yoke is easy, and his commandments are not grievous. And therefore none of his true disciples, since he had a church upon the earth, did or could satisfy themselves in their own faith and obedience, singularly and personally; but would venture their lives and all that was dear unto them for communion with others, and the associating themselves with them of the same spirit and way, for the observance of the commands of Christ. The martyrs of the primitive churches of old lost more of their blood and lives for their meetings and assemblies than for personal profession of the faith; and so also have others done under the Roman apostasy. It is a usual plea among them who engage in the persecution or punishment of such as differ from them, that if they please they may keep their opinions, their consciences, and faith unto themselves, without meetings for communion or public worship; and herein they suppose they deal friendly and gently With them. And this is our present case. It is true, indeed, as Tertullian observed of old, that men in these things have no power over us but what they have from our own wills: we willingly choose to be, and to continue, what they take advantage to give us trouble for. And it is naturally in our power to free ourselves from them and their laws every day. But we like it not; we cannot purchase outward peace and quietness at any such rate. But, as was said, the inward instinct of believers, from the same principles of faith, love, and all the graces of the Spirit in them all, doth efficaciously lead and incline them unto their joint exercise in societies, unto the glory of Christ, and their own edification, or increase of the same graces in them. When this appears to be under the guidance of the commands of Christ, as unto the ways of communion led unto, and to consist in a compliance therewithal, they find themselves under an indispensable obligation unto it. Nor hath the Lord Christ left them liberty to make a composition for their outward peace, and to purchase quietness with foregoing any part of their duty herein.

This, therefore, I say, is a means and cause on the part of believers themselves of the continuation of this church-state: for this instinct of believers, leading them unto communion, which is an article of our faith, in conjunction with the law and commands of Christ giving direction how and in what ways it is to be attained and exercised, binds and obliges them unto the continuation of this state; and the decay of this inward principle in them that profess Christian religion hath been the great and almost only ground of its neglect. (3.) The open evidence there is that sundry duties required of us in the gospel can never be performed in a due manner but where believers are brought into this state; which that they should enter into is, therefore, in the first place required of them. What these duties are will afterward appear.

On these sure grounds is founded the continuation of the gospel church-state, under ordinary officers, after the decease of the apostles; and so far secured as that nothing needs be added unto them for that end. Do but suppose that the Lord Christ yet liveth in heaven in the discharge of his mediatory office; that he hath given his word for a perpetual law unto all his disciples, and a charter to convey spiritual privileges unto them; that he abides to communicate gifts for the ministry unto men; and that there are any believers in the world who know it to be their duty to yield obedience unto all the commands of Christ, and have any internal principle inclining them to that which they profess to believe as a fundamental article of their faith, namely, the communion of saints; — and no man is desired to prove the certainty and necessity of the continuance of this state.

But there are some who maintain that the continuation and preservation of this church-state depends solely on a successive ordination of church-officers from the apostles, and so down throughout all ages unto the end of the world; for this, they say, is the only means of conveying church-power from one time to another, so as that if it fail, all church-state, order, and power must fail, never in this world to be recovered. There is, they say, a flux of power through the hands of the ordainers unto the ordained, by virtue of their outward ordination, whereon the being of the church doth depend. Howbeit those who use this plea are not at all agreed about those things which are essential in and unto this successive ordination. Some think that the Lord Christ committed the keys of the kingdom of heaven unto Peter

Chapter III.

only, and he to the *bishop of Rome* alone; from whose person, therefore, all their ordination must be derived. Some think, and those on various grounds, that it is committed unto all and only *diocesan bishops*; whose being and beginning are very uncertain. Others require no more unto it but that *presbyters* be ordained by presbyters, who are rejected in their plea by both the former sorts. And other differences almost innumerable among them who are thus minded might be reckoned up.

But whereas this whole argument about personal successive ordination hath been fully handled, and the pretences of it disproved, by the chiefest protestant writers against the Papists, and because I design not an opposition unto what others think and do, but the declaration and confirmation of the truth in what we have proposed to insist upon, I shall very briefly discover the falseness of this pretence, and pass on unto what is principally intended in this discourse.

1. The church is before all its ordinary officers; and therefore its continuation cannot depend on their successive ordination. It is so as essentially considered, though its being organical is simultaneous with their ordination. Extraordinary officers were before the church, for their work was to call, gather, and erect it out of the world; but no ordinary officers can be or ever were ordained, but to a church in being. Some say they are ordained unto the universal visible church of professors, some unto the particular church wherein their work doth lie; but all grant that the church-state whereunto they are ordained is antecedent unto their ordination. The Lord Christ could and did ordain apostles and evangelists when there was yet no gospel church; for they were to be the instruments of its calling and erection. But the apostles neither did nor could ordain any ordinary officers until there was a church or churches, with respect whereunto they should be ordained. It is, therefore, highly absurd to ascribe the continuation of the church unto the successive ordination of officers, if any such thing there were, seeing this successive ordination of officers depends solely on the continuation of the church. If that were not secured on other foundations, this successive ordination would quickly tumble into dust. (Yea, this successive ordination, were there any such thing appointed, must be an act of the church itself, and so cannot be the means of communicating church-power unto others. A successive ordination in some sense may be granted, — namely, that when

those who were ordained officers in any church do die, others be ordained in their steads; but this is by an act of power in the church itself, as we shall manifest afterward.)

2. Not to treat of papal succession, the limiting of this successive ordination, as the only way and means of communicating church-power, and so of the preservation of the church-state, unto diocesan prelates or bishops, is built on so many inevident presumptions and false principles as will leave it altogether uncertain whether there he any church-state in the world or no; as, — (1.) That such bishops were ordained by the *apostles*; which can never be proved. (2.) That they received power from the apostles to ordain others, and communicate *their whole power* unto them, by an authority inherent in themselves alone, yet still reserving their whole power unto themselves also, giving all and retaining all at the same time; which hath no more of truth than the former, and may be easily disproved. (3.) That they never did nor could, any of them, *forfeit* this power by any crime or error, so as to render their ordination invalid, and interrupt the succession pretended. (4.) That they all ordained others in such *manner* and way as to render their ordination valid, whereas multitudes were never agreed what is required thereunto. (5.) That whatever heresy, idolatry, flagitiousness of life, persecution of the true churches of Christ, these prelatical ordainers might fall into; by whatever arts, simoniacal practices, or false pretences unto what was not, they came themselves into their offices; yet nothing could deprive them of their right of *communicating all church-power* unto others by ordination. (6.) That persons so ordained, whether they have any call from the church or no; whether they have any of the qualifications required by the law of Christ in the Scripture to make them capable of any office in the church, or have received any *spiritual gifts* from Christ for the exercise of their office and discharge of their duty; whether they have any design or no to pursue the ends of that office which they take upon them; — yet all is one, being any way prelatically-ordained bishops, they may ordain others, and so the successive ordination is preserved. And what is this but to take the rule of the church out of the hand of Christ, to give law unto him, to follow with his approbation the actings of men besides and contrary to his law and institution, and to make application of his promises unto the vilest of men, whether he will or no? (7.) That it is not lawful for believers, or

the disciples of Christ, to yield obedience unto his commands without this episcopal ordination; which many churches cannot have, and more will not, as judging it against the mind and will of Christ. (8.) That one worldly, ignorant, proud, sensual beast, such as some of the heads of this successive ordination, as the popes of Rome, have been, should have more power and authority from Christ to preserve and continue a church state by ordination, than any the most holy church in the world that is or can be gathered according to his mind; with other unwarrantable presumptions innumerable.

3. The pernicious consequences that may ensue on this principle do manifest its inconsistency with what our Lord Jesus Christ hath ordained unto this end, of the continuation of his church. I need not reckon them up on the surest probabilities. There is no room left for fears of what may follow hereon, by what hath already done so. If we consider whither this successive ordination hath already led a great part of the church, we may easily judge what it is meet for. It hath, I say, led men, for instance in the church of Rome, into a presumption of a good church-state, in the loss of holiness and truth, in the practice of false worship and idolatry, in the persecution and slaughter of the faithful servants of Christ, — unto a state plainly antichristian. To think there should be a flux and communication of heavenly and spiritual power from Jesus Christ and his apostles, in and by the hands and actings of persons ignorant, simoniacal, adulterous, incestuous, proud, ambitious, sensual, presiding in a church-state never appointed by him, immersed in false and idolatrous worship, persecuting the true church of Christ, wherein was the true succession of apostolical doctrine and holiness, is an imagination for men who embrace the shadows and appearances of things, never once seriously thinking of the true nature of them. In brief, it is in vain to derive a succession, whereon the being of the church should depend, through the presence of Christ with the bishops of Rome, who for a hundred years together, from the year 900 to 1000, were monsters for ignorance, lust, pride, and luxury, as Baronius acknowledgeth, A.D. 912. 5, 8; or by the church of Antioch, by Samosatenus, Eudoxius, Gnapheus, Severus, and the like heretics; or in Constantinople, by Macedonius, Eusebius, Demophilus, Anthorinus, and their companions; or at Alexandria, by Lucius, Dioscorus, Ælurus, Sergius, and the rest of the same sort.

4. The principal argument whereby this conceit is fully discarded must be spoken unto afterward. And this is the due consideration of the proper subject of all church-power, unto whom it is originally, formally, and radically given and granted by Jesus Christ; for none can communicate this power unto others but those who have received it themselves from Christ, by virtue of his law and institution. Now, this is the whole church, and not any person in it or prelate over it. Look, whatever constitutes it a church, that gives it all the power and privilege of a church; for a church is nothing but a society of professed believers, enjoying all church-power and privileges, by virtue of the law of Christ. Unto this church, which is his spouse, doth the Lord Christ commit the keys of his house; by whom they are delivered into the hands of his stewards, so far as their office requires that trust, Now, this (which we shall afterward more fully confirm) is utterly inconsistent with the committing of all church-power unto one person by virtue of his ordination by another.

Nothing that hath been spoken doth at all hinder or deny but that, where churches are rightly constituted, they ought, in their offices, officers, and order, to be preserved by a successive ordination of pastors and rulers, wherein those who actually preside in them have a particular interest in the orderly communication of church-power unto them.

CHAPTER IV.

The especial nature of the gospel church-state appointed by Christ.

THE principal inquiry, which we have thus far prepared the way unto, and whereon all that ensues unto it doth depend, is concerning the especial nature of that church-state, rule, and order, which the Lord Christ hath instituted under the gospel, of what sort and kind it is; and hereunto some things must be premised:—

1. I design not here to oppose, nor any way to consider, such *additions as* men may have judged necessary to be added unto that church-state which Christ hath appointed, to render it, in their apprehension, more useful unto its ends than otherwise it would be. Of this sort there are many things in the world, and of a long season have been so. But our present business is to prove the truth, and not to disprove the conceits of other men. And so far as our cause is concerned herein, it shall be done by itself, so as not to interrupt us in the declaration of the truth.

2. Whereas there are great contests about communion with churches, or separation from them, and mutual charges of impositions and schisms thereon, they must be all regulated by this inquiry, — namely, What is that church-state which Christ hath prescribed? Herein alone is conscience concerned as unto all duties of ecclesiastical communion. Neither can a charge of schism be managed against any but on a supposition of sin with respect unto that church-state and order which Christ hath appointed. A dissent from any thing else, however pretended to be useful, yea, advantageous unto church ends, must come under other prudential considerations. All which shall be fully proved, and vindicated from the exceptions of Dr Stillingfleet.

3. There have been and are in the world several sorts of churches of great power and reputation, of several forms and kinds, yet contributing aid to each other in their respective sta-

tions; as, — (1.) The *papal* church, which pretends itself to be catholic or universal, comprehensive of all true believers or disciples of Christ, united in their subjection unto the bishop of Rome. (2.) There were of old, and the shadow of them is still remaining, churches called *patriarchal*, first three, then four, then five of them, whereinto all other churches and professed Christians in the Roman world were distributed, as unto a dependence on the authority, and subjection to the jurisdiction and order, of the bishops of five principal cities of the empire; who were thereon called patriarchs. (3.) Various divisions under them of *archiepiscopal* or metropolitical churches; and under them of those that are now called diocesan, whose bounds and limits were fixed and altered according to the variety of occasions and occurrences of things in the nations of the world. What hath been the original of all these sorts of churches, how from parochial assemblies they grew up, by the degrees of their descent now mentioned, into the height and centre of papal omnipotency, hath been declared elsewhere sufficiently.

4. Some there are who plead for a *national* church-state, arising from an association of the officers of particular churches, in several degrees, which they call *classical and provincial*, until it extend itself unto the limits of a whole nation; that is, one civil body, depending as such on its own supreme ruler and law. I shall neither examine nor oppose this opinion; there hath been enough, if not too much, already disputed about it. But, —

5. The visible church-state which Christ hath instituted under the New Testament consists in *an especial society or congregation of professed believers, joined together according unto his mind, with their officers, guides, or rulers, whom he hath appointed, which do or may meet together for the celebration of all the ordinances of divine worship, the professing and authoritatively proposing the doctrine of the gospel, with the exercise of the discipline prescribed by himself, unto their own mutual edification, with the glory of Christ, in the preservation and propagation of his kingdom in the world.*

The things observable in this description, and for the farther declaration of it, are, — (1.) The *material cause* of this church, or the matter whereof it is composed, which are *visible believers*. (2.) The *formal cause* of it, which is their voluntary coalescency into such a society or congregation, according to the mind of Christ. (3.) The *end of it* is, presential local communion, in all the ordinances and institutions of Christ, in obedience unto

Chapter IV.

him and [for] their own edification. (4.) In particular these ends are, — [1.] The *preaching of the word*, unto the edification of the church itself and the conversion of others; [2.] *Administration* of the sacraments, or all the mystical appointments of Christ in the church; [3.] The preservation and exercise of *evangelical discipline*, [4.] Visibly to profess their sub*jection* unto Christ in the world by the observation of his commands. (5.) The *bounds* and limits of this church are taken from the number of the members; which ought not to be so small as that they cannot observe and do all that Christ hath commanded in due order, nor yet so great as not to meet together for the ends of the institution of the church before mentioned. (6.) That this church, in its complete state, consists of *pastors*, or *a pastor and elders*, who are its guides and rulers; and the community of the faithful under their rule. (7.) That unto such a church, and every one of them, belong of right all the privileges, promises, and power that Christ doth give and grant unto the church in this world.

These, and sundry other things of the like nature, shall be afterward spoken unto in their order, according unto the method intended in the present discourse.

Two things I shall now proceed unto:—

First, To prove that Christ hath appointed this church-state under the gospel, — namely, of a particular or single congregation. Secondly, That he hath appointed no other church-state that is inconsistent with this, much less that is destructive of it:— First, Christ appointed that church-state which is meet and accommodated unto all the ends which he designed in his institution of a church. But such alone is that church form and order that we have proposed. In Christ's institution of the church, it was none of his ends that some men might be thereby advanced to rule, honour, riches, or secular grandeur, but the direct contrary, Matt. xx. 25–28. Nor did he do it that his disciples might be ruled and governed by force or the laws of men, or that they should be obstructed in the exercise of any graces, gifts, or privileges that he had purchased for them or would bestow on them. And to speak plainly (let it be despised by them that please), this cannot greatly value that church-state which is not suited to guide, excite, and direct the exercise of all evangelical graces unto the glory of Christ in a due manner; for to propose peculiar and proper objects far them, to give peculiar motives unto them, to limit the seasons and circumstances of their exercise, and regulate the manner of the performance of the duties that arise from them, is one principal end of its institution.

It would be too long to make a particular inquiry into all the ends for which the Lord Christ appointed this church-state; which, indeed, are all the duties of the gospel, either in themselves or in the manner of their performance. We may reduce them unto these three general heads:—

1. The *professed subjection* of the souls and consciences of believers unto his authority, in their observance of his commandments. He requireth that all who are baptized into his name be taught to do and observe "all things whatsoever he hath commanded," Matt. xxviii. 18–20. And God is to be glorified, not only in their subjection, but in their "professed subjection unto the gospel of Christ," 2 Cor. ix. 13. Having given an express charge unto his disciples to make public profession of his name, and not to be deterred from it by shame or fear of any thing that may befall them on the account thereof, and that on the penalty of his disowning them before his heavenly Father, Mark viii. 34–38, Matt. x. 33, he hath appointed this church-state as the way and means whereby they may jointly and visibly make profession of this their subjection to him, dependence on him, and freedom in the observation of all his commands.

He will not have this done singly and personally only, but in society and conjunction. Now, this cannot be done, in any church-state imaginable wherein the members of the church cannot meet together for this end; which they can only do in such a church as is congregational.

2. The *joint celebration* of all gospel ordinances and worship is the great and principal end of the evangelical church-state. How far this is directed unto by the law of nature was before declared. Man was made for society in things natural and civil, but especially in things spiritual, or such as concern the worship of God. Hereon depends the necessity of particular churches, or societies for divine worship. And this is declared to be the end of the churches instituted by Christ, Acts ii. 42; 1 Cor. v. 4, xi. 20; 2 Tim. ii. 1, 2; as also of the institution of officers in the church, for the solemn administration of the ordinances of his worship. And the reasons of this appointment are intimated in the Scripture; as, — (1.) That it might be a way for *the joint exercise* of the graces and gifts of the Spirit, as was in general before mentioned. The Lord Christ gives both his grace and his gifts in

Chapter IV.

great variety of measures, Eph. iv. 7, but "the manifestation of the Spirit is given unto every man to profit withal," 1 Cor. xii. 7–10. He gives neither of them unto any merely for themselves. Saving grace is firstly given for the good of him that receives it, but respect is had in it unto the good of others; and the Lord Christ expects such an exercise of it as may be to others' advantage. And the first end of gifts is the edification of others; and all that do receive them are thereby and so far "stewards of the manifold grace of God," 1 Pet. iv. 10. Wherefore, for the due exercise of these gifts and graces unto his glory and their proper ends, he hath appointed particular congregations, in whose assemblies alone they can be duly exercised. (2.) Hereby all his disciples are *mutually edified*; that is, increased in light, knowledge, faith, love, fruitfulness in obedience, and conformity unto himself. This the apostle affirms to be the especial end of all churches, their offices, officers, gifts, and order, Eph. iv. 12–16, and again, chap. ii. 19–22. No church-state that is not immediately suited unto this end is of his institution; and though others may in general pretend unto it, besides that of particular congregations, it were to be wished that they were not obstructive of it, or were any way fitted or useful unto it. (3.) That he might hereby express and testify his *promised presence* with his disciples unto the end of the world, Matt. xxviii. 20, xviii. 20; Rev. i. 13. It is in their church assemblies, and in the performance of his holy worship, that he is present with his disciples according unto his promise. (4.) In these churches, thus exercised in the holy worship of God, he gives us *a resemblance* and representation of the great assembly above, who worship God continually before his throne; which is too large a subject here to insist upon.

And to manifest that assemblies of the whole church, at once and in one place, for the celebration of divine worship, is of the essence of a church, without which it hath no real being; when God had instituted such a church-form as wherein all the members of it could not ordinarily come together every week for this end, yet he ordained that, for the preservation of their church-state, three times in the year the males (which was the circumcised church) should appear together in one place to celebrate the most solemn ordinances of his worship, Exod. xxiii. 14, xxxiv. 23; Deut. xvi. 16. All those difficulties which arose from the extent of the limits of that church unto the whole nation being removed, these meetings of the whole church for the worship of God become a continual duty; and when they cannot be observed in any church, the state or kind of it is not instituted by Christ.

3. The third end of the institution of the gospel church-state is the exercise and *preservation of the discipline* appointed by Christ to be observed by his disciples. The ancients do commonly call the whole religion of Christianity by the name of the "discipline of Christ," — that is, the faith and obedience which he hath prescribed unto them, in contradistinction and opposition unto the rules and prescriptions of all philosophical societies; and it is that without which the glory of Christian religion can in no due manner be preserved. The especial nature of it shall be afterward fully spoken unto. For the use of the present argument I shall only speak unto the ends of it, or what it is that the Lord Christ designeth in the institution of it; and these things may be referred unto four heads: —

(1.) *The preservation of the doctrine of the gospel in its purity*, and obedience unto the commands of Christ in its integrity. For the first, the Scripture is full of predictions, all confirmed in the event, that after the days of the apostles there should be various attempts to wrest, corrupt, and pervert the doctrine of the gospel, and to bring in pernicious errors and heresies. To prevent, or reprove and remove them, is no small part of the duty of the ministerial office, in the dispensation of the word. But whereas those who taught such perverse things did for the most part arise at first in the churches themselves, Acts xx. 30, 2 Pet. ii. 1, 1 John ii. 10, as the preaching of the word was appointed for the rebuke of the doctrines themselves, so this discipline was ordained in the church with respect unto the persons of them by whom they were taught, Rev. ii. 2, 14, 20, 3 John 8, 9; Gal. v. 12. And so also it was with respect unto schisms and divisions that might fall out in the church. The way of suppressing things of this nature by external force, by the sword of magistrates, in prisons, fines, banishments, and death, was not then thought of, nor directed unto by the Lord Jesus Christ, but is highly dishonourable unto him; as though the ways of his own appointment were not sufficient for the preservation of his own truth, but that his disciples must betake themselves unto the secular powers of this world, who for the most part are wicked, profane, and ignorant of the truth, for that end.

Chapter IV.

And hereunto belongeth the preservation of his commands in the integrity of obedience; for he appointed that hereby care should be taken of the ways, walkings, and conversations of his disciples, that in all things it should be such as became the gospel. Hence, the exercise of this discipline he ordained to consist in exhortations, admonitions, reproofs, of any that should offend in things moral or of his especial institution, with the total rejection of them that were obstinate in their offences; as we shall see afterward.

(2.) The second end of it was to *preserve love entire* among his disciples. This was that which he gave in especial charge unto all that should believe in his name, taking the command of it to be his own in a peculiar manner, and declaring our observance of it to be the principal pledge and evidence of our being his disciples; for although mutual love be an "old commandment," belonging both unto the moral law and sundry injunctions under the Old Testament, yet the degrees and measure of it, the ways and duties of its exercise, the motives unto it and reasons for it, were wholly his own, whereby it becomes a "new commandment" also. For the preservation and continuance of this love, which he lays so great weight upon, was this discipline appointed, which it is several ways effectual towards; as, — [1.] In the prevention or removal of offences that might arise among believers, to the impeachment of it, Matt. xviii. 15–17; [2.] In that watch over each other, with mutual exhortations and admonitions, without which this love, let men pretend what they please, will not be preserved. That which keepeth either life or soul in Christian love consists in the exercise of those graces mutually, and the discharge of those duties whereby they may be partakers of the fruits of love in one another. And, for the most part, those who pretend highly unto the preservation of love, by their coming to the same church who dwell in the same parish, have not so much as the carcase, nay, not a shadow of it. In the discipline of the Lord Christ it is appointed that this love, so strictly by him enjoined unto us, so expressive of his own wisdom and love, should be preserved, continued, and increased by the due and constant discharge of the duties of mutual exhortation, admonition, prayer, and watchful care over one another, Rom. xv. 14; 1 Thess. v. 11, 12; 2 Thess. iii. 15; Heb. iii. 12, 13, xii. 15, 16.

(3.) A third end of it is, that it might be *a due representation of his own love*, care, tenderness, patience, meekness, in the acting of his authority in the church. Where this is not observed and designed in the exercise of church-discipline, I will not say it is antichristian, but will say it is highly injurious, and dishonourable unto him; for all church-power is in him and derived from him. Nor is there any thing of that nature which belongs unto it, but it must be acted in his name, and esteemed, both for the manner and matter of it, to be his act and deed. For men, therefore, to pretend unto the exercise of this discipline in a worldly frame of spirit, with pride and passion, by tricks of laws and canons, in courts foreign to the churches themselves which are pretended to be under this discipline, it is a woful and scandalous representation of Christ, his wisdom, care, and love towards his church. But as for his discipline, he hath ordained that it shall be exercised in and with meekness, patience, gentleness, evidence of zeal for the good and compassion of the souls of men, with gravity and authority; so as that therein all the holy affections of his mind towards his church or any in it, in their mistakes, failings, and miscarriages, may be duly represented, as well as his authority acted among them, Isa. xl. 11; 2 Cor. x. 1; Gal. v. 22, 23; 1 Thess. ii. 7; 2 Tim. ii. 24–26; James iii. 17; 1 Cor. xiii.

(4.) It is in part appointed to be an evidence and pledge of *the future judgment*, wherein the whole church shall be judged before the throne of Christ Jesus; for in the exercise of this discipline Christ is on his own judgment-seat in the church: nor may any man pronounce any sentence but what he believeth that Christ himself would pronounce were he visibly present, and what is according to his mind as declared in his word. Hence Tertullian calls the sentence of excommunication in the church, "*Futuri judicii præjudicium,*" — a representation of the future judgment.

In all that degeneracy which the Christian professing church hath fallen into, in faith, worship, and manners, there is no instance can exceed the corruption of this *divine institution*: for that which was the honour of Christ and the gospel, and an effectual means to represent him in the glory of his wisdom and love, and for the exercise of all graces in the church, unto the blessed ends now declared, was turned into a domination, earthly and secular, exercised in a profane, litigious, unintelligible process, according unto the arts, ways, and terms of the worst of law courts, by persons for the most part remote from any just pretence of the least interest in church-power, on causes and for ends foreign unto the discipline of the gospel, by a tyranny over the consciences and over the persons of the disciples of Christ, unto the intolerable scandal of the gospel and rule of Christ in his church; as is evident in the state and rule of the church of Rome. As these are the general ends of the institution of a church-state under the gospel, and in order unto them, it is a great divine ordinance for the glory of Christ, with the edification and salvation of them that do believe. Wherefore, that church-state which is suited unto these ends is that which is appointed by Christ; and whatever kind of church or churches is not so, primarily and as such, are not of his appointment. But it is in congregational churches alone that these things can be done and observed; for unto all of them there are required assemblies of the whole church, which, wherever they are, that church is congregational. No such churches as those mentioned before, — papal, patriarchical, metropolitical, diocesan, or in any way national, — are capable of the discharge of these duties or attaining of these ends. If it be said, that what they cannot do in themselves, as that they cannot together in one place profess and express their subjection unto the commands of Christ, they cannot have personal communion in the celebration of gospel ordinances of worship, nor exercise discipline in one body and society, they can yet do the same things otherwise, partly in single congregations appointed by themselves, and partly in such ways, for the administration of discipline, as are suited unto their state and rule, — that is, by ecclesiastical courts, with jurisdiction over all persons or congregations belonging unto them, — it will not help their cause; for, — (1.) Those particular congregations wherein these things are to be observed are churches, or they are not. If they are churches, they are of Christ's appointment, and we obtain what we aim at; nor is it in the power of any man to deprive them of any thing that belongs unto them as such. If they are not, but inventions and appointments of their own, then that which they say is this, that "what is absolutely necessary unto the due observation of the worship of God, and unto all the ends of churches, being not appointed by Christ, is by them provided for, appointed, and ordained;" which is to exalt themselves in wisdom and care above him, and to place themselves in a nearer relation to the church than he. To grant that many of those things which are the ends for which any church-state under the gospel is appointed, cannot be performed or attained but in and by particular congregations, and yet to deny that those particular congregations are of Christ's institution, is to speak contradictions, and at the same time to affirm that they are churches and are not churches. (2.) A church is such a body or society as hath spiritual power, privileges, and promises annexed unto it and accompanying of it. That which hath not so, as such, is no church. The particular congregations mentioned have this power, with privileges and promises belonging to them, or they have not. If they have not, they are no churches, at least no complete churches; and there are no churches in the earth wherein those things can be done for which the being of churches was ordained, — as, namely, the joint celebration of divine worship by all the members of them. If they have such power, I desire to know from whence or whom they have it; if from Christ, then are they of his institution, and who can divest them of that power, or any part of it? That they have it from men, I suppose will not be pretended. (3.) As unto that way of the exercise of discipline suited unto any other church-state but that which is congregational, we shall consider it afterward. (4.) What is done in particular congregations is not the act of any greater church, as a diocesan, or the like; for whatever acts any thing, acts according unto what it is. But this of joint worship and discipline in assemblies is not the act of such a church according unto what it is; for so it is impossible for it to do any thing of that nature. But thus it is fallen out. Some men, under the power of a tradition that particular congregations were originally of a divine institution, and finding the absolute necessity of them unto the joint celebration of divine worship, yet finding what an inconsistency with their interest, and some other opinions which they have imbibed, should they still be acknowledged to be of the institution of Christ, seeing thereon the whole ordinary power given by Christ unto his church must reside in them, they would now have them to be only conveniences for some ends of worship of their own finding out. Something they would have like Christ's institution, but his it shall not be; which is an image.

Secondly, The very *notation of the word* doth determine the sense of it unto a particular congregation. Other things may in

Chapter IV.

churches, as we shall see afterward, both in the rule and administration of the duties of holy worship, be ordered and disposed in great variety; but whilst a church is such as that ordinarily the whole body, in its rulers and those that are ruled, do assemble together in one place for the administration of gospel ordinances and the exercise of discipline, it is still one single congregation, and can be neither diocesan, provincial, nor national: so that although the essence of the church doth not consist in actual assemblies, yet are they absolutely necessary unto its constitution in exercise.

Hence is the name of a church. קָהַל, the verb in the Old Testament, is to congregate, to assemble, to call and meet together, and nothing else. The LXX. render it mostly by ἐκκλησιάζω, to congregate in a church-assembly; and sometimes by other words of the same importance, as συνίστημι, συνάγω, ἐπισυνάγω. So they do the noun קָהָל by συναγωγή, ἐκκλησία, seldom by any other word; but where they do so it is always of the same signification. Wherefore, this word signifies nothing but a congregation which assembles for the ends and uses of it, and acts its duties and powers; so doth ἐκκλησία also in the New Testament. It may be sometimes applied unto that whose essence is not denoted thereby, as the church catholic invisible, which is only a mystical society or congregation. But where-ever it is used to denote an outward visible society, it doth connote their assembling together in one. It is frequently used for an actual assembly, Acts xix. 32, 39, 40, which was the signification of it in all Greek writers, 1 Cor. xiv. 4, 5; and sometimes it is expressly affirmed that it "met together in the same place," chap. xiv. 23. Wherefore, no society that doth not congregate, the whole body whereof doth not meet together, to act its powers and duties, is a church, or may be so called, whatever sort of body or corporation it may be.

In this sense is the word used when the first intimation is given of an evangelical church-state with order and discipline: Matt. xviii. 17, "if he shall neglect to hear them, tell the church," etc. There have been so many contests about the sense of these words and the interpretation of them, so many various and opposite opinions about them, and those debated in such long and operose discourses, that some would take an argument from thence that nothing can be directly proved from them, nor any certain account of the state and duty of the church be thence collected. But nothing can be insinuated more false and absurd, nor which more directly tendeth to the overthrow of the whole authority of the Scripture; for if when men are seduced, by their interests or otherwise, to multiply false expositions of any place of Scripture, and to contend earnestly about them, thereon, as unto us, they lose their instructive power and certain determination of the truth, we should quickly have no bottom or foundation for our faith in the most important articles of religion, nor could have so at this day. But all the various pretences of men, — some whereof would have the pope, others a general council, some the civil magistrate, some the Jewish synagogue, some a company of arbitrators, — are nothing but so many instances of what interest, prejudice, corrupt lusts, ambitious designs, with a dislike of the truth, will bring forth. To me it seems strange that any impartial man, reading the context, can take "the church" in this place in any other sense but for such a society as whereunto an offending and offended brother or disciple of Christ might and ought to belong, to the body whereof they might address themselves for relief and remedy, or the removal of offences, by virtue of the authority and appointment of Jesus Christ.

It were an endless task, and unsuited unto our present design, to examine the various pretensions unto the church in this place: enough, also, if not too much, hath been written already about them. I shall, therefore, observe only some few things from the context, which will sufficiently evidence what sort of church it is that is here intended:—

1. The rule and direction given by our Saviour in this place unto his disciples doth not concern *civil injuries* as such, but such sins as have *scandal* and offence in them, either causing other men to sin, or giving them grief and offence for sin; whereby the exercise of love in mutual communion may be impeded. Private injuries may be respected herein, but not as injuries, but so far as they are scandalous, and matter of offence unto them unto whom they are known. And this appears, —

(1.) From the proper signification of the phrase here used: Ἐὰν ἁμαρτήσῃ εἰς σέ· — "If thy brother sin against thee." Doing of an injury is expressed by ἀδικέω, and to be injured by ἀποστερέομαι, 1 Cor. vi. 7, 8, — that is, to be wronged, to be dealt unjustly withal, and to be defrauded or deprived of our right; but ἁμαρτάνω εἰς is not used but only for so to sin as to give scandal unto them against whom that sin is said to be, 1 Cor. viii. 11, 12. To be guilty of "sin against Christ," in the light of their consciences, is to "sin against them."

(2.) It is evident in the context. Our Saviour is treating directly about all sorts of scandals and offences, or sins, as occasions of falling, stumbling, and sinning, and so of perishing unto others, giving rules and directions about them from the eighth verse unto these words wherein direction is given about their cure and removal. And two things he ascribes unto these scandals, — first, That weak Christians are *despised in* them, verse 10; secondly, That they are in danger to be *destroyed* or lost for ever by them, verse 14; which gives us a true account of the nature of scandalous offences. Wherefore ἁμαρτάνω, to sin, is used here in the same sense with σκανδαλίζω before, to give offence by a scandalous miscarriage.

(3.) Where the same rule is again recorded, the words used enforce this application of them, Luke xvii. 1–3. The Lord Christ foretells his disciples that scandals and offences would arise, with the nature and danger of them, verse 1. And because that they obtain their pernicious effects mostly on them that are weak, he gives caution against them with especial respect to such among his disciples: "Better any one were cast into the sea," ἢ ἵνα σκαδαλίσῃ ἕνα τῶν μικρῶν τούτων, — "than that he should give scandal or offence unto one of these little ones," verse 2. And what he expresseth by σκανδαλίσῃ, verse 2, he expresseth by ἁμάρτῃ εἰς σέ, verse 3, "sin against thee;" and this is plain from the direction which he gives hereon, ἐπιτίμησον αὐτῷ, "rebuke him." The word is never used with respect unto private injuries, but as they are sins or faults; so is it joined with ἔλεγξον, 2 Tim. iv. 2. And ἐπιτιμία is the only word used for the rebuke given, or to be given, unto a scandalous offender, 2 Cor. ii. 6.

(4.) Another rule is given in case of private injuries that are only such; and that is, that we immediately forgive them.

(5.) It doth not seem a direction suited unto that *intense love* which the Lord Christ requireth in all his disciples one towards another, nor the nature of that love in its exercise, as it is described, 1 Cor. xiii., that for a private injury done unto any man, without respect unto sin against God therein, which is the scandal, he should follow his brother so far as to have him cast out of the communion of all Churches and believers; which yet, in case of sin unrepented of, is a necessary duty.

2. The rule here prescribed, and the direction given, were so prescribed and given for the use of all the disciples of Christ in all ages, and are not to be confined unto any present case or the present season. For, — (1.) There was no such case at present, no mutual offence among any of his disciples, that should require this determination of it; only respect is had unto what might afterward fall out in the church. (2.) There was no need of any such direction at that time, because Christ himself was then constantly present with them, in whom all church-power did reside both eminently and formally Accordingly, when any of them did offend unto scandal, he did himself rebuke them, Matt. xvi. 22, 23; and when any thing of mutual offence fell out among them, he instructed them and directed them into the way of love, doing what any church could do, and much more also, chap. xx. 24–28. (3.) This was a case which our Saviour foreknew and foretold that it would fall out in the church in future generations, even unto the end of the world. It doth so every day, and will do so whilst men are in an imperfect state here below. Nor is there any thing wherein the church, as unto its order, purity, and edification, is more concerned; nor can any of them be preserved without a certain rule for the cure and healing of offences, nor are so in any church where such a rule is not, or is neglected. It is therefore fond to suppose that our Saviour should prescribe this rule for that i season wherein there was no need of it, and not for those times wherein the church could not subsist in order without it.

3. The church here directed unto is a Christian church; for, — (1.) Whereas it hath been proved it concerned the times to come afterward, there was in those times nothing that could pretend unto the name of the church but a Christian church only. The Jewish synagogues had an utter end put unto them, so as that an address unto any of them in this case was not only useless but unlawful. And as unto magistrates or arbitrators, to have them called the church, and that in such a sense as that after the interposition of their authority or advice a man should be freed from the discharge of all Christian duties, such as are mutually required among the disciples of Christ, towards his brother, is a fond imagination: for, — (2.) It is such a church as can exercise *authority in the name of Christ* over his disciples, and

such as in conscience they should be bound to submit themselves unto; for the reason given of the contempt of the voice, judgment, and sentence of the church in case of offence, is their power of spiritual binding and loosing, which is committed by Christ thereunto, and so he adds immediately, Matt. xviii. 18, "Whatsoever ye shall bind on earth shall be bound in heaven, and whatsoever ye shall loose on earth shall be loosed in heaven;" [which] is the privilege of a Christian church only.

4. It is a visible *particular congregation* alone that is intended; for, — (1.) As unto "the church" in other acceptations of that name, either for the catholic invisible church, or for the whole body of professed believers throughout the world, it is utterly impossible that this duty should be observed towards it, as is manifest unto all. (2.) We have proved that the first and most proper signification of the word is of a *single* congregation, assembling together for its duties and enjoyments. Wherever, therefore, the church in general is mentioned, without the addition of any thing or circumstance that may lead unto another signification, it must be interpreted of such a particular church or congregation. (3.) The persons intended, offending and offended, must belong unto the *same society* unto whom the address is to be made, or else the one party may justly decline the judicatory applied unto, and so frustrate the process; and it must be such a church as unto whom they are known in their circumstances, without which it is impossible that a right judgment in sundry cases can be made in point of offence. (4.) It is a church of an easy address: "Go, tell the church;" which supposeth that free and immediate access which all the members of a church have unto that whole church whereof they are members. Wherefore, — (5.) It is said, Εἶπε τῇ ἐκκλησίᾳ, "Tell the church;" not a church, but *the* church, — namely, whereunto thou and thy brother do belong. (6.) One end of this direction is, that the offending and the offended parties may continue together in the communion of the same church, in love without dissimulation; which thing belongs unto a particular congregation. (7.) The meaning is not, "Tell the *diocesan bishop*," for whatever church he may have under his rule, yet is not he himself a church. Nor is it (8.) the chancellor's court that our Saviour intended. Be it what it will, it is a disparagement unto all churches to have that name applied thereunto. Nor, lastly, is it a presbytery, or association of the elders of many particular con-

gregations, that is intended; for the power proclaimed in such associated presbyteries is with respect unto what is already in or before particular congregations, which they have not either wisdom or authority, as is supposed, finally to order and determine. But this supposeth that the address in the first place be made unto a particular congregation; which, therefore, is firstly and properly here intended.

All things are plain, familiar, and exposed to the common understandings of all believers whose minds are any way exercised about these things, as, indeed, are all things that belong unto the discipline of Christ. Arguments pretendedly deep and learned, really obscure and perplexed, with logical notions and distinctions applied unto things thus plain and evident in themselves, do serve only to involve and darken the truth. It is plain in the place, — (1.) That there was a church-state for Christians then designed by Christ, which afterward he would institute and settle; (2.) That all true disciples were to join and unite themselves in some such church as might be helpful unto their love, order, peace, and edification; (3.) That among the members of these churches offences would or might arise, which in themselves tend unto pernicious events; (4.) That if these offences could not be cured and taken away, so as that love without dissimulation might be continued among all the members of the churches, an account of them at last was to be given unto that church or society whereunto the parties concerned do belong as members of it; (5.) That this church should hear, determine, and give judgment, with advice, in the cases so brought unto it, for the taking away and removal of all offences; (6.) That this determination of the church is to be rested in, on the penalty of a deprivation of all the privileges of the church; (7.) That these things are the institution and appointment of Christ himself, whose authority in them all is to be submitted unto, and which alone can cast one that is a professed Christian into the condition of a heathen or a publican.

These things, in the notion and practice of them, are plain, easy, and exposed to the understanding of the meanest of the disciples of Christ, as it is meet that all things should be wherein their daily practice is concerned; but it is not easily to be expressed into what horrible perplexities and confusions they have been wrested in the church of Rome, nor how those who depart from the plain, obvious sense of the words, and love not

Chapter IV.

the practice they direct unto, do lead themselves and others into ways and paths that have neither use nor end. From the corrupt abuse of the holy institution of our Lord Jesus Christ, here intended, so many powers, faculties, courts, jurisdictions, legal processes, with litigious, vexatious, oppressive courses of actions and trials, — whose very names are uncouth, horrid, foreign unto religion, and unintelligible without cunning in an artificial, barbarous science of the canon law, — have proceeded, as are enough to fill a sober, rational man with astonishment how it could ever enter into the minds of men to suppose that they can possibly have any relation unto this divine institution. Those who are not utterly blinded with interest and prejudice, wholly ignorant of the gospel and the mind of Christ therein, as also strangers from the practice of the duties which it requires, will hardly believe that in this context our Lord Jesus Christ designed to set up and erect an earthly domination in and over his churches, to be administered by the rules of the canon law and the Rota[4] at Rome. They must be spiritually mad and ridiculous who can give the least entertainment unto such an imagination.

Nor can the discipline of any diocesan churches, administered in and by courts and officers foreign to the Scripture, both name and thing, be brought within the view of this rule, nor can all the art of the world make any application of it thereunto; for what some plead concerning magistrates or arbitrators, they are things which men would never betake themselves unto, but only to evade the force of that truth which they love not. All this is fallen out by men's departing from the simplicity of the gospel, and a contempt of that sense of the words of the Lord Jesus which is plain and obvious unto all who desire not only to hear his words but also to observe his commands.

Thirdly, Our third argument is taken from the nature of the churches instituted by the apostles and their order, as it is expressed in the Scripture; for they were all of them congregational, and of no other sort. This the ensuing considerations will make evident:—

---

4 The Rota is an important ecclesiastical court at Rome, before which all suits in the territory of the church may be carried by appeal, and which takes cognizance of all beneficiary and patrimonial interests. Twelve prelates are the judges; of whom one must be a German, another a Frenchman, two Spaniards, and the rest Italians. — Ed.

1. There were *many churches* planted by the apostles in very small provinces. Not to insist on the churches of Galatia, Gal. i. 2, concerning which it is nowhere intimated that they had any one head or mother church, metropolitical or diocesan; nor of those of Macedonia, distinct from that of Philippi, whereof we have spoken before; upon the first coming of Paul after his conversion unto Jerusalem, which was three years, chap. i. 18, in the fourth year after the ascension of Christ, there were churches planted in all Judea, and Galilee, and Samaria, Acts ix. 31. Neither of the two latter provinces was equal unto one ordinary diocese; yet were there churches in both of them, and that in so short a time after the first preaching of the gospel as that it is impossible they should be conceived to be any other but single congregations. What is excepted or opposed hereunto by the Rev. Dr Stillingfleet shall be examined and disproved afterward by itself, that the progress of our discourse be not here interrupted.

2. These churches were such as that the apostles appointed in them *ordinary elders and deacons*, that might administer all ordinances unto the whole church, and take care of all the poor, Acts xiv. 23, xx. 17, 28. Now, the care, inspection, and labour of ordinary officers can extend itself no farther than unto a particular congregation. No man can administer all ordinances unto a diocesan church. And this "ordaining elders in every church" is the same with "ordaining them in every city," Tit. i. 5, — that is, in every town wherein there was a number converted unto the faith; as is evident from Acts xiv. 23. And it was in towns and cities ordinarily that the gospel was first preached and first received. Such believers being congregated and united in the profession of the same faith and subjection unto the authority of Christ, did constitute such a church-state as it was the will of Christ they should have bishops or elders and deacons ordained amongst them; and were, therefore, as unto their state, such churches as he owned.

3. It is said of most of these churches expressly that they respectively *met together in one place*, or had their assemblies of the whole church for the discharge of the duties required of them; which is peculiar unto congregational churches only: so did the church at Jerusalem on all occasions, Acts xv. 12, 22, xxi. 22; see chap. v. 11, vi. 2. It is of no force which is objected from the multitude of them that are said to believe, and so, consequently,

were of that church, so as that they could not assemble together; for whereas the Scripture says expressly that the "multitude" of the church did "come together," it is scarce fair for us to say they were such a multitude as that they could not come together. And it is evident that the great numbers of believers that are said to be at Jerusalem were there only occasionally, and were not fixed in that church; for many years after, a small village beyond Jordan could receive all that were so fixed in it. The church at Antioch gathered together in one assembly, chap. xiv. 27, to hear Paul and Silas. This church, thus called together, is called "The multitude," chap. xv. 30; that is, the whole brotherhood, at least, of that church. The whole church of Corinth did assemble together in one place, both for solemn worship and the exercise of discipline, 1 Cor. v. 4, 5, xi. 17, 18, 20, xiv. 23–26.

It is no way necessary to plead any thing in the illustration or for the confirmation of these testimonies. They all of them speak positively in a matter of fact, which will admit of no debate, unless we will put in exceptions unto the veracity of their authors. And they are of themselves sufficient to establish our assertion; for whatever may be the state of any church as unto its officers or rule, into what order soever it be disposed ordinarily or occasionally for its edification, so long as it is its duty to assemble in and with all its members in one place, either for the exercise of its power, the performance of its duty, or enjoyment of its privileges, it is a single congregation, and no more.

4. The duties prescribed unto all church-members in the writings of the apostles, to be diligently attended unto by them, are such as, either in their nature or the manner of their performance, cannot be attended unto and duly accomplished but in a *particular congregation only*. This I shall immediately speak distinctly unto, and therefore only mention it in this place.

These things being so plainly, positively, and frequently asserted in the Scripture, it cannot be questionable unto any impartial mind but that particular churches or congregations are of divine institution, and consequently that unto them the whole power and privilege of the church doth belong; for if they do not so, whatever they are, churches they are not. If, therefore, any other church-state be supposed, we may well require that its name, nature, use, power, and bounds be some or all of them declared in the Scripture. Reasonings drawn from the superiority of the apostles above the evangelists, of bishops above presbyters, or from church-rule in the hands of the officers of the church only, from the power of the Christian magistrate in things ecclesiastical, from the meetness of union among all churches, are of no use in this case; for they are all consistent with the sole institution of particular congregations, nor do in the least intimate that there is or needs to be any other church-state of divine appointment.

CHAPTER V.

The state of the first churches after the apostles, to the end of the second century.

IN confirmation of the foregoing argument, we urge the precedent and example of the primitive churches that succeeded unto those which were planted by the apostles themselves, and so may well be judged to have walked in the same way and order with them. And that which we allege is, —

That in no approved writers for the space of two hundred years after Christ is there any mention made of any other organical, visibly-professing church, but that only which is parochial or congregational.

A church of any other form, state, or order, — papal or œcumenical, patriarchal, metropolitical, diocesan, or classical, — they knew not, neither name nor thing, nor any of them appear in any of their writings.

Before I proceed unto the confirmation of this assertion by particular testimonies, I shall premise some things which are needful unto the right understanding of what it is that I intend to prove by them; as, —

1. All the churches at first planted by the apostles, whether in the greatest cities, as Jerusalem, Antioch, Corinth, Rome, etc., or those in the meanest villages of Judea, Galilee, or Samaria, were, as unto their church-state, in order, power, privilege, and duty, every way equal, — not superior or inferior, not ruling over or subject unto one another. No *institution* of any inequality between them, no instance of any *practice* supposing it, no *direction* for any compliance with it, no one word of intimation of it, can be produced from the Scripture; nor is it consistent with the nature of the gospel church-state.

2. In and among all these churches there was "one and the same Spirit, one hope of their calling, one Lord, one faith, one baptism;" whence they were all obliged mutually to seek and endeavour the good and edification of each other, to be helpful

to one another in all things, according unto that which any of them had received in the Lord. This they did by prayer, by advice and counsel, by messenger sent with salutations, exhortations, consolations, supplies for the poor, and on all the like occasions. By these means, and by the exercise of that mutual love and care which they were obliged unto, they kept and preserved unity and communion among themselves, and gave a common testimony against any thing that in doctrine or practice deviated from the rule and discipline of Christ. This order, with peace and love thereon, continued among them until pride, ambition, desire of rule and pre-eminence, in Diotrephes, and a multitude of the same spirit with him, began to open a door unto the entrance of "the mystery of iniquity," under pretence of a better order than this, which was of the appointment of Christ.

3. It must be acknowledged, that notwithstanding this equality among all churches, as unto their state and power, there were great differences between them, some real and some in reputation; which, not being rightly managed, proved an occasion of evil in and unto them all. For instance:—

(1.) Some were more eminent in *spiritual gifts* than others. As this was a privilege that might have been greatly improved unto the honour of Christ and the gospel, yet we know how it was abused in the church of Corinth, and what disorders followed thereon. So weak and frail are the best of men, so liable unto temptation, that all pre-eminence is dangerous for them, and often abused by them; which, I confess, makes me not a little admire to see men so earnestly pleading for it, so fearlessly assuming it unto themselves, so fiercely contending that all power and rule in the church belongs unto them alone. But, —

(2.) Reputation was given unto some by the long abode of some of the apostles in them. Of this advantage we find nothing in the Scripture; but certain it is it was much pleaded and contended about among the primitive churches, yea, so far, until by degrees disputes arose about the *places* where this or that apostle *fixed his seat*; which was looked on as a pre-eminence for the present and a security for the future. But yet we know how soon some of them degenerated from the church order and discipline wherein they were instructed by the apostles. See Rev. ii., iii.

(3.) The greatness, power, fame, or civil authority of the *place or city* where any church was planted, gave it an advantage and privilege in reputation above others; and the churches planted

Chapter V.

in such cities were quickly more numerous in their members than others were. Unless men strictly kept themselves unto the force of primitive institutions, it was very hard for them to think and judge that a church, it may be in a small village or town in Galilee, should be equal with that at Jerusalem or at Antioch, or afterward at Rome itself. The generality of men easily suffered themselves to be persuaded that those churches were advanced in state and order far above the other obscure, poor congregations. That there should be a church at Rome, the head city of the world, was a matter of great joy and triumph unto many; and the advancement of it in reputation they thought belonged unto the honour of our religion. Howbeit there is not in the Scripture the least regard expressed unto any of these things, of place, number, or possibility of outward splendour, either in the promises of the presence of Christ in and with his churches, or in the communication of power and privileges unto them. Yet such an improvement did this foolish imagination find, that after those who presided in the churches called in the principal cities had tasted of the sweetness of the bait which lay in the ascription of a pre-eminence unto them, they began openly to claim it unto themselves, and to usurp authority over other churches, confirming their own usurpations by canons and rules, until a few of them in the council of Nice began to divide the Christian world among themselves, as if it had been conquered by them. Hence proceeded those shameful contests that were among the greater prelates about their pre-eminency: and hence arose that pretence of the bishops of Rome unto no less a right of rule and dominion over all Christian churches than the city had over all the nations and cities of the empire; which being carried on by all sorts of evil artifices, as by downright forgeries, shameless intrusions of themselves, impudent laying hold of all advantages unto their own exaltation, prevailed at length unto the utter ruin of all church order and worship. There is no sober history of the rise and growth by several degrees of any city, commonwealth, or empire, that is filled with so many instances of ambitious seeking of pre-eminence as our church stories are.

By this imagination were the generality of the prelates in those days induced to introduce and settle a government in and among the churches of Christ answering unto the civil government of the Roman empire. As the civil government was cast into national, or diocesan, or provincial, in less or greater divisions, each of which had its capital city, the place of the residence of the chief civil governor; so they designed to frame an image of it in the church, ascribing an alike dignity and power unto the prelates of those cities, and a jurisdiction extending itself unto nations, dioceses, and provinces. Hereby the lesser congregations, or parochial churches, being weakened in process of time in their gifts and interest, were swallowed up in the power of the others, and became only inconsiderable appendices unto them, to be ruled at their pleasure. But these things fell out long after the times which we inquire into; only, their occasion began to present itself unto men of corrupt minds from the beginning. But we have before at large discoursed of them.

(4.) Some churches had a great advantage, in that the gospel, as the apostle speaks, "went forth from them" unto others. They in their ministry were the means, first, of the conversion of others unto the faith, and then of their gathering into a church-state, affording them assistance in all things they stood in need of. Hence these newly-formed churches, in lesser towns and villages, had always a great reverence for the church by whose means they were converted unto God and stated in church-order; and it was meet that so they should have. But in process of time, as these lesser churches decreased in spiritual gifts, and fell under a scarcity of able guides, this reverence was turned into obedience and dependence; and they thought it well enough to be under the rule of others, being unable well to rule themselves.

On these and the like accounts there was quickly introduced an inequality among churches; which, by virtue of their first institution, were equal as unto state and power.

4. Churches may admit of many *variations as* unto their outward form and order, which yet change not their state, nor cause them to cease from being congregational; as, —

(1.) Supposing that any of them might have many elders or presbyters in them, as it is apparent that most of them had, yea, all that are mentioned in the Scripture had so, Acts xi. 30, xiv. 23, xv. 6, 22, 23, xvi. 4, xx. 17, 18, 28, xxi. 18; Phil. i. 1; 1 Tim. v. 17; Tit. i. 5, — they might, and some of them did, choose out some one endued with especial gifts, that might in some sort preside amongst them, and who had quickly the name of bishop appropriated unto him. This practice is thought to have had its original at Alexandria, and began generally to be received in the third century. But this changed not the state of the church, though it had no divine warrant to authorize it; for this order may be agreed unto among the elders of a particular congregation, and sundry things may fall out inclining unto the reception of it. But from a distinct mention (if any such there be), in the writings of the second century, of bishops and presbyters, to fancy metropolitical and diocesan churches is but a pleasant dream.

(2.) The members of those churches that were great and numerous, being under the care and inspection of their *elders in common*, might, for the ordinary duty of divine worship, meet in parts or several actual assemblies; and they did so, especially in time of persecution. Nothing occurs more frequently in ecclesiastical story than the meetings of Christians in secret places, in private houses, yea, in caves and dens of the earth, when in some places it was impossible that the whole body of the church should so assemble together. How this disposition of the members of the church into several parts, in each of which some elder or elders of it did officiate, gave occasion unto the distinction of greater churches into particular titles or parishes, is not here to be declared; it may be so elsewhere. But neither yet did this alter the state of the churches from their original institution; for, —

(3.) Upon all extraordinary occasions, all such as concerned the whole church, — as the choice of elders or the deposition of them, the admission or exclusion of members, and the like, — the whole church continued to meet together; which practice was plainly continued in the days of Cyprian, as we shall see afterward. Neither doth it appear but that, during the first two hundred years of the church, the whole body of the church did ordinarily meet together in one place for the solemn administration of the holy ordinances of worship, and the exercise of discipline.

Wherefore, notwithstanding these and other the like variations from the original institution of churches, which came in partly by inadvertency unto the rule, and partly were received from the advantages and accommodations which they pretended unto, the state of the churches continued congregational only for two hundred years, so far as can be gathered from the remaining monuments of those times. Only, we must yet add, that we are no way concerned in testimonies or sayings taken from the writings of those in following ages, as unto the state, way, and manner of the churches in this season, but do appeal unto their own writings only. This is the great artifice whereby Baronius, in his Annals, would impose upon the credulity of men an apprehension of the antiquity of any of their Roman inventions; — he affixeth them unto some of the first ages, and giving some countenance unto them, it may be from some spurious writings, lays the weight of confirmation on testimonies and sayings of writers many years, yea, for the most part, ages afterward; for it was and is of the latter ages of the church, wherein use and custom have wrested ecclesiastical words to other significations than at first they were applied unto, to impose the present state of things among them on those who went before, who knew nothing of them.

I shall, therefore, briefly inquire into what representation is made of the state of the churches by the writers themselves who lived in the season inquired after, or in the age next unto it, which was acquainted with their practice.

That which first offereth itself unto us, and which is an invaluable testimony of the state of the first churches immediately after the decease of the apostles, is the epistle of Clemens Romanus unto the brethren of the church of Corinth. This epistle, according to the title of it, Irenæus ascribes unto the whole church at Rome, and calls it *"potentissimas literas:"* — *"Sub hoc Clemente dissensione non modica inter eos qui Corinthi erant fratres facta, scripsit quæ est Romæ ecclesia, potentissimas literas,"* lib. iii. cap. 3. By Eusebius it is termed μεγάλη καὶ θαυμασία, — "great and admirable;" who also affirms that it was publicly read in some churches, Eccles. Hist., lib. iii. cap. 16. And again he calls it ἱκανωτάτην γραφήν, — a "most powerful writing," lib. v. cap. 7.

There is no doubt but some things in the writing of it did befall him *"humanitus,"* that the work of such a companion of some of the apostles as he was might not be received as of divine institution, — such was the credit which he gives unto the vulgar fable of the phœnix; — but for the substance of it, it is such as every way becomes a person of an apostolical spirit, consonant unto the style and writings of the apostles themselves, a precious jewel and just representation of the state and order of the church in those days. And sundry things we may observe from it:—

Chapter V.

1. There is nothing in it that gives the least intimation of any other church-state but that which was *congregational*, although there were the highest causes and reasons for him so to do had there been any such churches then in being. The case he had in hand was that of ecclesiastical sedition or schism in the church of Corinth, the church or body of the brethren having unjustly deposed their elders, as it should seem, all of them. Giving advice herein unto the whole church, using all sorts of arguments to convince them of their sin, directing all probable means for their cure, he never once sends them to the bishop or church of Rome, as the head of unity unto all churches; makes no mention of any metropolitical or diocesan church and its rule, or of any single bishop and his authority. No one of any such order doth he either commend, or condemn, or once address himself unto, with either admonitions, exhortations, encouragements, or directions. He only handles the cause by the rule of the Scripture, as it was stated between the church itself and its elders. I take it for granted that if there were any church at Corinth consisting of many congregations, in the city and about it, or comprehensive, as some say, of the whole region of Achaia, that there was a single officer or bishop over that whole church; but none such is here mentioned. If there were any such, he was either deposed by the people or he was not. If he were deposed, he was only one of the presbyters; for they were only presbyters that were deposed. If he were not, why is he not once called on to discharge his duty in curing of that schism, or blamed for his neglect? Certainly there was never greater prevarication used by any man in any cause than is by Clemens in this, if the state of the church, its rule and order, were such as some now pretend; for he neither lets the people know wherein their sin and schism did lie, — namely, in a separation from their bishop, — nor doth once mention the only proper cure and remedy of all their evils. But he knew their state and order too well to insist on things that were not then *"in rerum natura,"* and wherein they were not concerned.

2. This epistle is written, as unto *the whole church* at Corinth, so in the name of *the whole church of Rome*: Ἐκκλησία τοῦ Θεοῦ ἡ παροικοῦσα Ῥώμην τῇ ἐκκλησίᾳ τοῦ Θεοῦ παροικούσῃ Κόρινθον· — "The church of God which dwelleth" (or sojourneth, as a stranger) "at Rome" (in the city of Rome) "to the church of God that dwelleth" (or sojourneth) "at Corinth." For

although that church was then in disorder, under no certain rule, having cast off all their elders, etc., yet the church of Rome not only allows it to be a sister church, but salutes the brethren of it in the following words: Κλητοῖς ἡγιασμένοις ἐν θελήματι Θεοῦ διὰ τοῦ Κυρίου ἡμῶν Ἰησοῦ Χριστοῦ· — "Called and sanctified through the will of God by our Lord Jesus Christ." The churches of Christ were not so ready in those days to condemn the persons, nor to judge the church-state and condition of others, on every miscarriage, real or supposed, as some have been and are in these latter ages.

3. This address being from the body of the church at Rome unto that at Corinth, without the least mention of the officers of them in particular, it is evident that the churches themselves, — that is, the whole entire community of them, — had communion with one another, as they were sister churches, and that they had themselves the transaction of all affairs wherein they were concerned, as they had in the days of the apostles, Acts xv. 1–3. It was the brethren of the church at Antioch who determined that Paul and Barnabas, and certain others, should go up to Jerusalem to consult the apostles and elders: see also chap. xxi. 22. This they did not, nor ought to do, without the presence, guidance, conduct, and consent of their elders or rulers, when they had any; but this they were now excluded from. And that church, the whole body or fraternity whereof doth advise and consult in those things wherein they are concerned, on the account of their communion with other churches, is a congregational church, and no other. It was the church who sent this epistle unto the Corinthians. Claudius Ephebus, Valerius, Bito, Fortunatus, are named[5] as their messengers: Τοὺς ἀπεσταλμένους ἀφ' ἡμῶν, — "That are sent by us," our messengers, our apostles in these matters; such as the churches made use of on all such occasions in the apostles' days, 2 Cor. viii. 23. And the persons whom they sent were only members of the church, and not officers; nor do we anywhere hear of them under that character. Now, they could not be sent in the name of the church but by its consent; nor could the church consent without its assembling together.

This was the state and order of the first churches. In that communion which was amongst them, according to the mind of Christ, they had a singular concern in the welfare and pros-

---

5   Page 73.

perity of each other, and were solicitous about them in their trials. Hence, those who were planted at a greater distance than would allow frequent personal converse with their respective members, did on all occasions send messengers unto one another; sometimes merely to visit them in love, and sometimes to give or take advice. But these things, as indeed almost all others that belong unto the communion of churches, either in themselves or with one another, are either utterly lost and buried, or kept above ground in a pretence of episcopal authority, churches themselves being wholly excluded from any concernment in them. But as the advice of the church of Rome was desired in this case by the whole church of Corinth (περὶ τῶν ἐπιζητουμένων παρ' ὑμῖν πραγμάτων), so it was given by the body of the church itself, and sent by messengers of their own.[6]

4. The description given of the state, ways, and walking of the church of Corinth,[7] — that is, that whole fraternity of the church, which fell afterward into that disorder which is reproved, — before their fall, is such as that it bespeaks their walking together in one and the same society, and is sufficient to make any good man desire that he might see churches yet in the world unto whom, or the generality of whose members, that description might be honestly and justly accommodated. One character which is given of them I shall mention only: Πλήρης πνεύματος ἁγίου ἔκχυσις ἐπὶ πάντας ἐγίνετο· μεστοίτε ὁσίας βουλῆς, ἐν ἀγαθῇ προθυμίᾳ μετ' εὐσεβοῦς πεποιθήσεως ἐξετείνατε τὰς χεῖρας ὑμῶν πρὸς τὸν παντοκράτορα Θεόν, ἱκετεύοντες αὐτὸν ἴλεως γενέσθαι, εἴτι ἄκοντες ἡμάρτετε. Ἀγὼν ἦν ὑμῖν ἡμέρας τε καὶ νυκτὸς ὑπὲρ πασῆς τῆς ἀδελφότητος εἰς τὸ σώζεσθαι μετ' ἐλέους καὶ συνειδήσεως τὸν ἀριθμὸν τῶν ἐκλεκτῶν αὐτοῦ — "There was a full" (or plentiful) "effusion of the Holy Ghost upon you all; so that, being full" (or filled) "with a holy will" (holiness of will) "and a good readiness of mind, with a pious devout confidence, you stretched out your hands in prayers to almighty God, supplicating his clemency" (or mercy) "for the pardon of your involuntary sins" (sins fallen into by infirmity, or the surprisals of temptations not consented to, nor delighted or continued in). "Your labour" (or contention of spirit, — Ἀγὼν ἦν ὑμῖν, as the apostle speaks, ἡλίκον ἀγῶνα

---

6 Page 1.

7 Pages 2–4.

ἔχω, Col. ii. 1) "was night and day" (in your prayers) "for the whole brotherhood" (that is, especially of their own church itself), "that the number of God's elect might be saved in mercy, through a good conscience towards him."

This was their state, this was their liturgy, this their practice: — (1.) There was on all the members of the church a plentiful effusion of the Holy Spirit in his gifts and graces; wherein, it may be, respect is had unto what was affirmed by the apostle before of the same church, 1 Cor. i. 4–7, the same grace being yet continued unto them. (2.) By virtue of this effusion of the Spirit on all of them, their wills and affections being sanctified, their minds were enabled to pour forth fervent prayers unto God. (3.) They were not such as lived in any open sin, or any secret sin, known to be so, but were only subject unto involuntary surprisals, whose pardon they continually prayed for. (4.) Their love and sense of duty stirred them up to labour mightily in their prayers, with fervency and constancy, for the salvation of the whole fraternity of elect believers, whether throughout the world, or more especially those in and of their own church.

He that should ascribe these things unto any of those churches which now in the world claim to be so only, would quickly find himself at a loss for the proof of what he asserts. Did we all sedulously endeavour to reduce and restore churches unto their primitive state and frame, it would bring more glory to God than all our contentions about role and domination.

4. It is certain that the church of Corinth was fallen into a sinful excess, in the deposition and rejection of their elders,[8] whom the church at Rome judged to have presided among them laudably and unblamably, as unto their whole walk and work amongst them. And this they did by the suggestion of two or three envious, discontented persons, and, as is probable from some digressions in the epistle, tainted with those, errors which had formerly infested that church, as the denial of the resurrection of the flesh; which is therefore here reflected on. But in the whole epistle, the church is nowhere reproved for assuming an authority unto themselves which did not belong unto them. It seems what Cyprian afterward affirmed was then acknowledged, — namely, that the right of choosing the worthy, and of rejecting the unworthy, was in the body of the people. But they are severely reproved for the abuse of their liberty and power;

---

8   Pages 57, 58, 62.

Chapter V.

for they had exercised them on ill grounds, by ill means, for ill ends, and in a most unjust cause. He therefore exhorts the body of the church to return unto their duty, in the restoration of their elders; and then prescribes unto them who were the first occasion of schism that every one would subject themselves unto the restored presbyters, and say, Ποιῶ τὰ προστασσόμενα ὑπὸ τοῦ πλήθους·[9] — "I will do the things appointed or commanded by the multitude," the church in the generality of its members. The "plebs," the multitude, the body of the fraternity in the church, — τὸ πλῆθος, as they are often called in the Scripture, Acts iv. 32, vi. 2, 5, xv. 12, 30, — had then right and power to appoint things that were to be done in the church, for order and peace. I do not say they had it without, or in distinction from, their officers, rulers, and guides, but in a concurrence with them, and subordination to them; whence the acts concluded on may be esteemed, and are, the acts of the whole church. This order can be observed, or this can fall out, only in a congregational church, all whose members do meet together for the discharge of their duties and exercise of their discipline. And if no more may be considered in it but the miscarriage of the people, without any respect to their right and power, yet such churches as wherein it is impossible that that should fall out in them as did so fall out in that church, are not of the same kind or order with it.

But, for the sake of them who may endeavour to reduce any church-state into its primitive constitution, that they may be cautioned against that great evil which this church, in the exercise of their supposed liberty, fell into, I cannot but transcribe a few of those excellent words which are used plentifully with cogent reasons in this epistle[10] against it: Ἀισχρὰ ἀγαπητοὶ, καὶ λίαν αἰσχρὰ, καὶ ἀνάξια τῆς ἐν Χριστῷ ἀγωγῆς ἀκούεται τὴν βεβαιοτάτην καὶ ἀρχαίαν Κορινθίων ἐκκλησίαν, δι' ἓν ἢ δύο πρόσωπα στασιάζειν πρὸς τοὺς πρεσβυτέρους· — "It is shameful, beloved, exceeding shameful, which is reported of you, that the most firm and ancient church of the Corinthians should, for the sake of one or two persons, seditiously tumultuate against their elders." And hereon he proceeds to declare the dreadful scandal that ensued thereon, both among believers and

---

9   Page 69.

10 Page 62.

infidels The instruction, also, which he adds hereunto is worthy the remembrance of all church-members: Ἤτω τὶς πιστὸς ἤτω δυνατὸς γνῶσιν ἐξειπεῖν ἤτω σοφὸς ἐν δικαίᾳ κρίσει λόγων ἤτω ἁγνὸς ἐν ἔργοις· τοσύτῳ μᾶλλον ταπεινοφρεῖν ὀφείλει, ὅσῳ δοκεῖ μᾶλλον μείζων εἶναι. It is blessed advice for all church-members that he gives: "Let a man be faithful; let him be powerful in knowledge" (or the declaration of it); "let him be wise to judge the words or doctrines; let him be chaste or pure in his works: the greater he seems to be, the more humble he ought to be, that so the church may have no trouble by him nor his gifts." But to return.

5. Having occasion to mention the officers of the church, he nameth only the two ranks of bishops and deacons,[11] as the apostle also doth, Phil. i. 1. Speaking of the apostles he says, Κατὰ χώρας καὶ πόλεις κηρύσσοντες, καθίστανον τὰς ἀπαρχὰς αὐτῶν, δοκιμάσαντες τῷ πνεύματι εἰς ἐπισκόπους καὶ διακόνους τῶν μελλόντων πιστεύειν· — "Preaching the word through regions and cities, they appointed the first-fruits" — as the house of Stephanas was the "first-fruits of Achaia," who therefore "addicted themselves to the ministry of the saints," 1 Cor. xvi. 15, — (or the first converts to the faith), "after a spiritual trial of them" (as unto their fitness for their work), "to be bishops and deacons of them that should afterward believe." Where there were as yet but a few converted, the apostles gathered them into church-order; and so soon as they found any fit among them, appointed and ordained them to be bishops and deacons; so that provision might be made for the guidance and conduct of them that should be converted and added unto them after they were left by the apostles. These bishops he affirms to be, and to have been, the presbyters or elders of the church,[12] even the same with those deposed by the Corinthians, in the same manner as the apostle doth, Acts xx. 28: Ἁμαρτία γὰρ οὐ μικρὰ ἡμῖν ἔσται, ἐὰν τοὺς ἀμέμπτως καὶ ὁσίως προσενέγκοντας τὰ δῶρα τῆς ἐπισκοπῆς ἀποβάλωμεν· μακάριοι δὲ προοδοιπορήσαντες πρεσβύτεροι, etc.; — "It is no small sin in us to reject or cast off them who have offered the gifts" (or discharged the duties) "of episcopacy holily and without blame. Blessed are the elders who went before!" — namely,

---

11 Pages 54, 55.

12 Pages 57, 58.

as he expresseth it, because they are freed from that amotion from their office which those elders now amongst them had undergone, after they had duly discharged the office of episcopacy. Other distinction and difference of ordinary officers, besides that of bishops or elders and deacons, the church at Rome in those days knew not. Such ought to be in every particular church. Of any one single person to preside over many churches, which is necessary unto the constitution of a church-state distinct from that which is congregational, Clemens knew nothing in his days, but gives us such a description of the church and its order as is inconsistent with such a pretence.

6. I shall add no more from this excellent epistle, but only the account given in it of the first constitution of officers in the churches: Καὶ οἱ ἀπόστολοι ἡμῶν ἔγνωσαν διὰ τοῦ Κυρίου ἡμῶν Ἰησοῦ Χριστοῦ ὅτι ἔρις ἔσται ἐπὶ τοῦ ὀνόματος τῆς ἐπισκοπῆς διὰ ταύτην οὖν τὴν αἰτίαν πρόγνωσιν εἰληφότες τελείαν κατέστησαν τοὺς προειρημένους καὶ μεταξὺ ἐπινομὴν δεδώκασιν ὅπως ἐὰν κοιμηθῶσιν διαδέξωνται ἕτεροι δεδοκιμασμένοι ἄνδρες, τὴν λειτουργίαν αὐτῶν, τοὺς οὖν κατασταθέντας ὑπ' ἐκείνων ἢ μεταξὺ ὑφ' ἑτέρων ἐλλογίμων ἀνδρῶν, συνευδοκησάσης τῆς ἐκκλησίας πάσης, κ. τ. λ. — "Our apostles, therefore, knowing by our Lord Jesus Christ that there would contention arise about the name of episcopacy" (that is, episcopacy itself); "for this cause, being endued with a perfect foresight of things, they appointed those forementioned" (their first converts, unto the office of the ministry), "for the future describing or giving order about the course of the ministry, that other approved men might succeed them in their ministry. These" (elders), "therefore, who were so appointed by them, and afterward by other famous men, with the consent of the whole church," etc.

Sundry things we may observe in this discourse:— 1. The apostles foresaw there would be strife and contention about *the name of episcopacy;* that is, the office itself, and those who should possess it. This episcopacy was that office which the deposed elders had well discharged in the church of Corinth. This they might foresee from the nature of the thing itself, the inclination of men unto pre-eminence, and the instance they had seen in their own days, in such as Diotrephes, with the former division that had been in this very church about their teachers, 1 Cor. i. 12. But, moreover, they were instructed in the knowledge of it by our Lord Jesus Christ, through his divine Spirit abiding with them and teaching them all things. This, therefore, they sought by all means to prevent, and that two ways:— (1.) In that, for the first time, themselves appointed approved persons unto the office of the ministry; not that they did it of themselves, without the consent and choice of the church whereunto any of them were appointed (for this was directly contrary unto their practice, Acts i. 15–26, vi. 1–6, xiv. 23), but that the peace and edification of the churches might be provided for, they themselves spiritually tried and approved of fit persons, so to lead the church in their choice. Wherefore, that which is added afterward, of "the consent of the whole church," is to be referred unto those who were ordained by the apostles themselves. (2.) They gave rules and orders, namely, in their writings, concerning the offices and officers that were to be in the church, with the way whereby they should be substituted in the place and room of them that were deceased, as we know they have done in their writings. (3.) After this was done by the apostles, other excellent persons, as the evangelists, did the same. These assisted the churches in the ordination and choice of their officers, according unto the rules prescribed by the apostles. And I know not but that the eminent pastors of other churches, who usually gave their assistance in the setting apart and ordination of others unto the ministry, be intended.

I have insisted long on this testimony, being led on by the excellency of the writing itself. Nothing remains written so near the times of the apostles, nor doth any that is extant which was written afterward give such an evidence of apostolical wisdom, gravity, and humility. Neither is there in all antiquity, after the writings of the apostles, such a representation of the state, order, and rule of the first evangelical churches. And it is no small prejudice unto the pretensions of future ages that this apostolical person, handling a most weighty ecclesiastical cause, makes not the least mention of such offices, power, and proceedings, as wherein some would have all church rule and order to consist.

The epistle of Polycarpus, and the elders of the church of Smyrna with him, unto the church of the Philippians, is the next on the roll of antiquity. Nothing appears in the whole to intimate any other church-state or order than that described by Clemens. The epistle is directed unto the whole church at Philippi, not unto any particular bishop: Πολύκαρπος καὶ οἱ

Chapter V.

σὺν αὐτῷ πρεσβύτεροι τῇ ἐκκλησίᾳ τοῦ Θεοῦ τῇ παροικούσῃ Φιλίππους. This was the usual style of those days. So was it used, as we have seen, by Clemens: Ἐκκλησία ἡ παροικοῦσα Ῥώμην. So it was used presently after the death of Polycarpus by the church at Smyrna, in the account they gave unto other churches of his death and martyrdom: Ἡ ἐκκλησία τοῦ Θεοῦ ἡ παροικοῦσα Σμύρναν τῇ ἐκκλησίᾳ παροικούσῃ ἐν Φιλομελίῳ. And the same was the inscription of the epistle of the churches at Vienne and Lyons in France, unto the churches in Phrygia, as we shall see immediately. And these are plain testimonies of that communion among the churches in those days which was held in and by the body of each church, or the community of the brotherhood; which is a clear demonstration of their state and order. And those whom the apostle, writing to the Philippians, calls their bishops and deacons, Polycarpus calls their presbyters and deacons. "It behoves you," saith he unto the church there, "to abstain from these things," ὑποτασσομένοις τοῖς πρεσβυτέροις καὶ διακόνοις, — "being subject unto the elders and deacons." Nor doth he mention any other bishop among the Philippians. And it may be observed, that in all these primitive writings there is still a distinction made, after the example of Scripture, between the church and the guides, rulers, bishops, or elders of it; and the name of *the church* is constantly assigned unto the body of the people as distinct from the elders, nowhere to the bishops or elders as distinct from the people, though the church, in its complete state, comprehendeth both sorts.

Unto this time, — that is, about the year 107 or 108, — do belong the epistles ascribed unto Ignatius, if so be they were written by him; for Polycarpus wrote his epistle to the Philippians after Ignatius was carried to Rome, having wrote his epistle before in Asia. Many are the contests of learned men about those epistles which remain, whether they are genuine, or the same that were written by him; for that he did write epistles unto sundry churches is acknowledged by all. And whereas there have in this age been two copies found and published of those epistles, wherein very many things that were obnoxious unto just exception in those before published do not at all appear, yet men are not agreed which of them ought to be preferred; and many yet deny that any of them were those written by Ignatius. I shall not interpose in this contest; only, I must say, that if any of his genuine writings do yet remain, yet the corruption and interpolation of them for many ages must needs much impair the authority of what is represented in them as his; nor am I delivered from these thoughts by the late either more sound or more maimed editions of them. And the truth is, the corruption and fiction of epistolical writings in the first ages was so intolerable, as that very little in that kind is preserved sincere and unquestionable. Hence Dionysius, the bishop of Corinth, complained that in his own time his own epistles were so corrupted, by additions and detractions, as that it seems he would have them no more esteemed as his, Eusebius Ecclesiast. Hist., lib. iv. cap. 23.

But yet, because these epistles are so earnestly contended for by many learned men as the genuine writings of Ignatius, I shall not pass by the consideration of them as unto the argument in hand. I do therefore affirm, that in these epistles (in any edition of them) there is no mention made or description given of any church or church-state but only of that which is congregational; that is, such a church as all the members whereof did meet, and were obliged to meet, for divine worship and discipline in the same place. What was the distinction they observed among their officers, of what sort they were, and what number, belongs not unto our present inquiry. Our concernment is only this, that they did preside in the same particular church, and were none of them bishops of more churches than one, or of any church that should consist of a collection or association of such particular churches as had no bishops, properly so called, of their own.

All these epistles, — that is, the seven most esteemed, — were written, as that of Clemens, unto the bodies or whole fraternity of the churches, unto whom they are directed, in distinction from their bishops, elders, and deacons, excepting that only unto Polycarpus, which is unto a single person. Under that consideration, — namely, of the entire fraternity in distinction from their officers, — doth he address unto them, and therein doth he ascribe and assign such duties unto them as could not be attended unto nor performed but in the assembly of them all. Such is the direction he gives unto the church of the Philadelphians, how and in what manner they should receive penitents returning unto the church, that they might be encouraged unto that duty by their benignity and patience; and many things of the like nature doth he deal with them about. And this assembling together in the same place, — namely, of the whole church, — he doth frequently intimate and express. Some instances hereof we may repeat: —

Πάντες ἐπὶ τὸ αὐτὸ ἐν τῇ προσευχῇ ἅμα συνέρχεσθε· μία δέησις ἔστω κοινή· — "Meet all of you together in the same place; let there be one prayer in common of all," Epist. ad Magnes. [cap. 7] This direction can be given unto no other but a particular church. And again to the Philadelphians [cap. 2]: Ὅπου ὁ ποιμήν ἐστιν, ἐκεῖ ὡς πρόβατα ἀκολουθεῖτε· — "Where your pastor is, there follow you as sheep." And how they may do so is declared immediately afterward [cap.4]: Θαρρῶν γράφω τῇ ἀξιοθέῳ ἀγάπῃ ὑμῶν, παρακαλῶν ὑμᾶς μιᾷ πίστει, καὶ ἑνὶ κηρύγματι καὶ μιᾷ εὐχαριστίᾳ χρῆσθαι· μία γάρ ἐστιν ἡ σάρξ τοῦ Κυρίου Ἰησοῦ, καὶ ἓν αὐτοῦ τὸ αἷμα τὸ ὑπὲρ ἡμῶν ἐκχυθέν, εἷς καὶ ἄρτος τοῖς πᾶσιν ἐθρύφθη καὶ ἓν ποτήριον τοῖς ὅλοις διενεμήθη ἓν θυσιαστήριον πάσῃ τῇ ἐκκλησίᾳ καὶ εἷς ἐπίσκοπος ἅμα τῷ πρεσβυτερίῳ καὶ τοῖς διακόνοις τοῖς συνδούλοις μου· — "I write with confidence unto your godly love, and persuade you to use one faith" (or the confession of it), "one preaching of the word, and one eucharist" (or administration of the holy sacrament). "For the flesh of Christ is one, and the blood of Christ that was shed for us is one: one bread is broken to all, and one cup distributed among all; there is one altar to the whole church, and one bishop, with the presbytery, and the deacons my fellow-servants." Nothing can be more evident than that it is a particular church, in its order and assembly for worship *in one place*, that he describes; nor can these things be accommodated unto a church of any other form. And towards the end of the epistle, treating about the churches sending their bishops or others on their occasions, he tells them in particular [cap. 10]: Πρέπον ἐστὶν ὑμῖν ὡς ἐκκλησίᾳ Θεοῦ χειροτονῆσαι ἐπίσκοπον, εἰς τὸ πρεσβεῦσαι ἐκεῖ Θεοῦ πρεσβείαν εἰς τὸ συγχωρηθῆναι αὐτοῖς ἐπὶ τὸ αὐτὸ γενομένοις, καὶ δοξάσαι τὸ ὄνομα τοῦ Θεοῦ· — "It becometh you as a church of God to choose or appoint a bishop, who may perform the embassy of God, that it may be granted unto them to glorify the name of God, being gathered together in one place." It is somewhat difficult [to conceive] how the church of Philadelphia should choose or ordain a bishop at this time, for they had one of their own, whom Ignatius greatly extols in the beginning of the epistle. Nor was it in their power or duty to choose or ordain a bishop for the church of Antioch, which was their own right and duty alone; nor had the church of Antioch any the least dependence on that at Philadelphia. It may be he intends only their assistance therein, as immediately before he ascribes the peace and tranquillity of the Antiochians unto the prayers of the Philadelphians. For my part, I judge he intends not the proper bishop of either place, but some elder, which they were to choose as a messenger to send to Antioch, to assist them in their present condition; for in those days there were persons chosen by the churches to be sent abroad to assist other churches on the like occasions. These were called ἀπόστολοι ἐκκλησιῶν, 2 Cor. viii. 23, — the especial "apostles of the churches;" as verse 19, it is said of Luke that he was χειροτονηθεὶς ὑπὸ τῶν ἐκκλησιῶν, — "chosen" and appointed "by the churches" for the service there mentioned. Such was this bishop, who was sent on God's errand to assist the church by his advice and counsel as unto the continuance of their assemblies, unto the glory of God, though at present their bishop was taken from them. In that epistle unto the Ephesians, he lets them know that he rejoiced at their πολυπλήθεια, their "numerous multitude;" whom he persuades and urgeth unto a common concurrence in prayer with their bishop [cap. 5]: Εἰ γὰρ ἑνὸς καὶ δευτέρου προσευχὴ τοσαύτην ἰσχὺν ἔχει ὥστε τὸν Χριστὸν ἐν αὐτοῖς ἑστάναι, πόσῳ μᾶλλον ἥ τε τοῦ ἐπισκόπου καὶ πάσης τῆς ἐκκλησίας προσευχὴ σύμφωνος; — "And if the prayers of one or two be so effectual that they bring Christ among them, how much more will the consenting prayer of the bishop and the whole church together?" So he again explains his mind towards the end of the epistle [cap. 13]: Σπουδάζετε οὖν πυκνότερον συνέρχεσθαι· ὅταν γὰρ συνεχῶς ἐπὶ τὸ αὐτὸ γένησθε καθαιροῦνται αἱ δυνάμεις τοῦ Σατανᾶ· "Do your diligence to meet together frequently; for when you frequently meet together in the same place, the powers of Satan are destroyed." And many other expressions of the like nature occur in those epistles. We are no way, at present, concerned in the controversy about that distinction of bishops and presbyters which the writer of those epistles doth assert; this only I say, that he doth in none of them take the least notice, or give the least intimation, of any church-state but such alone wherein the members of the whole church did constantly meet together in the same place, for the worship of God and communion among themselves. And not only so, but he

Chapter V.

everywhere, in all his epistles to them, ascribes such duties and rights unto the churches as cannot be observed and preserved but in particular churches only. Nor doth he leave any room for any other church-state whatever. Although, therefore, there might have been, and probably there were, some alterations in the order of the churches from what was of primitive institution, yet was there as yet no such change in their state as to make way for those greater alterations which not long after ensued; for they were not introduced until, through a defect in the multiplication of churches in an equality of power and order, — which ought to have been done, — they were increased into that multitude for number of members, and were so diffused as unto their habitations, as made an appearance of a necessity of another constitution of churches and another kind of rule than what was of original appointment.

Justin Martyr wrote his Second Apology for the Christians unto the Roman emperors about the year 150. It is marvellous to consider how ignorant not only the common sort of the Pagans, but the philosophers also, and governors of the nations, were of the nature of Christian churches, and of the worship celebrated in them. But who are so blind as those who will not see? Even unto this day not a few are willingly, or rather wilfully, ignorant of the nature of such assemblies, or what is performed in them, as were among the primitive Christians, that they may be at liberty to speak all manner of evil of them falsely. Hence were all the reports and stories among the heathen concerning what was done in the Christian conventicles; which they would have to be the most abominable villanies that were ever acted by mankind. Even those who made the most candid inquiry into what they were and did, attained unto very little knowledge or certainty concerning them and their mysteries; as is evident in the epistles of Trajan and Pliny, with the rescript of Adrian unto Minutius Fundanus about them.

In this state of things, this our great and learned philosopher, who afterward suffered martyrdom about the year 160, undertook to give an account unto Antoninus Pius and Lucius, who then ruled the Roman empire, of the nature, order, and worship of the Christian churches; and that in such an excellent manner, as that I know nothing material that can be added unto it, were an account of the same things to be given unto alike persons at this day. We may touch a little upon some heads of it:—

1. He declares *the conversion of men unto the faith as* the foundation of all their church order and worship: Ὅσοι ἂν πεισθῶσι καὶ πιστεύωσιν ἀληθῆ ταῦτα τὰ ὑφ' ἡμῶν διδασκόμενα καὶ λεγόμενα εἶναι, καὶ βιοῦν οὕτως δύνασθαι ὑπισχνῶνται, εὔχεσθαί τε καὶ αἰτεῖν νηστεύοντας παρὰ τοῦ Θεοῦ τῶν προημαρτημένων ἄφεσιν διδάσκονται ἡμῶν συνευχομένων καὶ συννηστευόντων αὐτοῖς· — "As many as are persuaded and do believe the things to be true which are taught and spoken by us, and take upon themselves that they are able to live according to that doctrine, they are taught to seek of God, by fasting and prayer, the pardon of their foregoing sins; and we also do join together with them in fasting and prayer for that end." And herein, — (1.) The only means of conversion which he insists upon is the preaching of the word, or truth of the gospel, wherein they especially insisted on the doctrine of the person and offices of Christ, as appears throughout his whole Apology. (2.) This preaching of the word, or declaration of the truth of the gospel, unto the conversion of the hearers, he doth not confine unto any especial sort of persons, as he doth afterward the administration of the holy things in the church; but speaks of it in general as the work of all Christians that were able for it, as doth the apostle, 1 Cor. xiv. 24, 25. (3.) Those who were converted did two things:— [1.] They *professed their faith* or assent unto the truth of the doctrine of the gospel; [2.] They took it on themselves to *live according to the rule of it*, — to do and observe the things commanded by Jesus Christ, as he appointed they should, Matt. xxviii. 18–20. (4.) To lay a sure and comfortable foundation of their future profession, they were taught to confess their former sins, and by earnest prayer, with fastings, to seek of God the pardon and forgiveness of them. And, — (5.) Herein (such was their love and zeal) those who had been the means of their conversion joined with them, for their comfort and edification. It is well known how this whole process is lost, and on what account it is discontinued; but whether it be done so unto the advantage of Christian religion, and the good of the souls of men, is well worth a strict inquiry.

2. In the next place he declares how those who were so converted were conducted unto *baptism*, and how they were initiated into the mysteries of the gospel thereby.

3. When any was so baptized, they brought him unto the church which he was to be joined unto: Ἡμεῖς δὲ μετὰ τὸ οὕτως

Chapter V.

λοῦσαι τὸν πεπεισμένον καὶ συγκατατεθειμένον ἐπὶ τοὺς λεγομένους ἀδελφοὺς ἄγομεν, ἔνθα συνηγμένοι εἰσί κοινὰς εὐχὰς ποιησόμενοι ὑπέρ τε ἑαυτῶν καὶ τοῦ φωτισθέντος καὶ ἄλλων πανταχοῦ πάντων εὐτόνως, κ. τ. λ. — "Him who is thus baptized, who believeth, and is received" (by consent) "among us" (or to be of our number), "we bring him unto those called the brethren, when they are met" (or gathered together) "for joint prayers and supplications for themselves, and for him who is now illuminated, and all others, with intension of mind," etc. We have here another illustrious instance of the care and diligence of the primitive church about the instating professed believers in the communion of the church. That hereon those who were to be admitted made their public confession we shall afterward declare. And the brethren here mentioned are the whole fraternity of the church, who were concerned in these things. And Justin is not ashamed to declare by what name they called one another among themselves, even to the heathen, though it be now a scorn and reproach among them that are called Christians.

4. He proceeds to declare the nature of their *church meetings* or assemblies, with the duties and worship of them. And he tells us, first, that they had frequent meetings among themselves: "They that have any wealth," saith he, "do help the poor," καὶ συνεσμὲν ἀλλήλοις αἰεί "and we are continually together;" that is, in the lesser occasional assemblies of the brethren, for so, in the next place, he adds immediately, Τῇ τοῦ ἡλίου λεγομένῃ ἡμέρᾳ πάντων κατὰ πόλεις καὶ ἀγροὺς μενόντων ἐπὶ τὸ αὐτὸ συνέλευσις γίνεται· — "On the day called Sunday there is a meeting of all that dwell in the towns and fields or villages about." This was the state, the order, the proceeding of the church in the days of Justin; whence it is undeniably evident that he knew no other church-state or order but that of a particular congregation, whose members, living in any town or city, or fields adjacent, did constantly, all of them, meet together in one place on the first day of the week, for the celebration of divine worship.

5. In this church he mentions only two sorts of officers, προεστῶτες and διάκονοι, "presidents and deacons." Of the first sort, in the duty of one of their assemblies, he mentions but one, ὁ προεστώς, "the president," the ruler, the bishop; to whom belonged the administration of all the holy mysteries.

And that we may not think that he is called the προεστώς with respect unto any pre-eminence over other ministers or elders, like a diocesan bishop, he terms him προεστὼς τῶν ἀδελφῶν, he that "presided over the brethren" of that church. Now, certainly that church wherein one president, elder, presbyter, or bishop, did administer the holy ordinances in one place unto all the members of it, was a particular congregation.

6. The things that he ascribeth unto this *leader*, to be done at this general meeting of the church every Lord's day, were, — (1.) That he *prayed*; (2.) That after the reading of the Scripture he *preached*; (3.) That he *consecrated the eucharist*, the elements of the bread and wine being distributed by the deacons unto the congregation; (4.) That he closed the whole worship of the day in prayer.

7. In the consecration of the sacramental elements, he observes that the president prayed at large, giving thanks to God: Εὐχαριστίαν ἐπὶ πολὺ ποιεῖται. So vain is the pretence of some, that in the primitive times they consecrated the elements by the repetition of the Lord's prayer only. After the participation of the eucharist there was a collection made for the poor, as he describeth it at large; what was so gathered being committed to the pastor, who took care for the distribution of it unto all sorts of poor belonging unto the church. Hereunto was added, as Tertullian observes, the exercise of discipline in their assemblies; whereof we shall speak afterward. The close of the administration of the sacrament Justin gives us in these words: Καὶ ὁ προεστὼς εὐχὰς ὁμοίως καὶ εὐχαριστίας ὅση δύναμυις αὐτῶ ἀναπέμπει — "The pastor again, according to his ability" (or power), "poureth forth" (or sends up) "prayers, the people all joyfully crying, Amen," etc. Ὅση δύναμις, — that is, as Origen expounds the phrase often used by himself, Κατὰ τὴν παροῦσαν καὶ δοθεῖσαν δύναμιν, lib. viii. ad Cels.; — "According unto the present ability given unto him."

This was the state, the order, and the worship of the church, with its method, in the days of Justin Martyr. This and no other is that which we plead for.

Unto these times belongs the most excellent epistle of the churches of Vienne and Lyons in France, unto the brethren in Asia and Phrygia, recorded at large by Eusebius, Hist., lib. v. cap. 1. Their design in it is to give an account of the holy martyrs who suffered in the persecution under Marcus Antoninus.

Chapter V.

I am no way concerned in what state Irenæus was in the church at Lyons, whereon, after the writing of this epistle, he was sent to Eleutherius, the bishop of Rome, which he gives an account of, cap. 4. He is, indeed, in that epistle called a presbyter of the church, although, as some suppose, it was sundry years after the death of Pothinus, whom they call bishop of Lyons, into whose room he immediately succeeded; and Eusebius himself, cap. 8, affirming that he would give an account of the writings of the ancient ecclesiastical presbyters, in the first place produceth those of Irenæus. But these things belong not unto our present contest. The epistle we intend was written by the brethren of those churches, and it was written to the brethren of the churches in Asia and Phrygia, after the manner of the Scripture; wherein the *fraternity or body of the church* was designed or intended in all such epistles. From them was this epistle, and unto those of the same sort was it written, — not from one bishop unto another. And as this manifests the concern of the brotherhood in all ecclesiastical affairs, so, with all other circumstances, it evidenceth that those churches were particular or congregational only. Nor is there any thing in the whole epistle that should give the least intimation of any other church-state known unto them. This epistle, as recorded by Eusebius, gives us a noble representation of the spirit and communion that was then among the churches of Christ; being written with apostolical simplicity and gravity, and remote from those titles of honour and affected swelling words, which the feigned writings of that age, and some that are genuine in those that followed, are stuffed withal.

Tertullian, who lived about the end of the second century, gives us the same account of the state, order, and worship of the churches, as was given before by Justin Martyr, Apol. ad Gen. cap. xxxix. The description of a church he first lays down in these words: "*Corpus sumus de conscientia religionis, et disciplinæ unitate, et spei fœdere;*" — "We are a body" (united) "in the conscience of religion" (or a conscientious observation of the duties of religion), "by an agreement in discipline" (whereby it was usual with the ancients to express universal obedience unto the doctrine and commands of Christ), "and in a covenant of hope." For whereas such a body or religious society could not be united but by a covenant, he calls it "a covenant of hope," because the principal respect was had therein unto the things hoped for. They covenanted together so to live and walk in the discipline of Christ, or obedience unto his commands, as that they might come together unto the enjoyment of eternal blessedness.

This religious body or society, thus united by covenant, did meet together in the same assembly or congregation: "*Corpus sumus, coimus in cœtum et congregationem, ut ad Deum quasi manu factÂ precationibus ambiamus orantes;*" and, "*Cogimur ad divinarum literarum commemorationem,*" etc. Designing to declare, as he doth in particular, "*Negotia Christianæ factionis,*" as he calls them, or the duties of Christian religion, which in their churches they did attend unto, he lays the foundation in their meetings in the same assembly or congregation.

In these assemblies there presided the elders, that, upon a testimony of their meetness unto that office, were chosen thereunto: "*President probati quique seniores, honorem istum non pretio sed testimonio adepti.*" And in the church thus met together in the same place, assembly, or congregation, under the rule and conduct of their elders, among other things they *exercised discipline*; that is, in the presence and by the consent of the whole: "*Ibidem etiam, exhortationes, castigationes, et censura divina. Nam et judicatur magno cum pondere, ut apud certos de Dei conspectu; summumque futuri judicii præjudicium est, si quis ita deliquerit, ut a communicatione orationis et conventus, et omnis sancti commercii relegetur.*" The loss of this discipline and the manner of its administration hath been one of the principal means of the apostasy of churches from their primitive institution.

To the same purpose doth Origen give us an account of the way of the gathering and establishing churches under elders of their own choosing, in the close of his last book against Celsus. And although in the days of Cyprian, in the third century, the distinction between the bishop in any church, eminently so called, and those who are only presbyters, with their imparity, and not only the precedency but superiority of one over others, began generally to be admitted, yet it is sufficiently manifest from his epistles that the church wherein he did preside was so far a *particular church as* that the whole body or fraternity of it was admitted unto all advice in things of common concernment unto the whole church, and allowed the exercise of their power and liberty in choosing or refusing the officers that were to be set over them.

Some few things we may observe from the testimonies insisted on; as, —

CHAPTER V.   149

1. There is in them a true and *full representation* of the state, order, rule, and discipline of the churches in the first ages. It is a sufficient demonstration that all those things wherein at the present the state and order of the church are supposed to consist are indeed later inventions; not merely because they are not mentioned by them, but because they axe not so when they avowedly profess to give an account of that state and order of the church which was then in use and practice. Had there been then among Christians metropolitan archbishops, or bishops diocesan, churches national or provincial, an enclosure of church power or ecclesiastical jurisdiction, in and for the whole rule of the church, unto bishops and officers utterly foreign unto any pretence of apostolical institution or countenance; had many churches, or many hundreds of churches, been without rule in or among themselves, subject to the rule of any one man standing in no especial relation unto any of them; with other things of the like nature been then invented, known, and in use, — how could they possibly be excused in passing them over without the least taking notice of them, or giving them the honour of being once mentioned by them? How easy had it been for their pagan rulers, unto whom they presented their accounts (some of them) of the state of their churches, to have replied that they knew well enough there were other dignities, orders, and practices than what they did acknowledge, which they were either afraid or ashamed to own! But besides this silence, on the other hand, they assert such things of the officers appointed in the church, — of the way of their appointment, of the duty of officers in the church, of the power and liberty of the people, of the nature and exercise of discipline, — as are utterly inconsistent with that state of these things which is by some pleaded for. Yea, as we have showed, whatever they write or speak about churches or their order can have no being or exercise in any other form of churches but of particular congregations.

2. That account which they give, that representation which they make, of the kind, state, and order of the churches among them, doth absolutely agree with and answer unto what we are taught in the divine writings about the same things. There were, indeed, before the end of the second century, some practices in and about some lesser things (such as sending the consecrated elements from the assembly unto such as were sick) that they had no warrant for from any thing written or done by the apos-

tles; but as unto the substance of what concerns the state, order, rule, discipline, and worship of evangelical churches, there is not any instance to be given wherein they departed from the apostolical traditions or institution, either by adding any thing of their own unto them, or omitting any thing that was by them ordained.

3. From this state the churches did by degrees and insensibly degenerate, so as that another form and order of them did appear towards the end of the third century; for some in the first churches not applying their minds unto the apostolical rule and practice, who "ordained elders in every church," and that not only in cities and towns, but, as Clemens affirms, κατὰ χώρας, in the country villages, many disorders ensued with respect unto such collections of Christians and congregations as were gathered at some distance from the first or city church. Until the time of Origen, the example of the apostles in this case was followed, and their directions observed; for so he writes: Ἡμεῖς ἐν ἑκάστῃ πόλει ἄλλο σύστημα πατρίδος κτισθὲν λόγῳ Θεοῦ ἐπιστάμενοι τοὺς δυνατοὺς λογῳ καὶ βίῳ ὑγιεῖ χρωμένους ἄρχειν ἐπὶ τὸ ἄρχειν ἐκκλησιῶν παρακαλοῦμεν. — Καὶ εἰ ἄρχουσιν οἱ καλῶς ἄρχοντες ἐν τῇ ἐκκλησίᾳ, ὑπὸ τῆς κατὰ θεὸν πατρίδος, λέγω δὲ τῆς ἐκκλησίας, ἐκλεγόμενοι· ἄρχουσι κατὰ τὰ ὑπὸ τοῦ Θεοῦ προτεταγμένα· — "And we, knowing that there are other congregations gathered in the towns up and down, by the preaching of the word of God" (or, that there is another heavenly city in any town, built by the word of God), "we persuade some that are sound in doctrine and of good conversation, and meet for their rule, to take on them the conduct or rule of those churches; and these, whilst they rule within the churches those societies of divine institution by whom they are chosen, they govern them according to the prescriptions" (or commands) "and rules given by God himself," Adver. Cels., lib. viii.

Those of whom he speaks, ἡμεῖς, were the pastors or principal members of the churches that were established. When they understood that, in any place distant from them, a number of believers were called and gathered into church-order by the preaching of the word, they presently, according unto their duty, took care of them, — inquired into their state and condition, assisting them, in particular, in finding out, trying, and recommending unto them persons meet to be their officers and rulers. These he acknowledgeth to be churches and cities of God, upon their collection by the preaching of the word, antecedently unto the constitution of any officers among them; as the apostles also did, Acts xiv. 22, 23. Wherefore, the church is essentially before its ordinary officers, and cannot, as unto its continuance, depend on any succession of theirs; which they have none but what it gives unto them. These officers thus recommended were *chosen,* as he tells us, by the churches wherein they were to preside, and thereon did govern them by the rule of God's word alone.

Hereby was the original constitution and state of the first churches for a good season preserved. Nor was there the least abridgment of the power either of these churches or of their officers, because, it may be, they were some of them planted in poor country villages; for as no man in the world can hinder but that every true church hath *"de jure"* all the rights and powers that any other church in the world hath or ought to have, or that every true officer, bishop, elder, or pastor hath all the power that Christ hath annexed unto that office (be they at Rome or Eugubium,[13]) so there was no abridgment of this power in the meanest of them as yet attempted.

But this course and duty in many places, not long after, became to be much omitted. Whether out of ignorance, or negligence, or unwillingness of men to undertake the pastoral charge in poor country churches, I know not, but so it was, that believers in the regions round about any city, ἐν χώραις, were looked on as those which belonged unto the city churches, and were not settled in particular congregations for their edification, which they ought to have been; and the councils that afterward ensued made laws and canons that they should be under the government of the bishops of those city churches. But when the number of such believers was greatly increased, so as that it was needful to have some always attending the ministry among them, they came, I know not how, to have *"chorepiscopi"* among them and over them. The first mention of them is in the synod of Ancyra in Galatia, about the year 314, can. 13; and mention is again made of them in a synod of Antioch, an. 341, and somewhat before at the council of Neocæsarea, can.

---

13 A small town about eighty miles from Rome. The expression is borrowed from Jerome ad Evang.: *"Ubicunque fuerit episcopus, sive Romæ, sive Eugubii,* etc." — ED.

13, and frequently afterward, as any one may see in the late collections of the ancient canons. I verily believe, nor can the contrary be proved, but that these *"chorepiscopi"* at first were as absolute and complete in the office of episcopacy as any of the bishops of the greater cities, having their name or denomination from the places of their residence (ἐπίσκοποι κατὰ χώρας), and not for an intimation of any inferiority in them unto other city bishops; but so it came to pass, that through their poverty and want of interest, their ministry being confined unto a small country parish, and perhaps through a comparative meanness of their gifts or abilities, the city bishop claimed a superiority over them, and made canons about their power, the bounding and exercising of it, in dependence on themselves. For a while they were esteemed a degree above mere presbyters, who accompanied or attended the bishop of the city church in his administrations, and a degree beneath the bishop himself, — in a posture never designed by Christ nor his apostles. Wherefore, in process of time, the name and thing were utterly lost, and all the country churches were brought into an absolute subjection unto the city churches, something being allowed unto them for worship, nothing for rule and discipline; whereby the first state of churches in their original institution, sacredly preserved in the first centuries, was utterly lost and demolished.

I shall add but one argument more to evince the true state and nature of evangelical churches herein, — namely, that they were only particular congregations; and that is taken from the duties and powers ascribed in the Scripture unto churches, and the members or entire brotherhood of them. It was observed before that the epistles of the apostles were written all of them unto the body of the churches, in contradistinction unto their elders, bishops, or pastors, unless it were those that were written unto particular persons by name. And as this is plain in all the epistles of Paul, wherein sometimes distinct mention is made of the officers of the church, sometimes none at all, so the apostle John affirms that he wrote unto the church, but that Diotrephes (who seems to have been their bishop) received him not, at once rejecting the authority of the apostle and overthrowing the liberty of the church; which example was diligently followed in the succeeding ages, 3 John 9. And the apostle Peter, writing unto the churches on an especial occasion, speaks distinctly of the elders, 1 Pet. v. 1, 2. See also Heb. xiii. 24, the body of the epistle

CHAPTER V.   153

being directed to the body of the churches. Wherefore, all the instructions, directions, and injunctions given in those epistles as unto the exercise of power or the performance of duty, they are given unto *the churches themselves*. Now, these are such, many of them, as cannot be acted or performed in any church by the body of the people, but that which is congregational only. It were too long here to insist on particulars, — it shall be done elsewhere; and it will thence appear that this argument alone is sufficient to bear the weight of this whole cause. The reader may, if he please, consider what representation hereof is made in these places compared together, Matt. xviii. 15–18; Acts i. 12, 23, ii. 1, 42, 44, 46, v. 11–13, xi. 21, 22, 25, 26, 28–30, xii. 5, 12, xiv. 26, 27, xv. 1–4, 6, 12, 13, 22, 23, 27, 28, 30, xx. 28; Rom. xv. 5, 6, 14, 25, 26, xvi. 1, 17, 18; 1 Cor. i. 4, 5, chap. v. throughout; xii. 4, 7–9, 11, 15, 18, 28–31, chap. xiv. throughout, xvi. 10, 11; 2 Cor. iii. 1–3, vii. 14, 15, viii. 22–24, ii. 6–11, viii. 5; Eph. ii. 19–22, v. 11, 12; Gal. vi. 1; Phil. ii. 25–28; Col. i. 1, 2, ii. 2, iii. 16, iv. 9, 12, 16, 17; 1 Thess. v. 11–14; 2 Thess. iii. 6, 7, 14, 15; Heb. x. 24, 25, xii. 15, 16. In these, I say, and other places innumerable, there are those things affirmed of and ascribed unto the apostolical churches, as unto their state, order, assemblies, duties, powers, and privileges, as evince them to have been only *particular congregations*.

CHAPTER VI.

Congregational churches alone suited unto the ends of Christ in the institution of his church.

HAVING given an account of that state and order of the gospel churches which are of divine institution, it is necessary that we declare also their *suitableness* and *sufficiency* unto all the ends for which the Lord Christ appointed such churches; for if there be any true proper end of that nature which cannot be attained in or by any church-state in this or that form, it must be granted that no such form is of divine appointment. Yea, it is necessary not only that such a state as pretends unto a divine original be not only not contradictory unto or inconsistent with such an end, but that it is effectually conducing thereunto, and in its place necessary unto that purpose. This, therefore, is that which we shall now inquire into, — namely, whether this state and form of gospel churches in single congregations be suited unto all those ends for which any such churches were appointed; which they must be on the account of the wisdom of Jesus Christ, the author and founder of them, or be utterly discarded from their pretence. Nor is there any more forcible argument against any pretended church-state, rule, or order, than that it is obstructive unto the souls of men in attaining the proper ends of their whole institution. What these ends are was in general before declared; I shall not here repeat them, or go over them again, but only single out the consideration of those which are usually pleaded as not attainable by this way of churches in single congregations only, or that at least they are not suited unto their attainment.

1. The first of these is *mutual love* among all Christians, all the disciples of Christ. By the disciples of Christ I intend them, and them only, who profess faith in his person and doctrine, and to hear him, or to be guided by him alone, in all things that appertain unto the worship of God, and their living unto him. If

there are any called Christians who in these things choose other guides, call other ministers, hear them in their appointments, we must sever them from our present consideration; though there are important duties required of us towards them also. But what is alleged is necessary unto the constitution of a true disciple of Christ. Unto all those his great command is, mutual love among themselves. This he calls in an especial manner "his commandment," and "a new commandment;" as for other reasons, so because he had given the first absolute great example of it in himself, as also discovered motives unto it and reasons for it which mankind before was in the dark unto. And such weight doth he lay on this command, that he declares the manifestation of the glory of God, his own honour, and the evidence to be given unto the world that we are his disciples, do depend on our obedience thereunto.

To express and exercise this love, in all the acts and duties of it, among his disciples, was one end of his appointing them to walk in church-relation one unto another, wherein this love is the bond of perfectness. And the loss of this love, as unto its due exercise, is no less a pernicious part of the fatal apostasy of the churches than is the loss of faith and worship: for hereon is Christendom, as it is usually called, become the greatest stage of hatred, rage, wrath, bloodshed, and mutual desolations that is in the whole world; so as that we have no way to answer the objection of the Jews arguing against us from the divine promises of love and peace in the kingdom of the Messiah, but by granting that all these things arise from a rebellion against his rule and kingdom. Now, this love in its exercise is eminently preserved in this order of particular churches; for, —

(1.) The principle of their collection into such societies, next unto that of faith in Christ Jesus, is *love unto all the saints*; for their conjunction being with some of them as such only, they must have a love unto all that are so. And none of them would join in such societies if their so doing did in any thing impair their love unto all the disciples of Christ, or impede it in any of its operations. And the communion of these churches among themselves is, and ought to be, such as that all of them do constitute as it were one body and common church; as we shall see afterward. And it is one principal duty of them to stir up themselves, in all their members, unto a continual exercise of love towards all the saints of Christ, as occasion doth require; and if they are defective in this catholic love, it is their fault, contrary to the rule and end of their institution.

(2.) Unto the constant expression and exercise of this love there are required, — [1.] *Present suitable objects* unto all the acts and duties of it; [2.] A *description and prescription* of those acts and duties; [3.] *Rules* for the right performance and exercise of them; [4.] An *end* to be attained in their discharge. All these things hath the Lord Christ provided for his disciples in the constitution and rule of these churches. And a due attendance unto them hath he appointed as the instance, trial, and experiment of their love unto all his disciples; for whereas they might pretend such a love, yet plead that they know not how nor wherein to express and exercise it, especially as unto sundry duties mentioned in the Scripture as belonging thereunto, he hath provided this way, wherein they cannot be ignorant of the duties of love required of them, nor of suitable objects, rules, and ends for their practice. It were too long to go over these things in particular. I shall only add (what is easily defensible) that gospel love will never be recovered and restored unto its pristine glory until particular churches or congregations are reformed and reduced to that exercise of love without dissimulation which is required in all their members among themselves; for whilst men live in envy and malice, be hateful and hating one another, or whilst they live in an open neglect of all those duties which the Lord Christ hath appointed to be observed towards the members of that society whereunto they do belong, as a pledge and evidence of their love unto all his disciples, no such thing can be attained. And thus is it in most parochial assemblies, who, in the midst of their complaints of the breach of love and union, by some men's withholding communion in some parts of divine worship with them, yet, besides the common duties of civility and neighbourhood, neither know nor practice any thing of that spiritual love, delight, and communion that ought to be amongst them as members of the same church.

We boast not ourselves of any attainments in this kind, — we know how short we come of that fervent love that flourished in the first churches; but this we say, that there is no way to recover it but by that state and order of particular churches which we propose, and, κατὰ τὴν δοθεῖσαν δύναμιν, do adhere unto.

But pretences unto the contrary are vehemently urged, and the clamours unto that end are loud and many: for this way, it is said, *of setting up particular congregations* is that which hath caused endless divisions, and lost all love and Christian affection among *us*, being attended with other mischievous consequents, such as the most rhetorical adversaries of it are scarce able to declare, nor could Tertullus himself do it if he were yet alive; for by this means, men not meeting as they used to do at the administration of the sacrament and common-prayer, *all love is lost among them*. I answer, —

[1.] This objection, so far as I am able to observe, is mostly managed by them who seem to know very little of the nature and duties of that love which our Lord Jesus Christ enjoins in the gospel, nor do give any considerable evidence of their living, walking, and acting in the power of it. And as unto what they fancy unto themselves under that name, whereas it is evident from common practice that it extends no farther but to peaceableness in things civil and indifferent, with some expressions of kindness in their mirth and feasting, and other jovial societies, we are not concerned in it.

[2.] This objection lies not at all against the thing itself, — namely, that all churches of divine institution are congregational, which alone at present is pleaded for, — but against the gathering of such societies or congregations in that state of things which now prevails amongst us. But whereas this depends on principles not yet declared and confirmed, the consideration of this part of the objection must be referred unto another place. I shall only say at present, that it is the greatest and most powerful engine in the hand of Satan, and men of corrupt secular interest, to keep all church reformation out of the world.

But if the way itself be changed (which alone, as absolutely considered, we at present defend), that change must be managed with respect unto some *principles* contrary unto love and its *due exercise*, which it doth assert and maintain, or some *practices* that it puts men upon of the same nature and tendency. But this hitherto hath not been attempted, at least not effected.

[3.] We do not find that *a joint participation of the same ordinances at the same time*, within the same walls, is in itself either an effect, or evidence, or duty of gospel love, or any means for the preservation or promotion of it; for it was diligently observed in the Papacy, When all true evangelical love, faith, and worship were lost. Yea, this kind of communion and conjunction, added unto an implicit dependence on the authority of the church, was substituted in their room; and multitudes were contented with them, as those which did bestead them in their neglect of all other graces and their exercise. And I wish it were not so among others, who suppose they have all the love that is required of them, if they are freed from such scandalous variances with their neighbours as should make them unfit for the communion.

[4.] If this be the only means of love, how do men maintain it towards any not of their own parish, seeing they never meet with them at the sacrament of the Lord's supper? And if they can live in love with those of other parishes, why can they not do so with those who, having the same faith and sacraments with them, do meet apart, for the exercise of divine worship, in such congregations as we have described? Wherefore, —

[5.] The *variance* that is pretended to be caused by the setting up of these particular congregations is a part of that variance which Christ came to send into the world: Matt. x. 34–36, "Think not that I am come to send peace on earth: I came not to send peace, but a sword. For I am come to set a man at variance against his father, and the daughter against her mother, and the daughter-in-law against her mother-in-law. And a man's foes shall be they of his own household." He was the Prince of Peace; he came to make peace between God and men, between men themselves, Jews and Gentiles; he taught nothing, enjoined nothing that in its own nature should have the least inconsistency with peace, or give countenance unto variance: but he declares what would ensue and fall out, through the sin, the darkness, unbelief, and enmity unto the truth that would continue on some under the preaching of the gospel, whilst others of their nearest relations should embrace the truth and profession of it. What occasion for this variance is taken from the gathering of these congregations, which the way itself doth neither cause nor give the least countenance unto, we are not accountable for. Whereas, therefore, there is with those among whom these variances, and loss of love thereby, are pretended, "one Lord, one faith, one baptism, one hope of their calling," — the same truth of the gospel preached, the same sacraments administered; and whereas both the principles of the way and the persons of those who assemble in distinct corporations for the celebration of divine worship, do lead unto love and the practice of it in all its known duties, — all the evils that ensue on this way must be charged on the enmity, hatred, pride, and secular interest of men; which it is not in our power to cure.

2. Another end of the institution of this state is, that the church might be the "pillar and ground of the truth," 1 Tim. iii. 15, — that is, that it might be the principal outward means to support, preserve, publish declare, and propagate the doctrine or truth of the gospel, especially that concerning the person and offices of Christ; which the apostle subjoins unto this assertion in the next words. That church-state which doth not answer this end is not of divine institution; but this the ministry of these churches is eminently suited unto. There are three things required in this duty, or required unto this end, theft the church be the pillar and ground of truth: — (1.) That it *preserve the truth in itself*, and in the profession of all its members, against all seducers, false teachers, and errors. This the apostle gives in special charge unto the elders of the church of Ephesus, adding the reasons of it, Acts xx. 28–31. This is in an especial manner committed unto the officers of the church, 1 Tim. v. 20; 2 Tim. i. 13, 14. This the ministry of these churches is meet and suited unto. The continual inspection which they may and ought to have into all the members of the church, added unto that circumspection about and trial of the doctrines preached by themselves, in the whole body of the church, fits them for this work. This is the fundamental means (on the matter the only outward means) that the Lord Christ hath appointed for the preservation of the truth of the gospel in this world, whereby the church is the pillar and ground of truth. How this can be done where churches are of that make and constitution that the officers of them can have no immediate inspection into or cognizance of either the knowledge, opinions, or practices of the members of their church, nor the body of the church know on any evident ground what it is that their principal officer believes and teaches, I know not. By this means was the truth preserved in the churches of the first two centuries, wherein they had no officers but what were placed in particular churches, so as that no considerable error made any entrance among them. (2.) That each church take care that the same truth be preserved entire, as unto the profession of it, in all other churches. Their communion among themselves (whereof afterward) is built upon their common ὁμολογία, or profession of the same faith. This, therefore, it is their duty, and was always their practice, to look after, that it was preserved en-

tire; for a change in the faith of any of them they knew would be the dissolution of their communion. Wherefore, when any thing of that nature fell out, as it did in the church of Antioch upon the preaching of the necessity of circumcision and keeping of the law, whereby the souls of many of the disciples were subverted, the church at Jerusalem, on the notice and knowledge of it, helped them with their advice and counsel. And Eusebius tells us, that upon the first promulgation of the heresies and frenzies of Montanus, the faithful, or churches in Asia, met frequently in sundry places to examine his pretences and condemn his errors; whereby the churches in Phrygia were preserved, Hist. Eccl., lib. v. cap. 14. So the same was done afterward in the case of Samosatenus at Antioch, whereby that church was delivered from the infection of his pernicious heresy, lib. vii. cap. 27, 28, 29. And this care is still incumbent on every particular church, if it would approve itself to be the pillar and ground of truth. And in like manner Epiphanius, giving an account of the original of the heresy of Noetus, a Patropassian, affirms that the holy presbyters of the church called him, and inquired of his opinion several times; whereon, being convicted before the presbytery of enormous errors, he was cast out of the church: Ἀλλὰ μεταξὺ τούτων (when he began to disperse his errors) ἀπὸ τῆς περὶ αὐτὸν ἐνηχήσεως οἱ μακάριοι πρεσβύτεροι τῆς ἐκκλησίας προσκαλεσάμενοι αὐτὸν ἐξητάζον περὶ τούτων ἁπάντων· — ὁ δὲ τὰ πρῶτα ᾑρεῖτο ἐπὶ τοῦ πρεσβυτερίου ἀγόμενος, Epiphanius, Hæres. cont. Noet., Hær. xxxviii. sec. 57.

Hence it was that the doctrine of the church, as unto the substance of it, was preserved entire during the first two centuries, and somewhat after. Indeed, as when the Israelites came out of Egypt, there came along with them a "mixed multitude" of other people, Exod. xii. 38, which fell to "lusting" for meat when they came into the wilderness, Num. xi. 4, to the danger of the whole congregation: so when Christianity was first preached and received in the world, besides those who embraced it sincerely, and were added unto the church, there was a great mixture of stubborn Jews, as the Ebionites; of philosophical Greeks, as the Valentinians and the Marcionites; of plain impostors, such as Simon Magus and Menander; who all of them pretended to be Christians, but they fell a lusting, and exceedingly troubled and perplexed the churches with an endeavour to seduce them unto their imaginations. Yet none of their abominations could force an entrance into the churches themselves; which, by the means insisted on, were preserved. But when this church-state and order was changed, and another gradually introduced in the room of it, errors and heresies got new advantages, and entered into the churches themselves, which before did only assault and perplex them; for, —

[1.] When prerogative and pre-eminence of any *single person in* the church began to be in esteem, not a few who failed in their attempts of attaining it, to revenge themselves on the church made it their business to invent and propagate pernicious heresies. So did Thebuthis at Jerusalem, Euseb., lib. iv. cap. 22; and Valentinus, Tertul ad Valentine, cap. iv.; and Marcion at Rome, Epiphan. Hæres. xlii. Montanus fell into his dotage on the same account; so did Novatianus at Rome, Euseb., lib. vi. cap. 43, and Arius at Alexandria. Hence is that censure of them by Lactantius, lib. iv. cap. 30: "*Ii quorum fides fuit lubrica, cum Deum nosse se et colere simularent, augendis opibus et honori studentes, affectabant maximum sacerdotium, et a potioribus victi, secedere cum suffragatoribus maluerunt, quam eos ferre præpositos quibus concupierant ipsi ante præponi.*"

[2.] When any of their bishops of the new constitution, whether *patriarchal or diocesan*, fell into heresies, which they did frequently, and theft numbers of them, they had so many advantages to diffuse their poison into the whole body of their churches, and such political interests for their promotion, as that the churches themselves were thoroughly infected with them. It is true, the body of the people in many places did oppose them, withdraw and separate from them; but it cannot be denied but that this was the first way and means whereby the churches ceased to be the ground and pillar of truth, many destructive errors being received into them, which did only outwardly assault them whilst they abode in their first institution. And had not the churches, in process of time, utterly lost their primitive state and order, by coalescing into one papal, pretended universal church, the faith itself could never have been so utterly corrupted, depraved, and lost among them, as in the issue it was.

(3.) To *propagate the gospel* is in like manner required hereunto. This, I acknowledge, doth more immediately concern the duty of persons in any church-order than the order itself; for it must be the work of some particular persons dedicating themselves unto their ministry, as it was in the first churches,3 John 5–8.

The like may be said of any other public acknowledged end of the institution of churches. If the way pleaded for be not consistent with them all, and the proper means of attaining them, if it be not suited unto their accomplishment, let it be discarded. I shall insist on one more only.

3. Our Lord Jesus Christ hath given that state unto his churches, hath instated them in that order, as that *his interest*, kingdom, and religion might be carried on in the world without prejudice or disadvantage *unto any of the lawful interests of men*, especially without any opposition unto or interfering with the civil authority or magistracy, which is the ordinance of God; and no church-way that doth so is of his institution. Wherefore, I shall briefly declare what are the principles of those of this way in these things, which are the principles of the way itself which they do profess:—

(1.) Our first general assertion unto this purpose is this: *The Lord Jesus Christ taught no doctrine, appointed no order in his church, gave it no power, that is opposite unto or inconsistent with any righteous government in this world, of what sort soever it be, of those whereinto government is distributed in reason and practice.* His doctrine, indeed, is opposed unto all unrighteousness in and of all men, magistrates and others; but not to *the legal rule of magistrates* that are unrighteous men. And this opposition is doctrinal only, confirmed with promises and threatenings of eternal things, refusing and despising all outward aids of force and restraint. This rule we allow for the trial of all churches and their state, whether they be according unto the mind of Christ.

But whereas the Lord Jesus Christ hath taught, commanded, appointed nothing that is contrary unto or inconsistent with righteous government of any sort, if rulers or magistrates shall forbid the observance of what he hath commanded, appointed, and ordered, and then charge it on him or his way that his disciples cannot, dare not, will not comply with that prohibition, and accuse them thereon of sedition and opposition unto government, they deal injuriously with him, whereof they must give an account; for, whereas "all power is given unto him in heaven and earth," all nations are his inheritance, all people in his absolute disposal, and it is his pleasure to set up his kingdom in the earth, without which the earth itself would not be

Chapter VI.

continued, he could not deal more gently with the righteous rulers of this world (and he did it because righteous rule is the ordinance of God), than to order all things so, that whether they receive his law and doctrine or no, nothing should be done in opposition unto them or their rule. And if any of them are not contented with this measure, but will forbid the observance of what he commands, where in he alone is concerned, and not they, this is left to be determined between him and them. In the meantime, when rulers are not able to fancy, much less give a real instance of, any one principle, doctrine, or practice, in any of the churches of Christ, or any belonging unto them, that is contrary unto, or inconsistent with, the rights or exercise of their rule and government, and yet shall not only prohibit the doing of those things which he hath commanded merely with respect unto the spiritual and eternal ends of his kingdom, but shall also punish and destroy those who will not disown his authority and comply with their prohibition, it doth scarce answer their interest and prudence; for to what purpose is it for any to provoke him who is mightier than they, when they have no appearance of necessity for their so doing, nor advantage thereby?

(2.) In particular, the Lord Christ hath ordained no *power or order in his church, no office or duty, that should stand in need of the civil authority*, sanction, or force to preserve it, or make it effectual unto its proper ends. It is sufficient to discharge any thing of a pretence to be an appointment of Christ in his church, if it be not sufficient unto its own proper end, without the help of the civil magistrate. That church-state which is either constituted by human authority, or cannot consist without it, is not from him. That ordinance which is in its own nature divine, or is pretended so to be, so far as it is not effectual unto its end without the aid of human authority is not of him; he needs it not. He will not borrow the assistance of civil authority to rule in and over the consciences of men, with respect unto their living to God and coming unto the enjoyment of himself.

The way of requiring the sanction of civil authority unto ecclesiastical orders and determinations began with the use of general councils in the days of Constantine; and when once it was engaged in and approved, so far as that what was determined in the synods, either as to doctrine or as unto the rule of the church, should be confirmed by the imperial authority, with penalties on all that should gainsay such determinations, it is deplorable to consider what mutual havoc was made among Christians upon the various sentiments of synods and emperors. Yet this way pleased the rulers of the church so well, and, as they thought, eased them of so much trouble, that it was so far improved amongst them, that at last they left no power in or about religion or religious persons unto the civil magistrate, but what was to be exercised in the execution of the decrees and determinations of the church.

It is necessary, from this institution of particular churches, that they have their subsistence, continuation, order, and the efficacy of all that they act and do as churches, from Christ himself; for whereas all that they are and do is heavenly, spiritual, and not of this world, so that it reacheth nothing of all those things which are under the power of the magistrate (that is, the lives and bodies of men, and all civil interests appertaining to them), and affects nothing but what no power of all the magistrates under heaven can reach unto (that is, the souls and consciences of men), — no trouble can hence arise unto any rulers of the world, no contests about what they ought and what they ought not to confirm; which have caused great disorders among many.

(3.) In particular, also, *there neither is nor can be in this church-state the least pretence of power or authority to be acted towards or over the persons of kings or rulers, which should either impeach their right or impede the exercise of their just authority*; for as Christ hath granted no such power unto the church, so it is impossible that any pretence of it should be seated in a particular congregation, especially being gathered on this principle, that there is no church-power properly so called but what is so seated, and that no concurrence, agreement, or association of many churches can add a new, greater, or other power or authority unto them than what they had singly before. And what power can such churches act towards kings, potentates, or rulers of nations? Have they not the highest security that it is utterly impossible that ever their authority, or their persons in the exercise of it, should be impeached, hindered, or receive any detriment from any thing that belongs to this church-state?

These principles, I say, are sufficient to secure Christian religion, and the state, order, and power of churches instituted therein, from all reflections of inconsistency with civil government, or of influencing men unto attempts of its change or ruin.

Chapter VI.

The sum is:— Let the outward frame and order of righteous government be of what sort it will, nothing inconsistent with it, nothing intrenching on it, nothing making opposition unto it, is appointed by Jesus Christ, or doth belong unto that church-state which he hath ordained and established.

Two things only must be added unto these principles, that we may not seem so to distinguish the civil state and the church as to make them unconcerned in each other; for, —

First, It is the unquestionable duty of the rulers and governors of the world, upon the preaching of the gospel, *to receive its truth*, and to yield obedience unto its commands. And whereas all power and offices are to be discharged for God, whose ministers all rulers be, they are bound, in the discharge of their office, to countenance, supply, and protect the profession and professors of the truth, — that is, the church, — according unto the degrees and measures which they shall judge necessary.

Secondly, It is the duty of the church, *materially* considered, — that is, of all those who are members of it, — in any kingdom or commonwealth, to be usefully subservient, even as Christians, unto that rule which is over them as men, in all those ways, and by all those means, which the laws, usages, and customs of the countries whereof they are do direct and prescribe. But these things are frequently spoken unto.

There are sundry other considerations whereby it may be evinced that this order and state of gospel churches is not only consistent with every righteous government in the world (I mean, that is so in its constitution, though, as all other forms, it be capable of maladministration), but the most useful and subservient unto its righteous administration, being utterly incapable of immixing itself, as such, in any of those occasions of the world or state affairs as may create the least difficulty or trouble unto rulers. With others it is not so. It is known that the very constitution of the papal church, as it is stated in the canons of it, is inconsistent with the just rights of kings and rulers, and ofttimes, in the exercise of its power, destructive unto their persons and dominions. And herein concurred the prelatical church-state of England, whilst it continued in their communion, and held its dependence on the Roman church; for although, they had all their power originally from the kings of this realm, — as the records and laws of it do expressly affirm, "That the church of England was founded in episcopacy by the king and his nobles," — yet they claimed such an addition of power and authority, by virtue of their office from the papal omnipotency, as that they were ringleaders in perplexing the government of this nation, under the pretence of maintaining what they called the "rights of the church." And hereunto they were enabled by the very constitution of their church-order, which gave them that power, grandeur, with political interest, that were needful to effectuate their design. And since they have been taken off from this foundation of contesting kings and princes on their own ecclesiastical authority, and deprived of their dependence on the power and interest of the papal see, having no bottom for or supportment of their church state and order but regal favour and mutable laws, there have, on such causes and reasons, which I shall not mention, ensued such emulations of the nobility and gentry, and such contempts of the common people, as leave it questionable whether their adherence unto the government be not note burdensome and dangerous unto it than were their ancient contests and oppositions.

CHAPTER VII.

No other church-state of divine institution.

It may be it will be generally granted, I am sure it cannot be modestly denied, that particular churches or congregations are of a divine original institution; as also, that the primitive churches continued long in that form or order. But it will be farther pleaded, that granting or supposing this divine institution of particular churches, yet there may be churches of another form and order also, as diocesan or national, that we are obliged to submit unto: for although the apostles appointed that there should be bishops or elders ordained κατὰ πόλιν, — that is, in every city and town where Christian religion was received; and Clemens affirmeth that they did themselves constitute bishops and deacons κατὰ χώρας καὶ πόλεις, — in the regions, or villages and cities; yet there was another form afterward introduced. Theodoret, bishop of Cyprus, affirms that there were eight hundred churches committed to his care, Epist. ciii., whereof many were in towns and cities having no bishop of their own. The whole country of Scythia, though there were in it many cities, villages, and fortresses, yet had but one bishop, whose residence was at Tomis, all other churches being under him; as Sozomen declares, lib. vi. cap. 20. So it is at this day in divers provinces belonging of old unto the Greek church; as in Moldavia and Wallachia, where they have one whom they call the ἡγούμενος, — the leader or ruler, that presides over all the churches in the nation. And this order of things, that there should not be a bishop in smaller churches, was first confirmed in the sixth canon of the council of Sardis, in the year 347.

In answer hereunto I shall do these two things:— First, I shall show that there is no church order, state, or church form of divine institution, that doth any way impede, take away, or overthrow the liberty, power, and order of particular congregations, such as we have described. Secondly, I shall inquire into the causes of churches of another state or order, as the power of magistrates and rulers, or their own choice and consent: —

1. *There is no form, order, or church-state, divinely instituted, that should annul the institution of particular congregations, or abridge them of their liberties, or deprive them of the power committed unto them.*

It is such a church-state alone that we are now concerned to quire after. Whatever of that kind either is or may be imagined that intrenches not on the state, liberty, and power of particular congregations, is not of our present consideration. Men may frame and order what they please; and what advantage they make thereby shall not be envied unto them, whilst they injure not any of the institutions, of Christ. But, —

(1.) These churches, *as they are churches*, are meet and able to attain the ends of churches To say they are churches, and yet have not in themselves power to attain the ends of churches, is to speak contradictions, or to grant and deny the same thing in the same breath; for a church is nothing but such a society as hath power, ability, and fitness to attain those ends for which Christ hath ordained churches: that which hath so is a church, and that which hath not so is none. Men may, if they please, deny them to be churches, but then I know not where they will find any that are so. For instance, suppose men should deny all the parochial churches in England to be such churches as are intrusted with church-power and administrations, what church, in the first instance, could they require our communion withal? Will they say, it is with the national or diocesan churches? Neither of these do or can, as such, administer sacred ordinances A man cannot preach nor hear the word but in a particular assembly; the Lord's supper cannot be administered but in a particular congregation; nor any presential, local communion of believers among themselves, like that described by the apostle, 1 Cor. xii. and xiv. be otherwise attained. No communion is firstly and immediately required, or can be required, with diocesan churches, as such. Wherefore, it is parochial, particular churches that we are required to hold communion with. We say, therefore, these parochial churches are either really and truly so endued with church power and liberty, or they are not. If they are, or are acknowledged so to be, we have herein obtained what we plead for; — if they are not, then are we required to join in church-communion with those societies that are not churches;

Chapter VII.

and if we refrain so doing, we are charged with schism, which is to turn religion into ridicule: for, —

(2.) It is utterly foreign to the Scripture, and a monster unto antiquity (I mean that which is pure and regardable in this cause), that there should be churches with a *part, half, more* or less, of church-power and not the whole, neither in right nor exercise; or that there should be church-officers, elders, presbyters, or bishops, that should have a partiary power, half or a third part, or less, of that which entirely belongeth unto the office they hold. Let one *testimony be* given out of the Scripture, or that antiquity which we appeal unto, unto his purpose, and we shall cease our plea But this is that which our understandings are set on rack withal every day; — there is a national church, that is intrusted with supreme church-power in the nation whereof it is. Here, at the entrance, we fall into a double disquietment.

For, — [1.] We know not as yet what this national church is, here (or in France), nor of what persons it doth consist. [2.] We know not whether this national church have all the power that Christ hath given unto the church, or that there is a reserve for some addition from beyond sea, if things were well accommodated. Then, that there are diocesan churches, whose original, with the causes and occasions of their bounds, limits, power, and manner of administration, I think God alone knows perfectly, we do but guess; for there is not one word mentioned of any of their concernments in the Scripture. And we know that these churches cannot be said to have all the power that Christ hath intrusted his church withal, because there is another church unto which they are in subjection, and on which they do depend; but it seems they have the next degree of power unto that which is uppermost. But whatever their power be, it is so administered by chancellors, commissaries, officials, in such ways and for such ends, that I shall believe a dissent from them and it to be schism when I believe it is midnight whilst the sun shines in his full strength and glory. And then we are told of parochial churches, who have this power only, that if we do not in them whatever is required of us, not by them but those that are put over them, they can inform against us, that we may be mulcted and punished.

(3.) It will be said that these churches, as such, were indeed originally intrusted and invested with all church rights, power, and authority, but for many weighty reasons are abridged in sundry things of the exercise of them; for who can think it meet that every single parish should be intrusted with the exercise of all church rule and power among themselves?

Ans. 1. Whose fault is it that these churches are not meet for the exercise of that power which Christ hath granted unto such churches? If it be from themselves, their negligence, or ignorance, or wickedness, it is high time they were reformed, and brought into that state and condition wherein they may be fit and able to answer the ends of their institution. 2. They are indeed sorry churches that are not as meet to exercise all church-power, according to the mind of Christ, as the chancellor's court. 3. There is no power pleaded for in congregational churches but what is granted unto them by the word and constitution of Christ. And who is he that shall take this from them, or deprive them of its exercise or right thereunto? (1.) It is not done, nor, ever was by Jesus Christ himself. He doth not pull down what himself hath built; nor doth any one institution of his in the least interfere with any other. It is true, the Lord Christ by his law deprives all churches of their power, yea, of their state, who walk, act, and exercise a power not derived from him, but set up against him, and used unto such ends as are opposite unto and destructive of the ends of church-order by him appointed; but to imagine that whilst a Church claims no power but what it receives from him, useth it only for him and in obedience unto his commands, he hath, by any act, order, or constitution, taken away that power or any part of it from such a church, is a vain supposition. (2.) *Such churches cannot by any act of their own deprive themselves of this right and power;* for, — [1.] It is committed unto them in a way of trust, which they falsify if by their own consent they part with it; [2.] Without it they cannot discharge many duties required of them. To part with this power is to renounce their duty; which is the only way whereby they may lose it. And if it be neither taken from them by any law, rule, or constitution of Christ, nor can be renounced or foregone by themselves, what other power under heaven can justly deprive them of it or hinder them in its execution? The truth is, the principal means which hath rendered the generality of parochial churches unmeet for the exercise of any church-power is, that their interest in it and right unto it hath been so long unjustly detained from them, as that they know not at all what belongs thereunto, being hidden from them by those who should instruct them in it. And might they be admitted, under the conduct of pious and prudent officers, unto any part of the practice of this duty in their assemblies, their understanding in it would quickly be increased.

That right, power, or authority which we thus assign unto all particular churches gathered according unto the mind of Christ, is that, and that only, which is necessary to their own preservation in their state and purity, and unto the discharge of all those duties which Christ requireth of the church.

2. Now, although they may not justly by any be deprived hereof, yet it may be inquired whether there may not an addition of ecclesiastical power be made unto that which is of original institution, for the good of the whole number of churches that are of the same communion. And this may be done, either by the power and authority of the supreme magistrate, with respect unto all the churches in his dominion; or it may be so by the churches themselves erecting a new power, in a combination of some, many, or all of them, which they had not in them singly and distinctly before.

For the power of the magistrate in and about religion, it: hath been much debated and disputed in some latter ages. For three hundred years there was no mention of it in the church, because no supreme powers did then own the Christian religion. For the next three hundred years there were great ascriptions unto supreme magistrates, to the exaltation of their power; and much use was made thereof among the churches by such as had the best interest in them. The next three hundred years was, as unto this case, much taken up with disputes about this power between the emperors and the popes of Rome; sometimes one side gaining the advantage in some especial instances, sometimes the other. But from that period of time, or thereabouts, the contest came to blows, and the blood of some hundred thousands was shed in the controversy, — namely, about the power of emperors and kings on the one side, and the popes of Rome on the other. In the issue, the popes abode masters of the field, and continued in actual possession of all ecclesiastical power, though sometimes mixed with the rebellion of one stubborn prince or other, as here frequently in England, who controlled them in some of their new acquisitions. Upon the public reformation of religion, many princes threw off the yoke of the papal rule, and, according to the doctrine of the reformers, assumed unto themselves the power which, as they judged, the godly kings of Judah of old and the first Christian emperors did exercise about ecclesiastical affairs. From that time there have been great and vehement disputes about the ecclesiastical power of sovereign princes and states. I shall not here undertake to treat concerning it, although it is a matter of no great difficulty to demonstrate the extremes that many have run into, some by granting too much, and some too little unto them. And I shall grant, for my part, that too much cannot well be assigned unto them whilst these two principles are preserved:— 1. That no supreme magistrate hath power to deprive or abridge the churches of Christ of any right, authority, or liberty granted unto them by Jesus Christ; 2. Nor hath any to coerce, punish, or kill any persons (being civilly peaceable and morally honest) because they are otherwise minded in things concerning gospel faith and worship than he is.

It hath not yet been disputed whether the supreme magistrate hath power to ordain, institute, and appoint any new form or state of churches, supposedly suited unto the civil interest, which were never ordained or appointed by Christ. It hath not, I say, been disputed under these terms expressly, though really the substance of the controversy lies therein. To assert this expressly would be to exalt him above Jesus Christ, at least to give him power equal unto his; though really unto the institution of the gospel church-state, and the communication of graces, offices, and gifts to make it useful unto its end, no less than all power in heaven and earth be required.

Some plead that there is no certain form of church-government appointed in the Scripture, — that there was none ordained by Christ, nor exemplified by the apostles; and therefore it is in the power of the magistrate to appoint any such form thereof as is suited unto the public interest. It would seem to follow more evidently that no form at all should by any be appointed; for what shall he do that cometh after the King? — what shall any one ordain in the church which, the Lord Christ thought not meet to ordain? And this is the proper inference from this consideration: Such a church-government as men imagine, Christ hath not appointed; therefore, neither may men to so. But suppose that the Lord Christ hath appointed a church-state, or that there should be churches of his disciples on the earth;

let them therein but yield obedience unto all that he hath commanded, and in their so doing make use of the light of nature and rules of common prudence, so as to do it unto their own edification (which to deny to be their duty is to destroy their nature as created of God), trusting in all things unto the conduct of the promised divine assistance of the Holy Spirit; — if any instance can be given of what is wanting unto the complete state and rule of the church, we shall willingly allow that it be added by the civil magistrate, or whomsoever men can agree upon, as was before declared. If it be said there is yet something wanting to accommodate these churches and their rule unto the state of the public interest and political government under which they are placed, whereon they may be framed into churches diocesan and metropolitical, with such a rule as they are capable of, I say, — 1. That in their original constitution they are more accommodated unto the interest of all righteous secular government than any arbitrary moulding them unto a pretended meetness to comply therewithal can attain unto. This we have proved before, and shall farther enlarge upon it if it be required. And we find it by experience, that those additions, changes, and alterations in the state, order, and rule of the churches, pretended for the end mentioned, have proved the cause of endless contentions; which have no good aspect on the public peace, and will assuredly continue for ever so to be. 2. It is granted that the magistrate may dispose of many outward concerns of these churches; may impart of his favour to them, or any of them, as he sees cause; may take care that nothing falls out among them that may occasion any public disturbance in and by itself; may prohibit the public exercise of worship idolatrous or superstitious; may remove and take away all instruments and monuments of idolatry; may coerce, restrain, and punish, as there is occasion, persons who, under pretence of religion, do advance principles of sedition, or promote any foreign interest opposite and destructive to his government, the welfare of the nation, and the truth of religion; with sundry things of the like nature. And herein lies an ample field, wherein the magistrate may exercise his power and discharge his duty.

It cannot well be denied but that the present pretences and pleas of some to reduce all things in the practice of religion into the power and disposal of the civil magistrate are full of offence and scandal. It seems to be only a design and contrivance to secure men's secular interests under every way of the profession of Christian religion, true or false, which may have the advantage of the magistrate's approbation. By this device conscience is set at liberty from concerning itself in an humble, diligent inquiry into the mind of God as unto what is its duty in his worship; and when it is so with the conscience of any, it will not be much concerned in what it doth attend unto or observe. What is, in divine things, done or practised solely on the authority of the magistrate is immediately and directly obedience unto him, and not unto God.

Whatever, therefore, the supreme power in any place may do, or will be pleased to do, for the accommodation of the outward state of the church and the exercise of its rule unto the political government of a people or nation, yet these two things are certain:—

1. That he can form, erect, or institute *no new church-state* which is not ordained and appointed by Christ, and his apostles by virtue of his authority; and what he doth of that nature appoint is called a church only equivocally, or by reason of some resemblance unto that which is properly so called.

2. To dissent from what is so appointed by the supreme power, in and about the state, form, rule, and worship of churches, whatever other evil it may be charged with or supposed liable unto, can have nothing in it of that which the Scripture condemns under *the name of schism*, which hath respect only unto what is stated by Christ himself.

That which in this place we should next inquire into is, what these particular churches themselves may do, by their own voluntary consent and act, in a way of association or otherwise, for the accumulation and exercise of a power not formally inherent in them as particular churches; but I shall refer it unto the head of the communion of churches, which must be afterward spoken unto.

CHAPTER VIII.

The duty of believers to join themselves in church-order.

UNTO some one or other of those particular congregations which we have described, continuing to be the pillar and ground of truth, it is the duty of every believer, of every disciple of Christ, to *join himself* for the due and orderly observation and performance of the commands of Christ, unto the glory of God and their own edification, Matt. xxviii. 18–20.

This, in general, is granted by all sorts and parties of men; the grant of it is the ground whereon they stand in the management of their mutual feuds in religion, pleading that men ought to be of, or join themselves unto, this or that church, — still supposing that it is their duty to be of one or another.

Yea, it is granted, also, that persons ought to choose what churches they will join themselves unto, wherein they may have the best advantage unto their edification and salvation. They are to choose, to join themselves unto, that church which is in all thugs most according to the mind of God.

This, it is supposed, is the liberty and duty of every man; for if it be not so, it is the foolishest thing in the world for any to attempt to got others from one church unto another; which is almost the whole business of religion that some think themselves concerned to attend unto.

But yet, notwithstanding these concessions, when things come to the trial in particular, there is very little granted in compliance with the assertion laid down; for besides that it is not a church of divine institution that is intended in these concessions, when it comes unto the issue where a man is born, and in what church he is baptized in his infancy, then all choice is printed, and in the communion of that church he is to abide, on the penalties of being esteemed and dealt withal as a schismatic. In what national church any person is baptized, in that national church he is to continue, or answer the contrary at his peril; and in the precincts of what parish his habitation falls to be, in that particular parish church is he bound to communicate in all ordinances of worship. I say, in the judgment of many, whatever is pretended of men's joining themselves unto the truest and purest churches, there is no liberty of judgment or practice in either of these things left unto any of the disciples of Christ.

Wherefore, the liberty and duty proposed being the foundation of all orderly evangelical profession, and that wherein the consciences of believers are greatly concerned, I shall lay down one proposition wherein it is asserted in the sense I intend, and then fully confirm it.

The proposition itself is this:—

It is the duty of every one who professeth faith in Christ Jesus, and takes due care of his own eternal salvation, voluntarily and by his own choice to join himself unto some particular congregation of Christ's institution, for his own spiritual edification, and the right discharge of his commands.

1. This duty is prescribed unto them only who *profess faith in Christ Jesus*, who own themselves to be his disciples, that call Jesus Lord; for this is the method of the gospel, that first men by the preaching of it be made disciples, or be brought unto faith in Christ Jesus, and then be taught to do and observe whatever he commands, Matt. xxviii. 18–20, — first to "believe," and then to be "added unto the church," Acts ii. 41, 42, 44, 46, 47. Men must first join unto the Lord, or give up themselves unto him, before they can give up themselves unto the church, according to the mind of Christ, 2 Cor. viii. 5. We are not, therefore, concerned at present as unto them who either do not at all profess faith in Christ Jesus, or else, through ignorance of the fundamental principles of religion and wickedness of life, do destroy or utterly render useless that profession. We do not say it is the duty of such persons, — that is, their immediate duty, — in the state wherein they are, to join themselves unto any church. Nay, it is the duty of every church to refuse them their communion whilst they abide in that state. There are other duties to be in the first place pressed on them, whereby they may be made meet for this. So in the primitive times, although in the extraordinary conversions unto Christianity that were made among the Jews, who before belonged unto God's covenant, they were all immediately added unto the church, yet afterward, in the ordinary way of the conversion of men, the churches did not immedi-

Chapter VIII.

ately admit them into complete communion, but kept them as catechumeners, for the increase of their knowledge and trial of their profession, until they were judged meet to be joined unto the church. And they are not to blame who receive not such into complete communion with them, unto whom it is not a present duty to desire that communion. Yea, the admission of such persons into church-societies, much more the compelling of them to be members of this or that church, almost whether they will or no, is contrary to the rule of the word, the example of the primitive churches, and a great expedient to harden men in their sins.

We do therefore avow, that we cannot admit any into our church-societies, as to complete membership and actual interest in the privileges of the church, who do not, by a profession of faith in and obedience unto Jesus Christ, no way contradicted by sins of life, manifest themselves to be such as whose duty it is to join themselves unto any church Neither do we injure any baptized persons hereby, or oppose any of their right unto and interest in the church; but only, as they did universally in the primitive churches, after the death of the apostles, we direct them into that way and method wherein they may be received, unto the glory of Christ and their own edification. And we do therefore alarm, that we will never deny that communion unto any person, high or low, rich or poor, old or young, male or female, whose duty it is to desire it.

2. It is added, in the description of the subject, that it is such *one who takes due care of his own salvation*. Many there are who profess themselves to be Christians, who, it may be, hear the word willingly, and do many things gladly, yet do not esteem themselves obliged unto a diligent inquiry into and a precise observation of all the commands of Christ. But it is such whom we intend who constantly fix their minds on the enjoyment of God as their chiefest good and utmost end; who thereon duly consider the means of attaining it, and apply themselves thereunto. And it is to be feared that the number of such persons will not be found to be very great in the world; which is sufficient to take off the reproach from some particular congregations of the smallness of their number. Such they ever were; and such is it foretold that they should be. Number was never yet esteemed a note of the true church by any, but those whose worldly interest

it is that it should so be; yet at present, absolutely in these nations, the number of such persons is not small.

3. Of these persons it is said that *it is their duty so to dispose of themselves*. It is not that which they may do as a convenience or an advantage, not that which others may do for them, but which they must do for themselves in a way of duty. It is an obediential act unto the commands of Christ; whereunto is required subjection of conscience unto his authority, faith in his promises, as also a respect unto an appearance before his judgment-throne at the last day. The way of the church of Rome, to compel men into their communion, and keep them in it, by fire and fagot, or any other means of external force, derives more from the Alcoran than the Gospel. Neither doth it answer the mind of Christ, in the institution, end, and order of church-societies, that men should become members of them partly by that which is no way in their own power, and partly by what their wills are regulated in by the laws of men; for it is, as was said, commonly esteemed that men being born and baptized in such a nation are thereby made members of the church of that nation, and by living within such parochial precincts as the law of the land hath arbitrarily established are members of this or that particular congregation. At least, they are accounted so far to belong unto these churches, as to render them liable unto all outward punishments that shall be thought meet to be inflicted on them who comply not with them. So far as these persuasions and actings according unto them do prevail, so far are they destructive of the principal foundation of the external being and order of the church. But that men's joining themselves in or unto any church-society is, or ought to be, a voluntary act, or an act of free choice, in mere obedience unto the authority and commands of Christ, is so sacred a truth, so evident in the Scripture, so necessary from its subject-matter, so testified unto by the practice of all the first churches, as that it despiseth all opposition. And I know not how any can reconcile the common practice of giving men the reputation or reality of being members of or belonging unto this or that church, as unto total communion, who desire or choose no such thing, unto this acknowledged principle.

4. There is *a double joining unto the church*:— (1.) That which is as unto *total communion* in all the duties and privileges of the church; which is that whereof we treat. (2.) An *adherence unto*

the church as unto the means of instruction and edification to be attained thereby. So persons may adhere unto any church who yet are not meet or free, on some present consideration, to confederate with it as unto total communion; see Acts v. 13, 14. And of this sort, in a peculiar manner, are the baptized children of the members of the church; for although they are not capable of performing church-duties or enjoying church-privileges in their tender years, nor can have a right unto total communion before *the testification of their own voluntary consent* thereunto and choice thereof, yet are they in a peculiar manner under the care and inspection of the church, so far as the outward administration of the covenant, in all the means of it, is committed thereunto; and their duty it is, according to their capacity, to attend unto the ministry of that church whereunto they do belong.

5. The proposition respects a *visible professing church*. And I intend such a church in general as avoweth authority from Christ, — (1.) For the *ministerial preaching* of the word; (2.) *Administration of the Sacraments*; (3.) For the *exercise of evangelical discipline*; and, (4.) To *give a public testimony* against the devil and the world, not contradicting their profession with any corrupt principles or practices inconsistent with it. What is required in particular, that any of them may be meet to be joined unto such a church we shall afterward inquire.

6. It is generally said that "*out of the church there is no salvation;*" and the truth hereof is testified unto in the Scriptures, Acts ii. 47; 1 Pet. iii. 20, 21; Matt. xvi. 18; Eph. v. 25-27; John x. 16.

7. This is true both positively and negatively of the *catholic church* invisible, of the elect; all that are of it shall be saved, and none shall be saved but those that belong unto it, Eph. v. 25–27; — of the catholic visible professing church negatively; that no adult person can be saved that doth not belong unto this church, Rom. x. 10.

8. This *position of truth* is abused by interest and pride, an enclosure of it being made by them who, of all Christians in the world, can lay the least and weakest claim unto it, — namely, the church of Rome; for they are so far from being that catholic church out of which there is no salvation, and wherein none can perish, like the ark of Noah, that it requires the highest charity to reckon them unto that visible professing church whereof the greatest part may perish, and do so undoubtedly.

9. Our inquiry is, what truth there is in this assertion with respect unto these particular churches or societies for the celebration of gospel worship and discipline whereof we treat; and I say, —

(1.) No church, of what *denomination soever*, can lay a claim unto this privilege as belonging unto itself alone. This was the ancient *Donatism*; they confined salvation unto the churches of their way alone. And after many false charges of it on others, it begins really to be renewed in our days; for some dispute that salvation is confined unto that church alone *wherein there is a succession of diocesan bishops*; which is the height of Donatism. The judgments and determinations made concerning the eternal salvation or damnation of men by the measures of some differences among Christians about churches, their state and order, are absurd, foolish, and impious; and for the most part used by them who sufficiently proclaim that they know neither what it is to be saved, nor do use any diligence about the necessary means of it. Salvation depends absolutely on no particular church-state in the world; he knows not the gospel who can really think it doth. Persons of believers are not for the church, but the church is for them. If the ministry of angels be for them who are heirs of salvation, much more is the ministry of the church so. If a man be an adulterer, an idolater, a railer, a hater and scoffer of godliness; if he choose to live in any known sin, without repentance, or in the neglect of any known duty; if he be ignorant and profane; a word, if he be not born again from above, be he of what church he will, and whatsoever place he possesses therein, he cannot be saved. And on the other side, if a man believe in Christ Jesus, — that is, know him in his person, offices, doctrine, and grace; trust unto him for all the ends of the wisdom and love of God towards mankind in him; if he endeavour to yield sincere and universal obedience unto all his commands, and to be conformed unto him, in all things following his example, having for these ends received of his Spirit, — though all the churches in the world should reject him, yet he shall undoubtedly be saved. If any shall hence infer that then it is all one of what church any one is, I answer, — [1.] That although the being of this or that or any particular church in the world will not secure the salvation of any men, yet the adherence unto some churches, or such as are so called, in their constitution and worship, may prejudice, yea, ruin the salvation

Chapter VIII.

of any that shall so do. [2.] The choice of what church we will join unto belongs unto the choice and use of the means for our edification; and he that makes no conscience hereof, but merely with respect unto the event of being saved at last, will probably come short thereof.

(2.) On this supposition, that there be no insuperable difficulties lying in the way of the discharge of this duty, — as that a person be cast by the providence of God into such a place or season as wherein there is no Church that he can possibly join himself unto, or that he be unjustly refused communion, by unwarrantable conditions of it, as it was with many during the prevalency of the Papacy in all the western empire, — it is the indispensable duty of every disciple of Christ, in order unto his edification and salvation, voluntarily, and of his own Choice, to join himself in and unto some particular congregation, for the celebration of divine worship, and the due observation of all the institutions and commands of Christ: which we shall now farther confirm: —

[1.] The foundation of this duty, as was before declared, doth lie in *the law and light of nature*. Man cannot exercise the principal powers and faculties of his soul, with which he was created, and whereby he is enabled to glorify God, which is the end of him and them, without a consent and conjunction in the worship of God in communion and society; as hath been proved before.

[2.] The Way whereby this is to be done God hath declared and revealed from the beginning, by the constitution of a church-state, through the addition of arbitrary institutions of worship unto what was required by the law of nature: for this gives the true state, and is the formal reason of a church, — namely, a divine addition of arbitrary institutions of worship unto the necessary dictates of the law of nature unto that end; and the especial nature of any church-state doth depend on the especial nature of those institutions, which is constitutive Of the difference between the church-state of the Old Testament and that of the New.

[3.] Such a church-state was constituted and appointed under the Old Testament, founded in and on an especial covenant between God and the people, Exod. xxiv. Unto this church every one that would please God and walk before him was bound to join himself, by the ways and means that he had appointed for that end, — namely, by circumcision, and their "laying hold on the covenant of God," Exod. xii. 48; Isa. lvi. 4. And this joining unto the church is called "joining unto the Lord," Isa. lvi. 6, Jer. l. 5; as being the means thereof, without which it could not be done. Herein was the tabernacle of God with men, and he dwelt among them.

[4.] As a new church-state is prophesied of under the New Testament, Ezek. xxxiv. 25-29, Isa. lxvi. 18-22, and other places innumerable, so it was actually erected by Jesus Christ; as we have declared. And whereas it is introduced and established in the place and room of the church-state under the Old Testament, which was to be removed at the time of reformation, as the apostle demonstrates at large in his Epistle to the Hebrews, all the commands, promises, and threatenings given or annexed unto that church-state, concerning the conjunction of men unto it and walking in it, are transferred unto this of the new erection of Christ. Wherefore, although the state of the church itself be reduced from that which was nation ally congregational unto that which is simply and absolutely so, and all the ordinances of its instituted worship are changed, with new rules for the observation of what we are directed unto by the light of nature, yet the commands, promises, and threatenings made and given unto it as a church are all in full force with respect unto this new church-state; and we need no new commands to render it our duty to join in evangelical churches for the ends of a church in general.

[5.] The Lord Christ hath *disposed all the ways and means of edification* unto these churches; so that ordinarily, and under an expectation of his presence in them and concurrence unto their efficacy, they are not otherwise to be enjoyed. Such are the ordinary dispensation of the word, and administration of the sacraments. For any disciple of Christ to live in a neglect of these things and the enjoyment of them according to his mind, is to despise his care and wisdom in providing for his eternal welfare.

[6.] He hath *prescribed sundry duties* unto us, both as necessary and as evidences of our being his disciples, such as cannot be orderly performed but as we are members of some particular congregation. This also hath been before declared.

[7.] The *institution of these churches* is the way which Christ hath ordained to render his kingdom visible or conspicuous, in

CHAPTER VIII.   183

distinction from and opposition unto the kingdom of Satan and the world. And he doth not, in a due manner, declare himself a subject in or unto the kingdom of Christ who doth not solemnly engage h this way. It is not enough to constitute a legal subject of the kingdom of England that he is born in the nation, and lives in some outward observance of the laws of it, if he refuse solemnly to express his allegiance in the way appointed by the law for that end. Nor will it constitute a regular subject of the kingdom of Christ that he is born in a place where the gospel is professed, and so professeth a general compliance therewith, if he refuse to testify his subjection by the way that Christ hath appointed for that end. It is true, the whole nation, in their civil relation and subordination according to law, is the kingdom of England; but the representation of the kingly power and rule in it is in the courts of all sorts, wherein the kingly power is acted openly and visibly. And he that lives in the nation, yet denies his homage unto these courts, is not to be esteemed a subject, So doth the whole visible professing church, in one or more nations or lesser precincts of people and places, constitute the visible kingdom of Christ; yet is no particular person to be esteemed a legal, true subject of Christ that doth not appear in these his courts with a solemn expression of his homage unto him.

[8.] The *whole administration of the rule and discipline appointed by Christ* is confined unto these churches, nor can they be approved by whom that rule is despised. I shall not argue farther in a case whose truth is of so uncontrollable evidence. In all the writings of the New Testament, recording things after the ascension of Christ, there is no mention of any of his disciples with approbation, unless they were extraordinary officers, but such as were entire members of these assemblies.

CHAPTER IX.

The continuation of a church-state and of the administration of evangelical ordinances of worship briefly vindicated.

THE controversy about *the continuation* of a church-state and the administration of gospel ordinances of worship is not *new* in this age, though some pride themselves as though the invention of the error whereby they are denied were their own. In former ages, both in the Papacy and among some of them that forsook it, there were divers who, on a pretence of a peculiar spirituality and imaginary attainments in religion, wherein these things are unnecessary, rejected their observation. I suppose it necessary briefly to confirm the truth, and vindicate it from this exception; because, though it be sufficiently weak in itself, yet what it is lies against the foundation of all that we are pleading about. But to reduce things into the lesser compass, I shall first confirm the truth by those arguments or considerations which will defeat all the pleas and pretences of them by whom it is opposed, and then confirm it by positive testimonies and arguments, with all brevity possible.

First, therefore, I shall argue from the removal of all causes whereon such a cessation of churches and ordinances is pretended; for it is granted on all hands that they had a divine original and institution, and were observed by all the disciples of Christ as things by him commanded. If now, therefore, they cease as unto their force, efficacy, and use, it must be on some of these reasons:—

1. *Because a limited time and season was fixed unto them*, which is now expired. So was it with the church-state and ordinances of old; they Were appointed unto the "time of reformation," Heb. ix. 10. They had a certain time prefixed unto their duration; according to the degrees of whose approach they waxed old, and at length utterly disappeared, Heb. viii. 13; until that time they were all punctually to be observed, Mal. iv. 4. But there

Chapter IX.

were many antecedent indications of the will of God concerning their cessation and abolition; whereof the apostle disputes at large in his Epistle unto the Hebrews. And from a pretended supposition that such was the state of evangelical ordinances, — namely, that they had a time prefixed unto their duration, — did the first opposition against them arise; for Montanus, with his followers, imagined that the appointments of Christ and his apostles in the gospel were to continue in force only unto the coming of the Paraclete, or the Comforter, promised by him. And adding a new frenzy hereunto, that that Paraclete was then first come in Montanus, they rejected the institutions of the gospel, and made new laws and rules for themselves. And this continues to be the principal pretence of them by whom the use of gospel ordinances is at present rejected, as that which is of no force or efficacy. Either they have received or do speedily look for such a dispensation of the Spirit or his gifts as wherein they are to cease and disappear. But nothing can be more vain than this pretence:—

(1.) It is so as unto the limitation of any time as unto their duration and continuance; for, — [1.] There is no intimation given of any such thing, either in the divine word, promise, declaration about them, or the nature of the institutions themselves. But whereas those of the Old Testament were in time to be removed, that the church might not be offended thereby, seeing originally they were all of immediate divine institution, God did by all manner of ways, as by promises, express declarations, and by the nature of the institutions themselves, fore-signify their removal; as the apostle proves at large in his Epistle to the Hebrews. But nothing of this nature can be pretended concerning the gospel church-state or worship. [2.] There is no *prediction* or intimation of any other way of worship, or serving God in this world, that should be introduced in the room of that established at first; so that upon a cessation thereof the church must be left unto all uncertainties and utter ruin. [3.] The principal reason why a church-state was erected of old, and ordinances of worship appointed therein, that were all to be removed and taken away, was that the Son, the Lord over his own house, might have the pre-eminence in all things. His glory it was to put an end unto the law, as given by the disposition of angels and the ministry of Moses, by the institution of a church-state and ordinances of his own appointment. And if his revelation of the will of God therein be not complete, perfect, ultimate, unalterable, if it be to expire, it must be that honour may be given above him unto one greater than he.

(2.) It is so *as unto their decay, or the loss of their primitive force and efficacy*; for their efficacy unto their proper ends depends on, — [1.] The *institution of Christ*. This is the foundation of all spiritual efficacy unto edification in the church, or whatever belongs thereunto. And, therefore, whatever church-state may be framed, or duties, ways, or means of worship appointed by men that have not his institution, how specious soever they may appear to be, have no spiritual force or efficacy as unto the edification of the church. But whilst this institution of Christ continues irrevocable, and is not abrogated by a greater power than what it was enacted by, whatever defect there may be as unto faith and obedience in men, rendering them useless and ineffectual unto themselves, however they may be corrupted by additions unto them or detractions from them, changing their nature and use, in themselves they continue to be of the same use and efficacy as they were at the beginning. [2.] On *the promise of Christ* that he will be present with his disciples, in the observation of his commands, unto the consummation of all things, Matt. xxviii. 20. To deny the continued accomplishment of this promise, and that on any pretence whatever, is the venom of infidelity. If, therefore, they have an irrevocable divine institution, if Christ be present in their administrations, as he was of old, Rev. ii. 1, there can be no abatement of their efficacy unto their proper ends, in the nature of instrumental causes. [3.] On the *covenant of God*, which gives an infallible, inseparable conjunction between the word, or the church and its institution by the word, and the Spirit, Isa. lix. 21. God's covenant with his people is the foundation of every church-state, of all offices, powers, privileges, and duties there unto belonging. They have no other end, they are of no other use, but to communicate, express, declare, and exemplify, on the one hand, the grace of God in his covenant unto his people, and, on the other, the duties of his people according unto the tenor of the same covenant unto him. They are the way, means, and instruments appointed of God for this end, and other end they have none; and hereon it follows, that if it be not in the power of men to appoint any thing that shall be a means of communication between God and his people, as unto the grace of the covenant on the one hand, or the duties of obedience which it requires on the other, they have no power to erect any new church-state, or enact any thing in divine worship not of his institution This being the state of churches and their ordinances, they cannot be altered, they cannot be liable unto any decay, unless the covenant whereunto they are annexed be altered or decayed; and therefore the apostle, to put finally and absolutely his argument unto an issue to prove that the Mosaical church-state and ordinances were changed, because useless and ineffectual, doth it on this ground, that the covenant whereunto they were annexed was changed and become useless. This, I suppose, at present, will not be said concerning the new covenant, whereunto all ordinances of divine worship are inseparably annexed.

Men might at a cheaper rate, as unto the eternal interest of their own souls, provide another covering for their sloth, negligence, unbelief, and indulgence unto proud, foolish imaginations, whereby they render the churches and ordinances of the gospel useless and ineffectual unto themselves; thereby charging them with a decay and uselessness, and so reflecting on the honour and faithfulness of Christ himself.

2. They do not cease because there is at present, or at least there is shortly to be expected, such *an effusion of the gifts and graces of the Spirit as to render all these external institutions needless, and consequently useless*. This, also, is falsely pretended. For, — (1.) The greatest and most plentiful effusion of the Holy Spirit in his gifts and graces was in the days of the apostles, and of the first churches planted by them; nor is any thing beyond it, or indeed equal unto it, any more to be expected in this world; — but yet then was the gospel church-state erected, and the use of all its ordinances of worship enjoined. (2.) The ministry of the gospel, which compriseth all the ordinances of church-worship as its object and end, is *the ministration of the Spirit*; and therefore no supplies or communication of him can render it useless. (3.) One of the principal ends for which the communication of the Spirit is promised unto the church is to make and render all the institutions of Christ effectual unto its edification. (4.) 1 John ii. 20, 27, is usually pleaded as giving countenance into this fond pretence. But, — [1.] The *unction* mentioned by the apostle was then upon all believers. Yet, — [2.] It is known that then they all walked in *church-order*, and in the sacred observation of all the institutions of Christ. [3.] If it takes away any thing, it is *the*

preaching of the word, or all manner of teaching and instruction; which is to overthrow the whole Scripture, and to reduce religion into barbarism. [4.] Nothing is intended in these words but the different way of teaching and degrees of success between that under the law and that now established in the gospel, by the plentiful effusion of the Spirit; as hath been evidenced at large elsewhere. Nor, —

3. Do they cease in their administration for *want either of authority or ability to dispense them,* which is pleaded unto the same end? But neither is this pretence of any force; it only begs the thing in question. (1.) The authority of office for the administration of all other ordinances is an institution; and to say that all institutions cease because none have authority to administer them is to say they must all cease because they are ceased. (2.) The office of the ministry, for the continuation of the church-state, and administration of all ordinances of worship, unto the end of the world, is sufficiently secured, — [1.] By the law, constitution, and appointment of our Lord Jesus Christ erecting that office, and giving warranty for its continuance to the consummation of all things, Matt. xxviii. 20; Eph. iv. 13. [2.] By his continuance, according unto his promise, to communicate spiritual gifts unto men, for the ministerial edification of the church. That this he doth so continue to do that it is the principal external evidence of his abiding in the discharge of his mediatory office, and of what nature these gifts are, I have declared at large in a peculiar discourse on that subject. [3.] On the duty of believers or of the church, which is to choose, call, and solemnly set apart unto the office of the ministry such as the Lord Christ by his Spirit hath made meet for it, according unto the rule of his word.

If all these, or any of them, do fail, I acknowledge that all ministerial authority and ability for the dispensation of gospel ordinances must fail also, and consequently the state of the church. And those who plead for the continuation of a successive ministry without respect unto these things, without resolving both the authority and office of it into them, do but erect a dead image, or embrace a dead carcase, instead of the living and life-giving institutions of Christ. They take away the living creature, and set up a skin stuffed with straw. But if these things do unalterably continue; if the law of Christ can neither be changed, abrogated, nor disannulled; if his dispensation of spiritual gifts according unto his promise cannot be impeded; if believers, through his grace, will continue in obedience unto his commands, — it is not possible there should be an utter failure in this office and office-power of this ministry. It may fail in this or that place, in this or that church, when the Lord Christ will remove his candlestick; but it hath a living root, whence it will spring again in other places and churches, whilst this world doth endure. Neither, —

4. Do they cease because they have been all of them *corrupted, abused, and defiled*, in the apostasy which fell out among all the churches in the latter ages, as it was fully foretold in the Scripture. For, — (1.) This supposition would make the whole kingdom of Christ in the world to depend on the corrupt lusts and wills of men, which have got by any means the outward possession of the administration of his laws and ordinances. This is all one as if we should say, that if a pack of wicked judges should for a season pervert justice, righteousness, and judgment, the being of the kingdom is so overthrown thereby as that it can never be restored. (2.) It would make all the duties and all the privileges of all true believers to depend on the wills of wicked apostates; for if they may not make use of what they have abused, they can never yield obedience to the commands of Christ, nor enjoy the privileges which he hath annexed unto his church and worship. (3.) On this supposition all reformation of an apostatized church is utterly impossible. But it is our duty to heal even Babylon itself, by a reduction of all things unto their first institution, if it would be healed, Jer. li. 9; and if not, we are to forsake her and reform ourselves, Rev. xviii. 4.

There is nothing, therefore, in all these pretences, that should in the least impeach the infallible continuation of the evangelical churches and worship, as to their right, unto the end of the world. And the heads of those arguments whereby the truth is invincibly confirmed may be briefly touched on: —

1. There are express testimonies of the will of Christ, and his promise for its accomplishment, that *the church and all its ordinances of worship should be continued always, unto the end of the world*. So as to the church itself, Matt. xvi. 18, Rev. xxi. 3; the ministry, Matt. xxviii. 20, Eph. iv. 13; baptism, Matt. xxviii. 19, 20; the Lord's supper, 1 Cor. xi. 26. As for other institutions, public prayer, preaching the word, the Lord's day, singing of God's praises, the exercise of discipline, with what belongs thereunto, they have their foundation in the law and fight of

nature, being only directed and applied unto the gospel church-state and worship by rules of especial institution; and they can no more cease than the original obligation of that law can so do.

If it be said, that notwithstanding what may be thus pleaded, yet, *"de facto,"* the true state of gospel churches and their whole worship, as unto its original institution, did fail under the papal apostasy, and therefore may do so again, I answer, — (1.) We do not plead that this state of things must be always *visible* and conspicuous; wherein all protestant writers do agree. It is acknowledged, that as unto public view, observation, and notoriety, all these things were lost under the Papacy, and may be so again under a renewed apostasy. (2.) I do not plead it to be necessary, "de facto," that there should be really at all times a true visible church, as the seat of all ordinances and, administrations in the world; but all such churches may fail, not only as unto visibility, but as unto their existence. But this supposition of a failure of all instituted churches and worship I grant only with these limitations:— [1.] That it is of necessity, from innumerable divine promises and the nature of Christ's kingly office, that there be always in the world *a number, greater or lesser, of sincere believers*, that openly profess subjection and obedience unto him; [2.] That in these persons there resides an *indefeasible right* always to gather themselves into a church-state, and to administer all gospel ordinances, which all the world cannot deprive them of: which is the whole of what I now plead for. And let it be observed, that all the ensuing arguments depend on this right, and not on any matter of fact. [3.] I do not know how far God may accept of churches in a very corrupt state, and of worship much depraved, until they have new means for their reformation; nor will I make any judgment of persons, as unto their eternal condition, who walk in churches so corrupted, and in the performance of worship so de-prayed: but as unto them who know them to be so corrupted and depraved, it is a damnable sin to join with them or not to separate from them, Rev. xviii. 4.

2. The nature and use of the gospel church-state require and prove *the uninterrupted continuance* of the right of its existence, and the observance of all ordinances of divine worship therein, with a power in them in whom that right doth indefeasibly reside, — that is, all true believers, — to bring it forth into exercise and practice, notwithstanding the external impediments which

in some places at some times may interrupt its exercise. In the observation of Christ's institutions and celebration of the ordinances of divine worship doth the church-state of the gospel, as professing, consist. It doth so in opposition, — (1.) Unto the *world* and the kingdom of Satan; for hereby do men call Jesus "Lord," as 1 Cor. xii. 3, and avow their subjection Unto his kingly power. (2.) Unto *the church-state of the Old Testament*, as the apostle disputes at large in his Epistle unto the Hebrews. And this state of the professing church in this world is unalterable, because it is the best state that the believing church is capable of; for so the apostle plainly proves, that hereby the believing church is brought εἰς τελείωσιν, which it was not under the law, — that is, unto its consummation, in the most complete perfection that God hath designed unto it on this side glory, Heb. vii. 11, 19. For Christ in all his offices is the immediate head of it; its constitution, and the revelation of the ways of its worship, are an effect of his wisdom; and from thence is it eminently suited unto all the ends of the covenant, both on the part of God and man, and is therefore liable to no intercision or alteration.

3. *The visible administration of the kingdom of Christ in* this world consists in this church-state, with the administration of his institutions and laws therein. A kingdom the Lord Jesus Christ hath in this world; and though it be not of the world, yet in the world it must be until the world shall be no more. The truth of all God's promises in the Scripture depends on this one assertion. We need not here concern ourselves what notions some men have about the exercise of this kingdom in the world, with respect unto the outward affairs and concerns of it; but this is certain, that this kingdom of Christ in the world, so far as it is external and visible, consists in the laws he hath given, the institutions he hath appointed, the rule or polity he hath prescribed, with the due observance of them. Now, all these things do make, constitute, and are the church-state and worship inquired after. Wherefore, as Christ always hath, and ever will have, an invisible kingdom in this world, in the souls of elect believers, led, guided, ruled by his Spirit, so he will have a visible kingdom also, consisting in a professed, avowed subjection unto the laws of his word, Rom. x. 10. And although this kingdom, or his kingdom in this sense, may, as unto the essence of it, be preserved in the external profession of individual persons,

and it may be so exist in the world for a season, yet the honour of it and its complete establishment consist in the visible profession of churches; which he will therefore maintain unto the end. But by *visible* in this discourse, I understand not that which is conspicuous and eminent unto all, through the church hath been so, and shall yet be so again; nor yet that which is actually seen or known by others; but only that which may be so, or is capable of being so known. Nor do I assert a necessity hereof, as unto a constant preservation of purity and regularity in order and ordinances, according to the original institution of them a in any place; but only of an *unalterable right and power in believers to render them visible*: which it becomes their indispensable duty to do when outward impediments are not absolutely insuperable. But of these things thus far, ὡς ἐν παρόδῳ.

CHAPTER X.

What sort of churches the disciples of Christ may and ought to join themselves unto as unto entire communion.

WE have proved before that it is the duty of all individual Christians to give themselves up unto the conduct, fellowship, and communion of some particular church or congregation. Our present inquiry hereon is, whereas there is a great diversity among professing societies in the world, concerning each whereof it is said, "Lo, here is Christ," and "Lo, there is Christ," what church, of what constitution and order, any one that takes care of his own edification and salvation ought to join himself unto. This I shall speak unto first in *general*, and then in the examination of one particular case or instance, wherein many at this day are concerned. And some things must b premised unto the right stating of the subject of our inquiry:—

1. The diversities and divisions among churches, which respect is to be had unto in the choice of any which we will or ought to join unto, are of two sorts:—

(1.) Such as are *occasioned* by the remaining weaknesses, infirmities, and ignorance of the best of men, whereby they know but in part, and prophesy only in part; wherein our edification is concerned, but our salvation not endangered.

(2.) Such as are in and about things *fundamental in faith*, worship, and obedience. We shall speak to both of them.

2. All Christians were *originally of one mind* in all things needful unto joint communion, so as that there might be among them all love without dissimulation. Howbeit there was great variety, not only in the measure of their apprehensions of the doctrines of truth, but in some doctrines themselves, — as about the continuance of the observations of the law, or at least of some of them; as also oppositions from without unto the truth by heretics and apostates: neither of which hindered the church-communion of true believers. But the diversity, differ-

ence, and divisions that are now among churches in the world is the effect of the great apostasy which befell them all in the latter ages, as unto the spirit, rule, and practice of those which were planted by the apostles; and will not be healed until that apostasy be abolished.

3. Satan having possessed himself of the *advantage of these divisions*, whereof he was the author, he makes use of them to act his malice and rage, in stirring up and instigating one party to persecute, oppress, and devour another, until the life, power, and glory of Christian religion is almost lost in the world. It requires, therefore, great wisdom to deport ourselves aright among these divisions, so as to contribute nothing unto the ends of malice designed by Satan in them.

4. In this state of things, until it may be cured, — which it will never be by any of the ways yet proposed and insisted on, — the inquiry is concerning the duty of any one who takes care of his own soul as unto a conjunction with some church or other. And on the negative part, I say, —

(1.) Such a one is bound not to *join* with any church or society where *any fundamental* article of faith is rejected or corrupted. There may be a fundamental error in a true church for a season, when the church erreth not fundamentally, 1 Cor. xv. 12; 2 Tim. ii. 18. But I suppose the error in or against the foundation is part of the profession of the church or society to be joined unto; for thereby the nature of the church is destroyed, — it doth not hold the Head, nor abide on the foundation, nor is the pillar and ground of truth. Wherefore, although the Socinians, under a pretence of love, forbearance, and mutual toleration, do offer us the communion of their churches, wherein there is somewhat of order and discipline commendable, yet it is unlawful to join in church fellowship or communion with them: for their errors about the Trinity, the incarnation Christ, and his satisfaction, are destructive of the foundation of the prophets and apostles; and idolatry, in the divine worship of a mere creature, is introduced by them.

(2.) Where there is in any church taught or allowed a mixture *of doctrines or opinions that are prejudicial unto gospel holiness and obedience*, no man that takes due care of his salvation can join himself unto it; for the original rule and measure of all church-communion is agreement in the doctrine of truth. Where, therefore, there is either not a stable profession of the same doctrine in all substantial truths of the gospel, but an uncertain sound is given, some saying one thing, some another, or that opposition is made unto any truths of the importance before mentioned, none can be bound or obliged to hold communion with it, nor can incur any blame by refraining from it: for it is the duty of a Christian in all things προτιμᾶν τὴν ἀλήθειαν, and to join with such a church would, — [1.] Stain their profession; [2.] Hinder their edification; [3.] Establish a new rule of communion, unknown to the Scriptures, — namely, besides truth; as might easily be manifested.

(3.) Where *the fundamentals of religious worship* are corrupted or overthrown, it is absolutely unlawful to join unto or abide in any church. So is it with the church of Rome. The various ways whereby the foundations of divine religious worship are overthrown in that church, by superstition and idolatry, have been sufficiently declared. These render the communion of that church pernicious.

(4.) Nor can any man be obliged to join himself with any church, nor can it be his duty so to do, where the eternally fixed rule and measure of religious worship, — namely, that it be of divine institution, — is varied or changed by any additions unto it or subtractions from it; for whereas one principal end of all churches is the joint celebration of divine worship, if there be not a certain stable rule thereof in any church of divine prescription, no man can be obliged unto communion therewith.

(5.) Where the fundamentals of church order, practice, and discipline are destroyed, it is not lawful for any man to join in church communion. These fundamentals are of two sorts, — [1.] Such as concern the *ministry of the church*; [2.] Such as concern the *church itself.*

[1.] There are four things that are *necessary fundamentals* unto the order of the church on the part of the ministry:—

1st. That all the ministers or officers of it be *duly chosen* by the church itself, and solemnly set apart in the church unto their office, according unto the rule and law of Christ. This is fundamental unto church-order, the root of it, from whence all other parts of it do spring. And it is that which is ῥητῶς, or expressly provided for in the Scripture, as we shall see. If there be a neglect herein, and no other relation required between ministers, elders, rulers, bishops, and the church, but what is raised and created by ways and rules of men's appointment; or if there be a temporary disposal of persons into a discharge of that office, without a solemn call, choice, ordination, and separation unto the office itself and its work, — the law of Christ is violated and the order of the church disturbed in its foundation.

2*dly.* That those who are called unto the office of the ministry be *duly qualified,* by their endowment with spiritual gifts, for the discharge of their duty, is fundamental unto the ministry. That the Lord Jesus Christ doth still continue his dispensation of spiritual gifts unto men, to fit and enable them unto the office and work of the ministry; that if he doth not do so, or should at any time cease so to do, the whole office of the ministry must cease, and the being of the church with it; that it is altogether useless for any churches or persons to erect an image of the gospel ministry by outward rites and ceremonies, without the enlivening force of these spiritual gifts, — I have proved sufficiently in my "Discourse of Spiritual Gifts, and their Continuance in the Church."[14] Wherefore, a communication of spiritual gifts, peculiarly enabling men unto the work of the ministry, antecedent unto their solemn separation unto the office, in some good measure, is absolutely necessary unto the due continuance of the office and its work. See Eph. iv. 7, 11–15. To suppose that the Lord Christ doth call and appoint men unto a certain office and work in his church, secluding all others from any interest in the one or other, and yet not endow them with peculiar gifts and abilities for the discharge of that office and work, is to ascribe that unto him which is every way unbecoming his wisdom

---

14 These words are printed in the original edition as if they were the title of a particular treatise by our author. His treatise under that title will be found in vol. iv. of his doctrinal works; but it seems to have been published in 1693, twelve years after the present work appeared. Such a discourse is promised in his preface to his treatise on "the Work of the Holy Spirit in Prayer," which was published in 1682, a year after the publication of the present work. There is some discussion on the subject of spiritual gifts in the first chapter of his great work on the Holy Spirit; but a special and separate treatise seems alluded to in the text above. To the "Discourse of Spiritual Gifts," as published in 1693, there is a preface by Nathaniel Mather; from which the reader is led to infer that it was then published for the first time. Perhaps the difficulty may be obviated by the supposition that Owen intended to publish it immediately, and refers to it in this work by anticipation.

and grace, with his love unto the church. But when men look on all church-order as a life-less machine, to be acted, moved, and disposed by external rules, laws, canons, and orders, without respect unto the actings of the Spirit of Christ going before in the rule of his word, to enliven every part of it, the true disciples of Christ will receive no advantage thereby.

3*dly*. It is of the same importance that persons so called do *take heed unto their ministry that they fulfil it*, — that they give themselves unto the word and prayer, that they labour continually in the word and doctrine, and all those other duties which in the Scripture are prescribed unto them; and this, not only as unto the matter of them, but as unto the manner of their performance, — with zeal, love, compassion, and diligence. Where there is a great defect in any of these things, on what pretence soever it be; where men esteem themselves exempted from this work, or not obliged unto it; when they suppose that they may discharge their office at a cheaper rate, and with less trouble as unto their present interest, by such ways as I shall not here express, — no man is, no man can be, obliged to confine his church-communion unto such a ministry.

4*thly*. It is required that they be *examples* unto the flock, in the expression of the nature and power of the doctrine which they preach, in their conversation, especially in zeal, humility, self-denial, and readiness for the cross.

Where these things are not, there is such a defect in the fundamentals of church-practice, as unto the ministry of it, that no man who takes care of his own edification can join himself unto a church labouring under it; for ministers and churches are nothing but institute, means of the conversion of sinners and the edification of believers. And when any of them, through their own default, cease so to be, there is no obligation unto any man to join or continue in their communion, nor do they contract any guilt in a peaceable departure from them, but discharge their duty. That this be done peaceably, without strife or contention, without judging of others, as unto their interest in Christ and eternal salvation, the law of moral obedience doth require; that it be done with love, and compassion, and prayer towards and for them who are left, is the peculiar direction of that moral duty by the gospel. Such a practice at present would fall under severe charges and accusations, as also brutish penalties, in some places. But when all church-craft shall be defeated, and the uses that are made of its imaginary authority be discarded, there will be little occasion of this practice, and none at all of offence.

[2.] Again; there are things fundamental unto church practice and order in the church itself, which, where they are neglected, no man ought of choice to join himself unto that church, seeing he cannot do without the prejudice of his edification, the furtherance whereof he ought to design in that duty. And these are, —

1st. That the *discipline of Christ be* duly exercised in it according unto his mind, and by the rules of his prescription. There never was any sect, order, or society of men in the world, designed for the preservation and promotion of virtue and things praiseworthy, but they had rules of discipline proper unto the ends of their design, to be observed in and by all that belong unto them. Where the erection of such societies is continued in the world, as it is much in the Papacy, both their constitution and their conversation depend on the especial rules of discipline which they have framed unto themselves. And this is done by them in great variety; for being ignorant of the discipline of the gospel, and so esteeming it insufficient unto their design, they have made no end of coining rules unto themselves. To suppose that our Lord Jesus Christ, who in his church-state, according to ms infinite wisdom, hath erected the most perfect society for the most perfect ends of religion, of obedience towards God, of love and usefulness among ourselves, hath not appointed a discipline, and given rules concerning its administration, for the preservation of that society and the attaining of those ends, is highly injurious unto his honour and glory.

Where, therefore, there is a church, or any society that pretends so to be, wherein there is an utter neglect of this discipline of Christ, or the establishment of another not administered by the laws and rules that he hath prescribed, no disciple of Christ can be obliged to join unto or to continue in the total, sole communion of such a church. And whereas there are two parts of this discipline of Christ, — that which is private, among the members of the church, for the exercise and preservation of love; and that which is public, in and by the authority of the rulers of the church, for the preservation of purity and order, — a neglect in either of them cloth much impeach the fundamental constitution of a church as unto its practice.

2dly. There are sundry other things which belong unto this *discipline* in general, which are of great consideration in the discharge of the duty we inquire into. Among them are, — (1st.) That *constant difference* be put between the good and the bad in all church administrations; (2dly) That persons *openly or flagitiously wicked* be not admitted into the society of the church, or a participation of its privileges; (3dly.) That *holiness*, love, and usefulness be openly avowed as the design and interest of the church. But they are all so comprised in the general head of discipline as that I shall not in particular insist upon them.

From what hath been thus declared, it will appear, on the other hand, what church it is that a disciple of Christ, who takes due care of his own edification and salvation, ought in duty to join himself unto in complete communion. To answer this inquiry is the end of all those discourses and controversies which have been about the notes of the true church. I shall briefly determine concerning it, according to the principles before evinced:—

(1.) It must be such a church as wherein all *the fundamental truths* of the gospel are believed, owned, and professed, without controversy, and those not borne withal by whom they are denied or opposed. Without this a church is not the pillar and ground of truth, it doth not hold the Head, it is not built on the foundation of the prophets and apostles. Neither is it sufficient that those things are generally professed, or not denied. A church that is filled with wranglings and contentions about fundamental or important truths of the gospel is not of choice to be joined unto; for these things subvert the souls of men, and greatly impede their edification. And although, both among distinct churches and among the members of the same church, mutual forbearance be to be exercised, with respect unto a variety in apprehensions in some doctrines of lesser moment, yet the incursion that hath been made into sundry protestant churches, in the last and present age, of novel doctrines and opinions, with differences, divisions, and endless disputes which have ensued thereon, have rendered it very difficult to determine how to engage in complete communion with them; for I do not judge that any man is or can be obliged unto constant, total communion with any church, or to give up himself absolutely unto the conduct thereof, wherein there are incurable dissensions about important doctrines of the gospel. And if any church shall publicly avow, countenance, or approve of doctrines contrary unto those which were the foundation of its first communion, the members of it are at liberty to refrain the communion of it, and to provide otherwise for their own edification.

(2.) It must be such a church as wherein *the divine worship instituted* or approved by Christ himself is diligently observed, without any addition made thereunto. In the observance of this worship, as unto all external, occasional incidences and circumstances of the acts wherein it doth consist, it is left unto the prudence of the church itself, according to the light of nature and general rules of Scripture; and it must be so, unless we shall suppose that the Lord Jesus Christ, by making men his disciples, doth unmake them from being rational creatures, or refuseth the exercise of the rational faculties of our souls in his service. But this is so remote from truth, that, on the contrary, he gives them an improvement for this very end, that we may know how to deport ourselves aright in the observance of his commands, as unto the outward discharge of them in his worship and the circumstances of it; and this he doth by that gift of spiritual wisdom whereof we shall treat afterward.

But if men, if churches, will make *additions* in or unto the rites of religious worship, unto what is appointed by Christ himself, and require their observance in their communion, on the force and efficacy of their being so by them appointed, no disciple of Christ is or can be obliged, by virtue of any divine institution or command, to join in total, absolute communion with any such church. He may be induced, on various considerations, to judge that something of that nature at some season may not be evil and sinful unto him, which, therefore, he will bear with or comply withal; yet he is not, he cannot be obliged, by virtue of any divine rule or command, to join himself with or continue in the communion of such a church. If any shall suppose that hereby *too much liberty* is granted unto believers in the choice of their communion, and shall thereon make severe declamations about the inconveniencies and evils which will ensue, I desire they would remember the principle I proceed upon; which is, that churches are not such *sacred machines* as some suppose, erected and acted for the outward interest and advantage of any sort of men, but only means of the edification, of believers, which they are bound to make use of, in obedience unto the commands of Christ, and no otherwise. Whereas, therefore, the disciples of Christ have not only a divine warranty justifying them in the doing of it, but an express command, making it their indispensable duty to join in the celebration of all that religious worship which the Lord Christ, the only lawgiver of the church, and who was faithful both in and over the house of God as the Son, hath instituted and commanded, but have no such warranty or command for any thing else, it is their duty to stand fast in the liberty wherewith Christ has made them free. And if by the same breath, in the same rule, law, or canon, they are commanded and obliged to observe in the worship of God what the Lord Christ hath appointed and what he hath not appointed, both on the same grounds, — namely, the authority of the church, — and on the same penalties for their omission, no man can be divinely obliged to embrace the communion of any church on such terms.

(3.) It is required that *the ministry of a church* so to be joined with is not defective in any of those things which, according to the rule of the gospel, are *fundamental* thereunto. What these are hath been declared. And because edification, which is the end of church-communion, doth so eminently depend on the ministry of the church, there is not any thing which we ought to have a more diligent consideration of in the joining of ourselves unto any such communion. And where the ministry of any church, be the church of what sort or size it will, is incurably ignorant or negligent, or, through a defect in gifts, grace, conscientious attendance unto their duty, is insufficient unto the due edification of the souls of them that believe, no man can account himself obliged unto the communion of the church but he that can be satisfied with a shadow and the names of things for the substance and reality of them.

If, therefore, it be granted, as I think it is, that edification is the principal end of all church-communion, it is not intelligible how a man should be obliged unto that communion, and that alone, wherein due edification cannot be obtained. Wherefore, a ministry enabled by spiritual gifts, and engaged by sense of duty, to labour constantly in the use of all means appointed by Christ for the edification of the church, or increase of his mystical body, is required in such a church as a believer may conscientiously join himself unto; and where it is otherwise, let men cry out "schism" and "faction" whilst they please, Jesus Christ will acquit his disciples in the exercise of their liberty, and accept them in the discharge of their duty.

If it he said, that if all men be thus allowed to judge of what is best for their own edification, and to act according unto the judgment which they make, they will be continually parting from one church unto another, until all things are filled with disturbance and confusion, I say, —

[1.] That the contrary assertion, — namely, that *men are not allowed to judge* what is meet and best for their own edification, or not to act according to the judgment they make herein, — may possibly keep *up some churches*, but is the ready way *to destroy all religion*.

[2.] That many of those by whom this liberty is denied unto professing Christians yet do indeed take it for granted that *they have such a liberty*, and that it is their duty to make use of it. For what are all the contests between the church of Rome and the church of England, so far as Christians that are not churchmen are concerned in them? Is it not, in whether of the churches edification may be best obtained? If this be not the ball between us, I know not what is. Now, herein do not all the writers and preachers of both parties give t heir reasons and arguments unto the people why edification is better to be had in the one church than in the other? And do they not require of them to form a judgment upon those reasons and arguments, and to act accordingly? If they do not, they do but make a flourish, and act a part, like players on a stage, without any determinate design.

[3.] All Christians *actually do so*. They do judge for themselves unless they are brutish; they do act according unto that judgment, unless they are hardened in sin; and therefore who do not so are not to be esteemed disciples of Christ. To suppose that in all things of spiritual and eternal concernment men are not determined and acted every one by his own judgment, is an imagination of men who think but little of what they are, or do, or say, or write. Even those who shut their eyes against the light and follow in the herd, resolving not to inquire into any of these things, do it because they *judge it is best for them so to do*.

[4.] It is commonly acknowledged by Protestants that private Christians have *a judgment of discretion* in things of religion. The term was invented to grant them some liberty of judgment, in opposition unto the blind obedience required by the church of Rome; but withal to put a restraint upon it, and a distinction of some superior judgment, it may be in the church or others. But if by *discretion* they mean the best of men's understanding, knowledge, wisdom, and prudence, in and about the things wherein it is exercised, I should be glad to be informed what other judgment than this of discretion, in and about the things of religion, this, or that, or any church in the world, can have or exercise. But to allow men a judgment of discretion, and not to grant it their duty to act according unto that judgment, is to oblige them to be fools, and to act not *discreetly*, at least not according unto their *own discretion*.

(4.) The same is to be spoken of *gospel discipline*, without which neither can the duties of church-societies be observed nor the ends of them attained. The neglect, the loss, the abuse hereof, is that which hath ruined the glory of Christian religion in the world, and brought the whole profession of it into confusion. Hereon have the fervency and sincerity of true, evangelical, mutual love been abated, yea utterly lost; for that love which Jesus Christ requireth among his disciples is such as never was in the world before amongst men, nor can be in the world but on the principles of the gospel, and faith therein. Therefore it is called his "new commandment." The continuation of it amongst the generality of Christians is but vainly pretended; little or nothing of the reality of it in its due exercise is found. And this hath ensued on the neglect of evangelical discipline in churches, or the turning of it into a worldly domination; for one principal end of it is the preservation, guidance, and acting of this love. That mutual watch over one another that ought to be in all the members of the church, the principal evidence and fruit of love without dissimulation, is also lost hereby. Most men are rather ready to say, in the spirit and words of Cain, "Am I my brother's keeper?" than to attend unto the command of the apostle, "Exhort one another daily, lest any of you be hardened through the deceitfulness of sin;" or comply with the command of our Saviour, "If thy brother offend thee, tell him of it between him and thee." By this means likewise is the purity of communion lost, and those received as principal members of churches who, by all the rules of primitive discipline, ought to be cast out of them. Wherefore this also is to be considered in the choice we are to make of what churches we will join ourselves unto, as unto constant, complete communion, and in whose communion we will abide; for these things are matters of choice, and consist in voluntary, free acts of obedience. With those unto whom they are not so, who would on the one hand have them to be things that men may be compelled unto, and ought so to be, or, on the other, that follow no other guidance in them but outward circumstances, from the times and places where they are born and inhabit, I will have no contest. It follows from hence, also, that where there are many churches wherein these things are found, whereon we may lawfully, and ought in duty, to join with some of them in particular, every one is obliged to join himself unto such a church as whose principles and practices are most suited unto his edification.

CHAPTER XI.

Of conformity and communion in parochial assemblies.

FROM what we have insisted on we may borrow some light into the determination of that case wherein multitudes are at this day concerned. And the case itself may be briefly stated in this inquiry, — namely, *Whether all Protestants, ministers and people, are bound to join a themselves unto the church of England, as now by law established in its parochial assemblies, as unto complete, constant communion, without the use of any other church means for their own edification, so as if they do not so do they are guilty of schism*? This is that which is called "conformity unto the church of England;" which, as unto private persons, can be expressed only in constant, complete communion in parochial assemblies, according to their present constitution, without the use or exercise of any other church worship or discipline but what is by law established in them. Refraining from an absolute compliance herein is called *schism*. But whereas ecclesiastical schism, whatever it be in particular, in its general nature hath respect only unto divine institutions, this, which respecteth only the laws, rules, and determinations of men, can have no alliance thereunto. Yet it is not only charged as such, without the least countenance from Scripture or antiquity, so far as it may be allowed of authority with us, but the supposition of it is accumulated with another evil, — namely, that those who are so guilty (of it), in the judgment of them who are intrusted with secular power, though peaceable and orthodox, ought to be punished with various penalties, gradually coming unto the loss of goods, liberty, and in some cases of life itself; — an opinion *ignominious unto Christian religion*, however vapoured withal by young men, whose wit flies above all serious consideration of things and their circumstances, and countenanced by others, from an influence of interest, who otherwise would, not be imposed on by such an anti-evangelical presumption. I shall, therefore, at the utmost distance from interest or passion, briefly consider the case proposed, and give an account of my thoughts concerning it.

1. One or two things are usually premised unto the consideration of this case; as, namely, —

(1.) That those who refrain from that communion with the church of England which we insist upon do yet agree therewith in all important doctrines of faith; which is the foundation, the life and soul of church union and communion. This I freely grant, but with this limitation, that this agreement respects the doctrine as declared at the first reformation, and explained in the age next ensuing thereon. If there be a change made in or of these doctrines, or any of them, by any in or of the church of England, we profess our disagreement from them, and do declare that thereby the foundation of our communion with them is weakened, and the principal bond of it loosened.

(2.) That not only as Christians, but as reformed Protestants, we do agree in the renunciation of the doctrines and worship of the church of Rome; which are opposed by the common consent of all those who are usually so called. Yet this must be added thereunto, that if any in or of the church of England should make an accession unto any parts of the doctrine and worship of the Roman church, not avowed or warranted by the consent of the church in its first reformation, we are not, we cannot be, obliged unto communion with them therein; and by their so doing, the original bond of our communion is weakened if not dissolved.

2. These things being premised, we shall inquire, in the first place, what is the rule of that communion with the church of England in its parochial assemblies which is required of us. If this be pleaded to be a rule of divine prescription, we acknowledge that great diligence and humility are required unto the consideration of it, that we be not mistaken. And if it prove to be according to the mind of Christ, — that is, of his institution, — if we fail of a compliance with it, we are guilty of schism. But if the rule prescribing, limiting, and exacting this communion, be not so much as pleaded to be of divine institution, whatever fault there may be in our dissent from it, schism it is not: for ecclesiastical schism neither hath nor can have respect unto any thing but divine institutions; for if it hath, it is in the power of an sort of men to make schismatics of whom they please, as,

practically and in pretence, it is come to pass at this day in the world. Now, the rule of the communion required is, the *law of the land, the Book of Canons,* with the *rubric of the Common Prayer.* If, according to the prescriptions, directions, and commands given in them, we do join ourselves in communion with parochial assemblies, then are we judged conformable to the church of England, and not else. By and according unto these are all inquiries made concerning communion with the church; and if they are observed, the return is, "*omnia bene.*" Now, this rule hath no divine warrant for its institution, no example in the primitive churches, especially considering what are the things which it obliges us unto, nor can be made consistent with the liberty wherewith Christ hath made his disciples free. A dissent from this rule is as far from schism as any man need desire it; for nothing is so but what respects some command or institution of Christ, which immediately affects the conscience. It is true, the Lord Christ hath commanded that love, union, peace, and order, whereof schism is a disturbance, and whereunto it is opposite; but they are that love, union, and order which he hath appointed. To suppose that he hath left it unto men to invent and appoint a new kind of union and order, — which is done in the rule we treat of, — which he never required, and then to oblige his disciples unto the observation of it, be it what it will, so as that their dissent from it should be criminal, and that for this reason, that it is so appointed of men, is no small mistake. And if all that love, union, peace, and order, which the Lord Jesus hath enjoined his disciples, may be punctually observed without any respect unto this rule as a rule of church-communion, to dissent from it, whatever fault of another kind it may be, is no more schism than it is adultery. And if, on some men's arbitrary constitution of this rule, and the dissent of others from it, such differences and divisions ensue as seem to have the general nature of schism, the evil of them belongs unto those alone by whom the rule is framed. If, indeed, some should frame such a rule of church-communion because they suppose they see cause for it, and would then leave it unto others to observe as they see cause, if it be not o use, it would not be liable unto much abuse. But whereas our Lord Jesus Christ hath given one and the same rule equally unto all his disciples in these things, — namely, that they should observe and do all that he hath commanded them, — for some of them, on any pretence or plea whatever, as of their being the church, or the like, arbitrarily to frame a rule of their own, as an addition unto his, obliging all others unto a strict observance of it because they have so framed it, is that which neither the Scripture nor primitive antiquity knows any thing of.

I will not inquire what is that power and authority whereby this rule constituted and confirmed, nor in whom it doth reside. The name of the church is usually pretended and pleaded. But before any can be concerned herein, all that hath been pleaded for the true state and nature of evangelical churches must be overthrown; which will not be done speedily. Railings, revilings, and reproaches will not do it. But until this is done, it will be believed that every particular congregation is indispensably obliged in itself to observe and do all the commands of Christ, and is left at liberty so to regulate the outward circumstances of its worship and order as is best for its own edification, whereof itself is the most competent judge. But as for a church of another sort, invested with authority to make a rule, not only as rote the outward circumstances of those actions wherein church order and worship do consist, but as unto sundry religious rites and observances, which thereby are added unto it, and impose the observance of it on a great multitude of other congregations, without their consent, whether they judge the things enjoined to be for their edification or otherwise, it is apparently not from heaven, but of men. Wherefore, leave Christians and churches at that liberty which Christ hath purchased for them, wherewith he hath made them free, and then let those who first break union and order bear the charge of schism; which they cannot avoid.

3. The church-communion required by virtue of this rule is *constant and complete*, exclusive unto any other church-order or means of public edification. It doth not command or appoint that men should communicate in parochial assemblies when there is occasion, when it is for their edification, when scandal would arise if they should refuse it; but absolutely and completely. And whereas there are many things relating unto church-order and divine worship enjoined in that rule, there is no distinction made between them, — some things that are always necessary (that is, in the seasons of them), and some things wherein men may forbear a compliance, — but they are all equally required in their places and seasons, though perhaps

on different penalties. And whoever fails in the observation of any ceremony, time, or place, appointed therein, is in the power of them who are intrusted with the administration of church power or jurisdiction; for the discipline of the church it cannot be called. Suppose a man would comply with all other things, only he esteems the use of one rite or ceremony, as the cross in baptism, or the like, to be unlawful; if he forbear the use of it, or to tender his child unto baptism where it is used, he is to be cut off as a schismatic from the communion of the church, no less than if he had absolutely refused a compliance with the whole rule. And, therefore, whatever condescension and forbearance a some things is pretended, he that doth not in all things observe the whole rule is in *"misericordia cancellarii;"* which oft proves an uneasy posture. If any men think that the Lord Christ hath given them such a power and authority over the souls and consciences of his disciples, as that they can bind them unto the religious observance of every rite and ceremony that they are pleased to appoint, on the penalty of excision from all church-communion and the guilt of schism, I shall only say that I am not of their mind, nor ever shall be so.

4. This communion contains a virtual *approbation* of all that is contained in the rule of it, as good for the edification of the church. It is certain that nothing is to be appointed in the church but what is so; even order itself, which these things it is said are framed for, is good only with respect thereunto. Now, it is to be judged that whatever a man practiseth in religion, that he approveth of; for if he do not, he is a vile hypocrite. Nor is he worthy the name of a Christian who will practice any thing in religion but what he approveth. The disputes that have been amongst us about doing things with a doubting conscience, upon the command of superiors, and consenting unto the use of things which we approve not of in themselves, tend all to atheism and the eternal dishonour of Christian religion begetting a frame of mind which an honest heathen would scorn. Wherefore, unless men be allowed to declare what it is they approve and what they do not, their practice is their profession of what they approve, which is the whole rule of communion prescribed unto them.

These things being premised, I shall propose some of those reasons on the account whereof many cannot conform unto the church of England, by joining in constant, complete communion with parochial assemblies, so as by their practice to approve the rule of that communion obliging themselves to use no other public means for their own edification:—

I. The church of England in its parochial assemblies stands in need of reformation; for it is apparent that either they fail in their original institution or else have degenerated from it. What hath already been discoursed concerning the original institution of churches, with men's voluntary coalescency into such sacred societies, with what shall be afterward treated concerning their essential parts in matter and form, will sufficiently evidence their present deviation from the rule of their first institution. Neither, so far as I know, is it pleaded that they are distinct churches of divine institution, but secular appointments, as for other ends, so for an accommodation of men in the performance of some parts of divine worship. And if they are found no more, they can have no concernment into the inquiry about schism; for withholding church-communion from such societies as are not churches is a new kind of schism, unknown to all antiquity. And for that which takes itself to be a church by a divine warranty, suppose it be so, to command constant, complete communion, exclusive unto all other church-communion, with that or them which are no churches, determining a refusal thereof to be schism, is to undertake a cause which needs not only great parts but great power also to defend it.

But let these parochial assemblies be esteemed churches (without a supposition whereof I know not what ecclesiastical concernment we can have in them), three things will be said thereon:— 1. That the church of England, as in other things so in these *parochial assemblies*, stands in need of reformation. 2. That they neither do, nor will, nor can *reform themselves*. 3. On this supposition, it is lawful for any of the disciples of Christ to yield obedience unto him by joining in such societies for their edification as he hath appointed; which is the whole of the cause in hand. Nor doth any necessity from hence ensue of a departure from communion with the church of England in faith and love, or the profession of the same faith, and the due exercise of all the acts and duties of Christian love.

1. Unto the proof of the first assertion some things are to be premised; as, —

(1.) Churches instituted, planted, ruled according to the mind of Christ in all things, *may degenerate* into a corrupt state,

Chapter XI.

such as shall stand in need of reformation; in a neglect whereof they must perish as unto their church-state and privileges. This needs no confirmation; for besides that it is possible, from all the causes of such an apostasy and defection, that so it should be, and it is frequently foretold in the Scripture that so it would be, the event in and among all churches that had originally a divine institution doth make uncontrollably evident. The seven churches of Asia, most of them within few years of their first plantation, were so degenerated that our Lord Jesus Christ threatened them with casting off unless they reformed themselves. What a woful apostasy all other churches, both of the east and west, were involved in, is known unto and confessed by all Protestants. But yet the case of none of them was deplorable or desperate, until, through pride and carnal interest, they fell some of them into a persuasion that they needed no reformation, nor could be reformed; which is become a principal article of faith in the Roman church. There was a reformation attempted, and attained in some measure, by some nations or churches in the last ages, from the corruption and impositions of the church of Rome. However, none of them ever pretended that it was complete or perfect, according to the pattern of the Scripture, as unto the institution and discipline of the churches; no, nor yet to the example of the primitive church c f after ages, as is acknowledged by the church of England in the beginning of the "commination against sinners." But suppose it to be complete, to conclude that because an outward rule of it was established, so long as that outward rule is observed there can be no need of reformation, is a way to lead churches into a presumptuous security unto their ruin; for whereas men, being secured in their interest by that rule, are prejudiced against any progress in reformation beyond what they have attained, — which that it should be a duty is contrary unto the whole nature of Christian religion, which is the conduct of a spiritual life, in the growth and increase of light and a suitable obedience, — so they are apt to think that whilst they adhere unto that rule they can stand in no need of reformation, which, is but a new name for trouble and sedition, though it be the foundation on which they stand. But generally churches think that others stand in need of reformation, but they need none themselves. If they would but give them leave to reform themselves who judge that it is needful for them, without the least prejudice unto their church profession or secular interest, it is all that is desired of them.

(2.) Where churches do so stand in need of reformation, and will not reform themselves, being warned of their duty, the Lord Christ threatens to leave them, and assuredly will do so in the time that he hath limited unto his patience. This is the subject of five of his epistles or messages unto the churches of Asia, Rev. ii., iii. And where the Lord Christ doth, on any cause or provocation, withdraw his presence, in any kind or degree, from any church, it is the duty of any of the members of that church to remove from themselves the guilt of that provocation, though it cannot be done without a separation from that church. It is safer leaving of any church whatever than of Jesus Christ. I suppose most men think that if they had a warning from Christ charging their defection and calling for reformation, as those churches of Asia had, they would repent and reform themselves. But whereas it doth not appear that some of them did so, — whereon they were, not long after, deserted and destroyed, — it is like that there are others who would follow their steps though one should rise from the dead to warn them of their danger. But this instruction, that churches who lose their first faith, love, and works, who are negligent in discipline, and tolerate offensive evils in doctrines and manners among them, who are lukewarm as unto zeal, and dead, for the greatest part of their members, as unto the life of holiness, are disapproved by Christ, and in danger of being utterly deserted by him, is given unto all churches, no less divinely than if they had an immediate message from heaven about these things. Those, therefore, who, being under the guilt of them, do not reform themselves, cannot claim the necessity of a continuance in their communion from any disciples of Christ, as we shall see afterward.

(3.) Reformation respects either doctrine and worship, or obedience becoming the gospel. The debates about such a reformation as concerns the retaining or removing of certain ceremonies, we concern not ourselves in at present; nor shall we in this place insist on what concerns doctrine and worship, which may afterward be spoken unto. But we shall confine ourselves here unto the consideration of gospel obedience only. And we say, —

That the church of England, in the generality of its parochial assemblies, and in itself, stands in need of reformation, by reason of the woful degeneracy of the generality of its members,

Chapter XI.

— that is, the inhabitants of the land, — from the rule of the gospel and commands of Christ, as unto spiritual light, faith, love, holiness, charity, and abounding n the fruits of righteousness unto the praise of God by Jesus Christ. These things are the immediate ends of church societies, the principal means whereby God is glorified in the world. Where they are neglected, where they are not attained, where they are not duly improved by the generality of the members of any church, that church, I think, stands in need of reformation.

This assertion may seem somewhat importune and severe; but when the sins of a church or nation are come to that height, in all ranks, sorts, and degrees of men, that all persons of sobriety do fear daily that desolating judgments from God will break in upon us, it cannot be unseasonable to make mention of them, when it is done with no other design but only to show the necessity of reformation, or how necessary it is for some, if all will not comply therewith; for if a city be on fire, it is surely lawful for any of the citizens to save and preserve, if they can, their own houses, though the mayor and aldermen should neglect the preservation of the whole city in general.

It might be easily demonstrated what great numbers [there are] amongst us, — [1.] Who have imbibed *atheistical opinions*, and either vent them or speak presumptuously, according unto their influence and tendency every day; [2.] Who are *profane scoffers* at all true Christian pigsty and the due expressions of the power of godliness, — an evil not confined unto the laity, — such things being uttered and published b them as should be astonishable unto all that know the fear of the Lord and his terror; [3.] Who are *profoundly ignorant* of the mysteries of the gospel, or those doctrines of Christian religion whose knowledge is of the highest importance and necessity; [4.] Who are openly *flagitious in their lives*, whence all sorts of gross immoralities do fill the land from one end unto the other; [5.] Who live in a *constant neglect* of all more private holy duties, whether in their families or in personal retirement; [6.] Who are evidently under *the power of pride*, vanity, covetousness, profaneness of speech in cursed oaths and swearing; [7.] Who *instruct the worst of men* unto an approbation of themselves in such ways as these, by petulant scoffing at the very name of the Spirit and grace of Christ, at all expectation of his spiritual aids and assistances, at all fervency in religious duties, or other acts of a holy converse.

These, and such like things as these, do sufficiently evidence the necessity of reformation; for where they are continued, the use and end of church-societies is impaired or lost. And it is in vain to pretend that this is the old plea of them who caused schisms in the church, — namely, that bad men were mixed with the good, for which cause they rejected those churches wherein that was allowed as no true churches of Christ; for no such thing is included in what we assert, nor doth follow thereon. We do own that wicked hypocrites may be joined in true churches, and be made partakers of all the privileges of them. Neither is this a cause of withdrawing communion from any church, much less of condemning it as no true church of Christ. But this we say, that if such hypocrites discover themselves in open scandalous sins, — which upon examination will prove to be of a larger extent than some suppose, with respect unto sins of omission as well as of commission, — if they are not dealt withal according as the discipline of Christ doth require in such cases, the church wherein they are allowed, especially if the number of such persons be many, or the most, the generality of the people, and their sins notorious, doth stand in need of reformation; as the church of England doth acknowledge in the "commination against sinners."

The substance of what is proposed under this consideration may be expressed in the ensuing observations:— (1.) The generality of the inhabitants of this nation are joined and do belong unto the church of England, in its parochial assemblies. (2.) That many walk and live without any visible compliance unto the rule of Christ in gospel obedience: yea, — (3.) Great, notorious, provoking sins do abound among them, for which it ought to be feared continually that the judgments of God will speedily follow; as is acknowledged in the "commination." (4.) That hereon they all stand in need of reformation, without which the principal ends of church-communion cannot be obtained among them. (5.) That this reformation is the duty of these churches themselves; which if it be neglected, they live in a contempt of the commands of Christ; for, — (6.) Unto them, in the preaching of the word and exercise of discipline, are the means of this reformation committed: for we treat not at present of the power or duty of the supreme magistrate in these things. (7.) That this state of churches cannot hinder, nor ought so to do, if continued in, the true disciples of Christ from reforming themselves, by endeavouring the due observance of all his commands.

2. In this state the church of England doth not, and it is to be feared *will not, nor can reform itself.* But although the weight of the whole argument in hand depends very much on this assertion, yet I shall not insist on its particular confirmation, for sundry reasons not now to be mentioned. It is enough that no such work hath been a yet attempted, nor is at this day publicly proposed, notwithstanding all the mercies that some have received, the losses which the church for want of it hath sustained, the judgments for sins that are feared; which ought to be motives thereunto. Yea, the generality of ecclesiastical persons seem to judge that all things among them are as they ought to be, that there is no crime or disorder but only in complaining of their good estate, and calling upon them for reformation.

3. This being the state of the parochial churches in England, the inquiry is, Whether *every believer in England be indispensably obliged, by virtue of any law, rule, or direction of a divine original, to continue in constant, complete communion with them, so as not to make use of any other ways and means of Christ's appointment for their own edification, on the penalty of the guilt of schism*? Now, although we do not (as we shall see immediately) lay the weight of refraining from their communion on this consideration, yet is there enough in it to warrant any man in his so doing; for a man in his conforming thereunto makes it a part of his religious profession, not only that the church wherein he is joined is a true church, but that there is in its state and actings a due representation of the mind of Christ, as unto what he requireth of his churches, and what he would have them to be. The Lord Christ is the "apostle and high priest of our profession:" and in all things that belong thereunto we declare that we do it in compliance with his will; and we do so, or we are hypocrites. This no man can do in such a church-state who is convinced of its defects, without reflecting the greatest dishonour on Christ and the gospel.

More weight will be added unto this consideration when we shall treat of the matter of gospel churches, or of what sort of persons they ought to consist. In the meantime, those who pretend a reverence unto antiquity in those things wherein they suppose countenance to be given unto their interest, may do well sometimes to consider what *was the discipline of the prim-*

itive churches, and what were the manners, the lives, the heavenly conversations of their members. Because in the third and fourth centuries there is mention made of bishops distinct from presbyters, with some ecclesiastical practices and ceremonies in worship not mentioned in the Scripture nor known unto the apostolical churches, shall we judge ourselves obliged to conform thereunto as our rule and pattern, so as that in the judgment of some they are to be esteemed no churches who conform not their outward state and practice unto the same rule? and shall we judge ourselves at liberty to reject all that they did in the exercise of discipline, and in the preservation of purity of life and holiness in the churches, and that according to the command of Christ and rule of the Scripture? Who knows not upon what diligent trial, and experience first obtained of their knowledge, faith, and godliness, they admitted members into their churches? Yea, such was their care and severity herein that they would not admit a Roman emperor unto communion with them, unless he first confessed his sins, and joined amongst other penitents before his admission, Euseb., lib. vi. cap. 33. Who knows not with what diligence they watched over the walkings and conversations of all that were admitted among them, and with what severity they animadverted on all that fell into scandalous sins? What was hereon their conversation, in all holiness, righteousness, temperance, usefulness unto the world, in works of charity and benevolence, as in all other Christian virtues, we have sufficient testimony. The heathen who were morally sober and virtuous, desired no more than that they might find out among them an indulgence unto any sort of sin, crime, or wickedness; which because they could not charge any of them withal, they invented those brutish and foolish lies about their nightly meetings. But when a sober inquiry was made concerning them, their enemies were forced to confess that they were guilty of no open sin, no adulteries, no swearings or perjuries; as is evident in the epistles of Pliny and Trajan the emperor. In particular, they utterly rejected from their communion all that resorted unto public stage-plays or other spectacles; a solemn renunciation whereof was required of them who were admitted unto baptism when they were adult. See Clem. Pedag., lib. iii. cap. 12. If the reader would have an account of the lives and manners of the first churches in their members, he may find it in Clem. Epist. ad Cor. pp. 2–4; Justin Mart. Apol. ii.; Tertullian in his Apol. and lib. ii. ad Uxor. et de cultu fœminarum; Cyprian, Epist. ii. et xii.; Euseb. Hist. lib. ix., cap. 8; Athanas. Epist. ad Solit., et Epiphan. lib. iii. t. 2, sect. 24; and the multiplied complaints of Chrysostom concerning the beginning of degeneracy in this matter, with others. If the example of the primitive churches had been esteemed of any value or authority in these things, much of our present differences had been prevented.

II. The constitution of these parochial assemblies is not from heaven, but of men. There is almost nothing which is required unto the constitution of evangelical churches found in them; nor are they looked on by any as complete churches, but only as conveniencies for the observance of some parts of the worship of God. What some have in their wisdom found out for conveniency, others are engaged unto a compliance therewithal by necessity; for being born within the precincts of the parish makes them to belong unto the assemblies of it, whether they will or no. To refrain from the communion of such churches, whose bond of relation consists only in cohabitation within the precincts of a political constitution, is a new kind of schism, which may be cured by a removal out of those precincts. If it be said that these parochial assemblies have their foundation in the light of nature, and are directed unto in the institution of particular churches in the Scripture, — that they are not men's inventions for convenience, but have somewhat divine in them, — I say, let them be left unto the warranty which they have from these causes and principles, let nothing be mixed in their constitution which is contrary unto them, nor let them be abridged of what they direct unto, and there will be no more contending about them, as unto their constitution. For instance, whatever there is of warranty in the light of nature, or direction in evangelical institutions for such assemblies, they absolutely suppose these three things:—

1. That a conjunction in them is a *voluntary act* of free choice in them that so join together in them. Other kind of assemblies for the worship of God neither the one nor the other doth give the least countenance unto.

2. That they have in themselves sufficient *right, power, and authority* unto the attaining all the ends of such assemblies in holy worship and rule. Other kind of churches they know nothing of.

3. That they are enabled to *preserve their own purity* and continue their own being.

But all these things are denied unto our parochial assemblies by law; and therefore they can claim no warranty from either of those principles. Wherefore, there can be no obligation upon any believer to join himself with such churches in constant communion as are judged none by them that appoint them, or only partially and improperly so, or are of such a constitution as hath in its essentially constituent, parts no warranty either from the light of nature or Scripture direction, so as that his dissent from them should be esteemed schism. How far communion with them for some duties of worship, — which is, indeed, all that they can pretend unto, — may be admitted, we do not now inquire.

III. There is not in them (and therefore not in the church of England, as unto its present profession) a *fixed standard of truth*, or rule of faith to be professed, which every believer may own, and have his part or interest therein. This I grant is not from the original constitution of the church, nor from what is established by any law therein, but from persons who at present have the declaration of its profession, committed unto them. But from what cause soever it be, it is sufficient to warrant any man who takes care of his own edification and salvation to use his own liberty in the choice of the most effectual means unto those ends. Wherefore some things may be added in farther explanation of this consideration; as, —

1. It is the duty of every church *to be the pillar and ground of truth*, to hold fast the form of wholesome words, or to keep the truth pure and uncorrupted from all mixture of false doctrines, errors, heresies, or the speaking of perverse things in it, unto the hurt of the disciples of Christ, 1 Tim. iii. 15; 2 Tim. ii. 2; Acts xx. 28–30, etc. When any church ceaseth so to be, the obligation unto communion with it is dissolved.

2. This is the *principal end* of the ministry of the church in particular, Eph. iv. 11–13; 1 Tim. vi. 20. And where those who possess and exercise it do eminently fail herein, it is the duty of others to withdraw from them; for, —

3. Every private man's confession is included in the public profession of the church or assembly whereunto he belongs. And, —

4. Oneness or agreement in the truth, whereby we come to have "one Lord, one faith, one baptism," is the foundation of all church-communion; which if it be taken away, the whole fabric of it falls to the ground. If the trumpet in any church, as unto these things, gives an uncertain sound, no man knows how to prepare himself for the battle, or to "fight the good fight of faith."

It will be said that this cannot be justly charged on the church of England, yea, not without open wrong and injustice; for she hath a fixed, invariable standard of truth in the Thirty-nine Articles, which contain its public profession of faith and the rule of its communion. Wherefore I say, that it is not the *primitive constitution* of the church nor its *legal establishment* that are reflected on, but only the present practice of so many as makes it necessary for men to take the care of their own edification on themselves. But here also some things are to be observed:—

1. These articles at present are exceeding defective, in their being a fixed standard of the profession of truth, with respect unto those errors and heresies which have invaded and pestered the churches since their framing and establishment. We know it was the constant, invariable custom of the primitive churches, upon the emergency of any new errors or heresies, to add unto the rule and symbol of their confession a testimony against them, so as to preserve themselves from all communion in them or participation of them. And a usage it was both necessary and laudable, as countenanced by Scripture example, however afterward it was abused; for no writing, such as all church-confessions are, can obviate unforeseen heresies, or errors not broached at the time of its writing, but only that which is · of divine institution, wherein infinite wisdom hath stored up provision of truth, for the destruction of all errors that the subtlety or folly of man can invent. When these articles of the church of England were composed, neither Socinianism nor Arminianism, which have now made such an inroad on some protestant churches, were n the world, either name or things. Wherefore, in their confession no testimony could be expressly given against them, though I acknowledge it is evident, from what is contained in the articles of it, and the approved exposition they received for a long time in the writings of the most eminent persons of the church, that there is a virtual condemnation of all these errors included therein. But in that state where-

unto things are come amongst us, some more express testimony against them is necessary to render any church the pillar and ground of truth.

2. Besides, a distinction is found out, and passeth current among us, that the articles of this confession are *not articles of faith*, but of outward agreement for peace' sake among ourselves: which is an invention to help on the ruin of religion; for articles of peace in religion, concerning matters of faith, which he that subscribes doth it not because they are true or articles of faith, are an engine to accommodate hypocrisy, and nothing else. But according unto this supposition they are used at men's pleasure, and turned which way they have mind to. Wherefore,

3. Notwithstanding this standard of truth, differences in important doctrines, wherein the edification of the souls of men is highly concerned, do abound among them who manage the public profession of the church. I shall not urge this any farther by instances; in general it cannot modestly be denied. Neither is this spoken to abridge ministers of churches of their due liberty in their management o the truths of the gospel; for such a liberty is to be granted as:—

(1.) Ariseth from the *distinct gifts* that men have received; for "unto every one is given grace according to the measure of the gift of Christ," Eph. iv. 7. "As every man hath received the gift, even so minister the same one to another, as good stewards of the manifold grace of God," 1 Pet. iv. 10.

(2.) As followeth on that *spiritual wisdom* which ministers receive in great variety, for the application of the truths of the gospel unto the souls and consciences of men. Hereon great variety in public church-administrations will ensue, but all unto edification.

(3.) Such as consists in a *different exposition* of particular places of Scripture, whilst the analogy of faith is kept and preserved, Rom. xii. 6.

(4.) Such as admits of *different stated apprehensions* in and about such doctrines as wherein the practice and comfort of Christians are not immediately nor greatly concerned.

Such a liberty, I say, as the dispensation of spiritual gifts, and the different manner of their exercise, as the unsearchable depths that are in the Scripture, not to be fathomed at once by any church or any sort of persons whatever, and our knowing the best of us but in part, with the difference of men's capacities and understandings in and about things not absolutely necessary unto edification, must be allowed in churches and their ministry. But I speak of that variety of doctrines, which is of greater importance. Such it is as will set men at liberty to make their own choice in the use of means for their edification. And if such novel opinions about the person, grace, satisfaction, and righteousness of Christ, about the work of the Holy Spirit of God in regeneration, or the renovation of our nature into the image of God, as abound in some churches, should at any time, by the suffrage of the major part of them who by law are intrusted with its conduct, be declared as the sense of the church, it is and would be sufficient to absolve any man from an obligation unto its communion by virtue of its first institution and establishment.

IV. *Evangelical discipline* is neither observed nor attainable in these parochial assemblies, nor is there any relief provided by any other means for that defect. This hath in general been spoken unto before; but because it belongs in an especial manner unto the argument now in hand, I shall yet farther speak unto it. For, to declare my mind freely, I do not judge that any man can incur the guilt of schism who refrains from the communion of the church wherein the discipline of the gospel is either wholly wanting or is perverted into rule and domination, which hath no countenance given unto it in the word of truth. And we may observe, —

1. The *discipline of the church* is that alone for which any rule or authority is given unto it or exercised in it. Authority is given unto the ministers of the church to dispense the word and administer the sacraments; which, I know not why, some call the "key of order." But the only end why the Lord Christ hath given authority, or rule, or power for it unto the church, or any in it, is for the exercise of discipline, and no other. Whatever power, rule, dignity, or pre-eminence is assumed in the churches, not merely for this end, is usurpation and tyranny.

2. The outward means appointed by Jesus Christ, for the preservation of his churches in order, peace, and purity, consists in this discipline. He doth by his word give directions and commands for this end; and it is by discipline alone that they are executed. Wherefore, without it the church cannot live in its health, purity, and vigour. The word and sacraments are its

spiritual food, whereon its life doth depend; but without that exercise, and medicinal applications unto its distempers which are made by discipline, it cannot live a healthy, vigorous, faithful life in the things of God.

3. This discipline is either private or public: —

(1.) That which is *private* consists in the mutual watch that all the members of the church have over one another, with admonitions, exhortations, and reproofs, as their edification doth require. The loss of this part of the discipline of Christ in most churches hath lost us much of the glory of Christian profession.

(2.) That which is public, in the rulers of the church, with and by its own consent. The nature and acts of it will be afterward considered.

4. There are three things considerable in this discipline: — (1.) The power and authority whereby it is exercised; (2.) The manner of its administration; (3.) The especial object of it, both as it is susceptive of members and corrective; whereunto we may add its general end: —

(1.) The *authority* of it is only a power and liberty to act and ministerially exercise the authority of Christ himself. As unto those by whom it is exercised, it is in them an act of obedience unto the command of Christ; but with respect unto its object, the authority of Christ is exerted in it. That which is exercised on any other warranty or authority (as none can exert the authority of Christ but by virtue of his own institutions), whose acts are not acts of obedience unto Christ, whatever else it be, belongs not unto the discipline of evangelical churches.

(2.) As unto the *manner* of its administration, it is that which the Lord Christ hath appointed to express his love, care, and tenderness towards the church. Hence the acts of it which are corrective are called "lamenting" or "bewailing" of them towards whom they are exercised, 2 Cor. xii. 20. Whatever, therefore, is done in it that is not expressive of the love, care, patience, and holiness of Christ, is dishonourable unto him.

(3.) The *object* of it, as it is *susceptive of members*, is professed believers; and as it is *corrective*, it is those who stubbornly deviate from the rule of Christ, or live in disobedience of his commands. Wherefore, the general end of its institution is, to be a representation of the authority, wisdom, love, care, and patience of Christ towards his church, with a testimony unto the certainty, truth, and holiness of his future judgment. The especial nature of it shall be afterward considered.

Unto this discipline, either as unto its right or exercise, there is no pretence in parochial assemblies, yea, it is expressly forbidden unto them. Whereas, therefore, it is a matter of so great importance in itself, so subservient unto the glory of Christ, so useful and necessary into the edification of his disciples, so weighty a part of our professed subjection unto him, without which no church can be continued in gospel purity, order, and peace, the total want or neglect of it is a sufficient cause for any man who takes care of his own salvation, or is concerned in the glory and honour of Christ, to refrain the communion of those churches wherein it is so wanting or neglected, or at least not to confine himself thereunto.

It will be said that this defect is supplied, in that the administration of church-discipline is committed unto others, — namely, the bishops and their officers, that are more meet and able for it than the ministers and people of parochial assemblies; what, therefore, is wafting in them is supplied fully another way, so that no pretence can be taken from hence for refraining communion in them. But it will be said, —

1. That this discipline is not to be placed where and in what hands men please, but to be left where Christ hath disposed it.

2. That one reason of the unmeetness of parochial churches for the exercise of this discipline is because they have been unjustly deprived of it for so many ages.

3. It is to be inquired, whether the pretended discipline doth in any thing answer that which Christ hath plainly and expressly ordained. For if a discipline should be erected whose right of exercise is derived from secular power, whose administration is committed unto persons who pretend not in the least unto any office of divine institution, as chancellors, commissaries, officials, etc., every way unknown unto antiquity, foreign unto the churches over which they rule, exercising their pretended power of discipline in a way of civil jurisdiction, without the least regard unto the rules or ends of evangelical discipline, managing its administration in brawlings, contentions, revilings, fees, pecuniary mulcts, etc., in open defiance of the spirit, example, rule, and commands of our Lord Jesus Christ, — it would be so far from supplying this defect, that it would exceedingly aggravate the evil of it. God forbid that any Christian should look

on such a power of discipline, and such an administration of it, to be that which is appointed by Jesus Christ, or any way participant of the nature of it! Of what expediency it may be unto other ends I know not, but unto ecclesiastical discipline it hath no alliance; and therefore in its exercise, so far as it is corrective, it is usually applied unto the best and most sober Christians.

Wherefore, to deal plainly in this case, whereas there is neither the power nor exercise of discipline in parochial assemblies or their ministry, not so much by their own neglect as because their right thereunto is denied and its exercise wholly forbidden by them in whose power they are; and whereas, in the supply that is made of this defect, a secular power is erected, coercive by pecuniary and corporal penalties, administered by persons no way relating unto the churches over which they exercise this power, by rules of human laws and constitutions, in litigious and oppressive courts, in the room of that institution of Christ, whose power and exercise is spiritual, by spiritual means, according to the Scripture rules, — it is lawful for any in m who takes care of his own salvation and of the means of it to withdraw from the communion of such churches, so far as it hinders or forbids him the use of the means appointed by Christ for his edification. Men may talk what they please of schism, but he that forsakes the conduct of his own soul, in things of so plain an evidence, must answer for it at his own peril.

V. This defect in parochial churches, that they are intrusted by law with no part of the rule of themselves, but are wholly governed and disposed of by others at their pleasure, in the ways before mentioned, — which shakes their very being as churches, though there be in them assemblies for divine worship, founded in common right and the light of nature, wherein men may be accepted with God, — is accompanied with such other wants and defects also as will weaken any obligation unto complete and constant communion with them. I shall give one only instance hereof: The *people's free choice of all their officers*, bishops, elders, pastors, etc., is, in our judgment, of divine institution, by virtue of apostolical example and directions. It is also so suitable unto the light of nature, — namely, that in a society absolutely founded in the *voluntary consent* of them who enter into it, and [which] doth actually exist thereby, without any necessity imposed on them from prescription, former usage, or the state of being born in and under such rules and laws, as it is with men in their political societies, the people should have the election of them who are to rule among them and over them, there being no provision of a right unto a successive imposition of any such rulers on them without their own consent, — that nothing can rationally be pleaded against it. And, therefore, whereas in all ordinarily settled governments in the world, setting aside the confusion of their originals, by war and conquests, the succession of rulers is either by *natural generations*, the rule being confined unto such a line, or by a *popular election*, or by a temperature of both; there hath been a new way invented for the communication of power and rule in churches, never exemplified in any political society, — namely, that it shall neither be successive, as it was under the Old Testament, nor elective, nor by any temperature of these two ways in one, but by a strange kind of flux of it through the hands of men who pretend to have so received it themselves from others. But whether hereon the people of the church can have that respect and devotion unto them as they would have unto hereditary rulers (long succession in rulers being the great cause of veneration in the people), especially such as had a succession one unto another by a natural descent through divine appointment, as the priests had under the law, or as unto those whom, on the account of their worth, ability, and fitness for the work of the ministry among them, they do choose themselves, they may do well to consider who are concerned. The necessity there is of maintaining a reputation and interest by secular grandeur, pomp, and power, of ruling the people of the church in church-matters by external force, with many other inconveniencies, do all proceed from this order of things, or rather disorder, in the call of men unto the ministry. And hence it is that the city of God and the people of Christ therein, — which is, indeed, the only true, free society in the world, — have rulers in and over them, neither by a natural right of their own, as in paternal government, nor by hereditary succession, nor by election, nor by any way or means wherein their own consent is included, but are under a yoke of an imposition of rulers on them above any society on the earth whatever. Besides, there is that relation between the church and its guides that no law, order, or constitution, can create without their mutual voluntary consent; and therefore, this right and liberty of the people, in every church, to choose their own spiritual officers, was for many ages preserved sacredly in the primitive times. But hereof there is no shadow remaining in our parochial churches; sundry persons, as patrons and ordinaries, have a concurring interest into the imposing of a minister, or such whom they esteem so, upon any such church, without the knowledge, consent, or approbation of the body of the church, — either desired or accepted. If there be any who cannot comply with this constitution of things relating unto the ministry, because it is a part of their profession of the gospel which they are to make in the world, which yet really consists only in an avowed subjection unto the commands of Christ, they can be no way obnoxious unto any charge of schism upon their refusal so to do; for a schism that consists in giving a testimony unto the institutions of Christ, and standing fast in the liberty where with he hath made his disciples free, is that whose guilt no man need to fear.

VI. What remaineth of those reasons whereon those who cannot comply with the conformity under consideration are cleared, in point of conscience, from any obligation thereunto, and so from all guilt of schism whatever, belongs unto the head of impositions on their consciences and practice, which they must submit unto. These being such as many whole books *have* been written about, the chief whereof have r o way been answered, — unless railings and scoffings, with contempt and fierce reproaches, with false accusations, may pass for answers, — I shall not here again insist upon them. Some few things of that nature I shall only mention, and put an end unto this dispute:—

1. The *conformity* required of ministers consists in a public *assent and consent* unto the Book of Common Prayer, with the rubric, in it, which contains all the whole practice of the church of England, in its commands and prohibitions. Now, these being things that concern the worship of God in Christ, the whole entire state, order, rule, and government of the gospel church, whoever gives solemnly this assent and consent, unless he be allowed to enter his protestation against those things which he dislikes, and of the sense wherein he doth so assent and consent, — which by law is allowed unto none, — the said assent and consent is his public profession that all these things, and all contained in them, are according to the mind of Christ, and that the ordering of them, as such, is part of their professed subjection unto his gospel. Blessed be God, most ministers are too

wise and honest to delude their consciences with distinctions, equivocations, and reservations; and do thereon rather choose to suffer penury and penalty than to make the least intrenchment upon their own consciences, or the honour of the gospel in their profession! What they do and declare of this nature they must do it in sincerity, as in the sight of God, as approving what they do; not only as pardonable effects of necessity, but as that which is the best they have or can do a the worship of God, with a solemn renunciation of whatever is contrary unto what they do so approve. And whether this be a meet imposition on the consciences of ministers, with reference unto a great book or volume of a various composition, unto things almost without number, wherein exceptions have been given of old and lately, not answered nor answerable, with rules, laws, orders, not pretending to be scriptural prescriptions, is left unto the judgment of all who have due thoughts of their approaching account before the judgment-seat of Jesus Christ.

2. The conformity that is required of others being precise, and without power of dispensation in them by whom it is required, to answer the rule or law of it before declared, every man by his so conforming doth thereby take it on his conscience, and make it *part of his Christian profession*, that all which he so conforms unto is not only what he may do, but what he ought to do, both in matter and manner, so far as the law, or any part of it, doth determine or enjoin them. No man is allowed to make either distinction or protestation with respect unto any thing contained in the rules; and, therefore, whatever he doth in compliance therewith is interpretable, in the sight of God and man, as an approbation of the whole. Sincerity and openness in profession is indispensably required of us in order unto our salvation. And, therefore, to instruct men, as unto the worship of God, to do what they do not judge to be their duty to do, but only hope they may do without sin, or to join themselves in and unto that performance of it which either they approve not of as the best in the whole, or not lawful or approvable in some parts of it, is to instruct them unto the debauching of their consciences and ruin of their own souls. "Let every man be persuaded in his own mind;" for "what is not of faith is sin."

3. There is in this conformity required a *renunciation* of all other ways of public worship or means of edification that may be made use of for they are all expressly forbidden in the rule of

that conformity. No men, therefore, can comply with that rule, but that a renunciation of all other public ways of edification as unlawful is part of the visible profession which they make. "*Video meliora proboque, Deteriora sequor,*" is no good plea in religion. It is uprightness and integrity that will preserve men, and nothing else. He that shall endeavour to cheat his conscience by distinctions and mental reservations, in any concernment of religious worship, I fear he hath little of it, if any at all, that is good for aught.

On these suppositions, I say, the imposition of the things so often contended about on the consciences and profession of Christians, — as, namely, the constant, sole use of the liturgy in all church administrations, in the matter and manner prescribed; the use and practice of all canonical ceremonies; the religious observation of stated holidays, with other things of the like nature, — is sufficient to warrant any sober, peaceable disciple of Christ, who takes care of his own edification and salvation, to refrain the communion required in this rule of conformity, unless he be fully satisfied in his own mind that all that it requires is according to the mind of Christ, and all that it forbids is disapproved by him. And whereas the whole entire matter of all these impositions are things whereof the Scripture and the primitive churches know nothing at all, nor is there any rumour of them to be imposed in or on any church of Christ for some centuries of years, I can but pity poor men who must bear the charge and penalties of schism for dissenting from them, as well as admire the fertility of their inventions who can find out arguments to manage such a charge on their account.

But whereas the dissent declared from that communion with parochial assemblies is that whereon we are so fiercely charged with the guilt of schism, and so frequently called schismatics, I shall divert a little to inquire into the nature and true notion of schism itself; and so much the rather, because I find the author of the "Unreasonableness of Separation" omit any inquiry thereinto, that he might not lose the advantage of any pretended description or aggravation of it.

CHAPTER XII.

Of schism.

ALTHOUGH it be no part of my present design to treat of the nature of schism, yet with respect unto what hath already been discoursed, and to manifest our unconcernment in the guilt of it, I shall, as was said divert to give a plain and brief account of it. And in our inquiry I must declare myself wholly unconcerned in all the discords, divisions, and seditions, that have fallen out among Christians in the latter ages about things that were of their own invention. *Schism is sin against Christian love*, with reference unto the deportment of men in and about the institutions of Christ, and their communion in them. As for contentions, divisions, or separations amongst men, about that order, agreement, unity, or uniformity which are of their own appointment, whatever moral evil they have had in them, they do not belong unto that church-schism which we inquire after. Such have been the horrid divisions and fightings that have prevailed at seasons in the church of Rome; a departure from whose self-constituted state, order, and rule, hath not the least affinity unto schism. It will not, therefore, be admitted that any thing can fall under the note and guilt of schism which hath not respect unto some church-state, order, rule, unity, or uniformity that is of Christ's institution.

There are three notions of schism that deserve our consideration:—

1. The first is that of *divisions among the members of the same church*, all of them abiding still in the same outward communion, without any separation into distinct parties. And unto schism in this notion of it three things do concur:—

(1.) Want of that *mutual love*, condescension, and forbearance, which are required in all the members of the same church; with the moral evils of whisperings, back-bitings, and evil surmises, that ensue thereon.

(2.) All *undue adherence* unto some church offices above others, causing disputes and janglings.

(3.) *Disorder* in the attendance unto the duties of church assemblies, and the worship of God performed in them. This is the only notion of schism that is exemplified in the Scripture, the only evil that is condemned under that name. This will appear unto any who shall with heedfulness read the Epistles of Paul the apostle unto the Corinthians; wherein alone the nature of this evil is stated and exemplified. But this consideration of schism hath been almost utterly lost for many ages. Whatever men do in churches, so that they depart not from the outward communion of them, it would be accounted ridiculous to esteem them schismatics. Yet this is that which, if not only, yet principally, the consciences of men are to regard, if the will avoid the guilt of schism. But this notion of it, as was said, being not suited unto the interest or advantages of any sort of men, in the charge of it on others, nor any way subservient to secure the inventions and impositions of the most, is on the matter lost in the world.

2. The second instance of ecclesiastical schism was given us in the same church of the Corinthians afterward; an account whereof we have in the epistle of Clemens, or of the church of Rome unto them about it; the most eminent monument of primitive antiquity, after the writings by divine inspiration. And that which he calls schism in that church, he calls also "strife, contention, sedition, tumult" And it may be observed concerning that schism, as all the ancients call it, —

(1.) That the church continued its state and outward communion: There is no mention of any that *separated from it*, that constituted a new church; only in the same church they agreed not, but were divided among themselves. Want of love and forbearance, attended with strife and contention among the members of the same church, abiding in the same outward communion, was the schism they were guilty of.

(2.) The effect of this schism was, that the body of the church, or *multitudes of the members*, by the instigation of *some few disorderly persons, had deposed their elders and rulers* from their offices, and probably had chosen others in their places; though that be not mentioned expressly in the epistle.

(3.) That the church itself is not blamed for assuming a power unto themselves to depose their elders, much less that they had done it without the consent, advice, or authority of any bishop or other church but only that they had dealt unjustly with those whom they had deposed; who, in the judgment of the church of Rome, unto which they had written for advice, were esteemed not only innocent, but such as had *laudably, and profitably discharged their office*; whereon the whole blame is cast on those who had instigated the church unto this procedure.

(4.) There was not yet, nor in a hundred and fifty years after, the least mention or intimation of any schism in a dissent from any humanly-invented rules or canons for order, government, or worship in any church, or religious ceremonies imposed on the practice of any in divine service, — that is, on any church or any of the members of it. There is not the least rumour of any such things in primitive antiquity, no instance to be given of any man charged with schism for a dissent from such a rule. Any such rule, and any ecclesiastical censure upon it, is apocryphal, not only unto the Scripture, but unto that which I call primitive antiquity. The first attempt of any thing a this kind was in reference unto *the time and day of the observation of Easter*. This was the first instance among Christians of an endeavour to impose the observation of human or church constitutions or groundless traditions on any churches or persons in them. And whereas that which was called a schism between the churches of Italy and Asia, or some of them, did ensue thereon, we have a most illustrious testimony from the best, the wisest, and the holiest of that age (for Irenæus in France and Polycrates in Asia were not alone herein), that the blame of all that division and schism was to be charged on them who attempted to deprive the churches of their liberty, and imposed on them a necessity of the observation of the time and season which they had determined on. After a rebuke was given unto the attempt of the Judaizing Christians to impose the observation of Mosaical ceremonies, from the pretence of their divine institution, on the churches of the Gentiles, by the apostles themselves, this was the original of all endeavours to impose human constitutions, for which there was no such pretence, upon the practice of any. And as it was an original not unmeet for the beginning and foundation of such impositions, being in a matter of no use unto the edification of the church, so it received such a solemn rebuke at its first entrance and attempt, that had it not been for the ignorance, pride, interest, and superstition of some in the following ages, it had perished without imitation. The account hereof is given in Eusebius, lib. v. cap. 21–23; as also of the rule which then prevailed, though afterward shamefully forsaken, — namely, that an *agreement in the faith was the only rule of communion*, which ought to be kept under any diversity in voluntary observations. And the discourse of Socrates on this occasion, lib. v. cap. 21, concerning the non-institution of any days of fastings or feastings, or other rites or ceremonies then in use, with the liberty which is therefore to be left in such things unto all Christians, is the plain truth, whatever some except against it, declared with much judgment and moderation.

This beginning, I say, had the imposition of unscriptural, uninstituted rites, ceremonies, and religious observations, among the churches of Christ, and this solemn rebuke was given unto it. Howbeit the ignorance, superstition, and interest of following ages, with the contempt of all modesty, brake through the boundaries of this holy rebuke, until their own impositions and observations became the substance of all their church-discipline, unto the total subversion of Christian liberty.

Wherefore, to allow church-rulers, or such as pretend so to be, a liberty and power to appoint a rule of communion, — comprising institutions and commands of sundry things to be constantly observed in the whole worship and discipline of the church, not warranted in themselves by divine authority, — and then to charge believers, abiding firm in the doctrines of the faith, with schism, for a non-compliance with such commands and appointments, is that which, neither in the Scripture nor in primitive antiquity, hath either instance, example, precedent, testimony, rumour, or report, to give countenance unto it. The pedigree of this practice cannot be derived one step higher than the fact of Victor, the bishop of Rome, in the excommunication of the churches and Christians of Asia; which was solemnly condemned as an intrenchment on Christian liberty.

3. After these things the notion of schism began to be managed variously, according unto the interest of them who seemed to have the most advantage in the application of it unto those who dissented from them. It were an endless thing to express the rise and declare the progress of these apprehensions; but after many loose and declamatory discourses about it, they are generally issued in two heads. The first is, that *any kind of dissent from the pope and church of Rome is schism*, all the schism that is

CHAPTER XII. 233

or can be in the world, the other is, that a causeless separation from a true church is schism, and this only is so. But whereas, in this pretended definition there is no mention of any of its internal causes nor of its formal reason, but a bare description of it by an outward effect, it serves only for a weapon in every man's hand to perpetuate digladiations about it; for every church esteems itself true, and every one that separates himself esteems himself to have just cause so to do.

In the following times, especially after the rise and prevalency of the Arian heresy, it was ordinary for those of the orthodox persuasion to forsake the communion of those churches wherein Arian bishops did preside, and to gather themselves into separate meetings or conventicles for divine worship; for which they were accused of schism and in sundry places punished accordingly, yea, some of them unto the loss of their lives. Yet I suppose there are none nosy who judge them to have been *schismatics*.

The separation of Novatus and Donatus from the communion of the whole catholic visible church, on unwarrantable pretences, is that which makes the loudest noise about schism in antiquity. That there was in what was done by them and their followers the general nature and moral evil of causeless schisms and divisions, will be easily granted. But it is that wherein we are not concerned, be the especial nature of schism what it will. Nor did they make use of any one reason whereon the merit of the present cause doth depend. The Novatians[15] (the modester sect of the two) pretended only a defect in discipline, in granting church-communion unto such as they would not have received, though they were apparently in the wrong, proceed-

---

15   Novatianus, or, as the name is given by Eusebius, Novatus, protested against the choice of Cornelius as bishop of Rome in A.D. 251, on the ground of his leniency towards those who, during the Decian persecution, had lapsed into a denial of Christ. He withdrew from communion with Cornelius, and procured his own ordination as bishop of Rome. At first, the Novatians, as those who joined him were called, held simply that no man who had shrunk from avowing Christ under the terrors of martyrdom should be admitted again into the church, whatever evidence he gave that he had repented of the sin. Latterly, they adopted a principle of African origin, that all who had lapsed into gross sins after baptism should be subjected to perpetual exclusion from the communion of the church. — ED.

ing on mistaken principles. The Donatists pleaded only some personal crimes in some few bishops, fallen into in the time of persecution which they could never prove, and thereon grew angry with all the world, who would not condemn them and renounce their communion as well as they. These slight pretences they made the occasion and reason of renouncing the communion of the whole visible catholic church, in all its distributions for communion, — that is, all particular churches, — and confined sacraments and salvation absolutely unto their own parties. And hereon they fell into many other woful miscarriages, especially those of the latter sort. It is indifferent by what name any are pleased to call this evil and folly. A sin and evil it was, schism, or what you please to term it, and justly condemned by all Christians not joining with them in those days. And that which was the animating principle of the tumult of the Donatists[16] was a supposition that the continuation of the true church-state depended on the successive ordination of bishops; which having, as they thought (unduly enough), failed in one or two instances, it became the destruction of a church-state, not only in the churches where such mistakes had happened, as they surmised, but unto all the churches in the world that would hold communion with them.

But in these things we have no concernment. Other notions of schism besides those insisted on we acknowledge not, nor is any other advanced with the least probability of truth. Nor are we to be moved with outcries about schism, wherein, without regard to truth or charity, men contend for their own interest. Of those notions of it which have been received by men sober and learned we decline a trial by none, that only excepted, that the refusal of obedience unto the pope and church of Rome is all that is schism in the world; which, indexed, is none at all.

That which is now so fiercely pleaded by some concerning different observations of external modes, rites, customs, some

---

16 When the archdeacon Cæcilian was elected bishop at Carthage in A.D. 811, a party rose up against him, who chose Majorinus, and latterly, in A.D. 818, Donatus, as their bishops, in preference to Cæcilian; against whom they objected that his ordination as bishop was not valid, as Felix, bishop of Aptunga, who had ordained, had been a traditor; in other words, during the time of persecution, had delivered up the Scriptures to the heathen magistrates to be burned. — Ed.

more, or none at all, to make men schismatics, is at once to judge all the primitive churches to be schismatical. Their differences, varieties, and diversities among hem about these things cannot be enumerated; and so, without any disadvantage unto the faith or breach of love, they continued to be until all church order and power was swallowed up in the papal tyranny, ten thousand times more pernicious than ten thousand such disputes.

For a close unto this whole discourse concerning the original, nature, and state of gospel churches, I shall use that liberty which love of the truth puts into my possession. Churches mentioned in the Scripture, ordained and appointed by the authority of Jesus Christ, were nothing but a certain number of men and women converted to God by the preaching of the gospel, with their baptized seed, associating themselves, in obedience unto Christ's commands and by the direction of his apostles, for the common profession of the same faith, the observance and performance of all divine institutions of religious worship, unto the glory of God, their own edification, and the conversion of others. These believers, thus associated in societies, knowing the command and appointment of Jesus Christ by his apostles for that end, did choose from among themselves such as were to be their rulers, in the name and authority of Christ, according to the law and order of his institutions, — who in the Scripture are called, on various considerations, elders, bishops, pastors, and the like names of dignity, authority, and office, — who were to administer all the solemn ordinances of the church among them. Unto this office they were solemnly appointed, ordained, or set apart by the apostles themselves, with fasting, prayer, and imposition of hands, or by other ordinary officers after their decease.

This was the way and method of the call and setting apart of all *ordinary officers* in the church, both under the Old Testament and in the New. It is founded in the light of nature. In the first institution of ordinary church-rulers under the law, the people looked out and chose fit persons, whom Moses set apart to the office, Deut. i. 13–15. And in the call of deacons, the apostles use the same words, or words of the same importance, unto the church as Moses did to the people, Acts vi. 3, asserting the continuation of the same way and order in their call. And whereas he who was first to be called to office under the New Testament after the ascension of Christ fell under a double consideration,

— namely, of an officer in general, and of an apostle, which office was extraordinary, — there was a threefold act in his call: The people chose two, one of which was to be an officer, Acts i. 23; God's immediate determination of one, as he was to be an apostle, verses 24, 25; and the obedient consent of the people in compliance with that determination, verse 26.

The foundation of these churches was generally in *a small number* of believers. But that church-state was not complete until they were supplied with all ordinary officers, as bishops and deacons. The former were of several sorts, as shall be proved hereafter; and of them there were many in every church, whose number was increased as the members of the church were multiplied. So God appointed in the church of the Jews, that every ten families should have a peculiar ruler of their own choice, Deut. i. 13–15. For there is no mention in the New Testament of any one single bishop or elder in any church, of any sort whatever, either absolutely or by way of pre-eminence. But as the elders of each church were many, at least more than one, so there was a parity among them, and an equality in order, power, and rule. Nor can any instance be given unto the contrary.

Of these churches one only was originally planted, in *one city*, town, or village. This way was taken from conveniency for edification, and not from any positive institution; and it may be otherwise where conveniency and opportunity do require it. The number in these churches multiplying daily, there was a necessity for the multiplication of bishops or elders among them. Hereon the advantage of some one person in priority of conversion, or of ordination, in age, gifts, and races, especially in ability for preaching the gospel and administering the holy ordinances of the church, with the necessity of preserving order in the society of the elders themselves, gave him peculiar dignity, pre-eminence, and title. He was soon after *the bishop*, without any disadvantage to the church.

For in those churches, in some of them at least, evangelists continued for a long season, who had the administration of church-affairs in their hands. And some there were who were of note among the apostles, and eminently esteemed by them, who had eminent, yea, apostolical gifts as to preaching of the word and prayer, which was the peculiar work of the apostles These were the ἄνδρες ἐλλόγιμοι mentioned by Clemens. Of the many other elders who were associated in the rule of the church, it may be not many had gifts for the constant preaching of the word, nor were called thereunto. Hence Justin Martyr seems to assign the constant public administration of sacred ordinances unto one president. And this also promoted the constant presidency of one, in whom the apostolical aid by evangelists might be supplied. These churches, thus fixed and settled in one place (each of them), city, town, or village, were each of them intrusted with all the power and privileges which the Lord Christ hath granted unto or endued his church withal. This power is called the "power of the keys," or of "binding and loosing;" which hath respect only unto the consciences of men as unto things spiritual and eternal, being merely ministerial.

Every one of these churches were bound by the command of Christ to live in peace and unity, through the exercise of peculiar, sincere, and fervent love among all their members; as also to walk in peace and useful communion with all other churches in the world, according as they had opportunity of converse with them. And when on any occasion any division or schism fell out among any of their members in this church-state, it was severely rebuked by the apostles.

All these churches, and all the members of them, were obliged, by virtue of divine institution, to *obey their guides*, to honour and reverence them; and by their voluntary contribution to provide for their *honourable subsistence* and maintenance, according to their ability. Other church-state neither the Scripture nor antiquity unto the end of the second century doth know any thing of; which I shall hereafter more fully manifest, Neither was there any thing known then to be schism or so esteemed, but a division falling out in some one of these churches: which happened for the most part, if not only, by some of their teachers falling into heresy and drawing away disciples after them Acts xx. 30; or by various opinions about their guides, 1 Cor. i. 12; or the ambition of some in seeking the power and authority of office among them. To seek for any thing among those churches, wherein our present contest about schism is concerned, is altogether in vain. There was then no such subordination of churches, of many unto one, as is now pleaded; no such distinction of officers into those who have a plenary and those who have a partiary power only, in the rule of the church; no church with a single officer over it, comprehending, in a subjection unto its jurisdiction, a multitude of other churches. No invention, no imposition of any orders, forms of prayer, or ceremonies of worship not of divine institution, were once thought of; and when any thing of that nature was first attempted, it caused great troubles amongst them. In a word, the things on the account of a noncompliance wherewithal we are vehemently charged with schism were then neither laid nor hatched, neither thought of nor invented.

To erect new kinds of churches; to introduce into them new orders, new rules, rites and ceremonies; to impose their observation on all churches and all members of them; and to charge their dissent with the guilt of schism, that schism which is prohibited and condemned in the Scripture, — hath much of an assumed authority and severity in it, nothing of countenance from the Scripture or primitive antiquity.

But after that churches began to depart from this original constitution by the ways and means before declared, every alteration produced a new supposition of church unity and peace, whereto every church of a new constitution laid claim. New sorts of schism were also coined and framed; for there was a certain way found out and carried on, in a mystery of iniquity, whereby those meek, holy, humble churches or societies of Christ's institution, who, as such, had nothing to do with the things of the world, in power, authority, dignity, jurisdiction, or wealth, in some instances wherein they got the advantage one of another, became in all these things to equal kingdoms and principalities, yea, one of them to claim a monarchy over the whole world!

During the progression of this apostasy, church-unity and schism declined from their centre, and varied their state according unto the present interest of them that prevailed. Whoever had got possession of the name of the church in a prevailing reputation, though the state of it was never so corrupt, made it bite and devour all that disliked it, and would swear that submission unto them in all things was church-unity, and to dissent from them was schism. Unto that state all the world know that things were come in the church of Rome. Howbeit, what hath been disputed about or contended for, of power, privileges, authority, pre-eminence, jurisdiction, catholicism, ways of worship, rule, and discipline, which the world is filled with such a noise about, and in the dispute whereof so many various hypotheses are advanced that cannot be accommodated unto such Christian congregations as we have described, are but the effects of the prudence or imprudence of men; and what it will prove the event will show.

Things of this nature being once well understood will deliver the world from innumerable fruitless, endless contests, sovereign princes from all disturbance on the account of religion, and private persons from the fatal mistake of intrusting the eternal concernments of their souls unto their relation unto one church and not unto another. I am not so vain as at this time to expect the reduction of Christian religion unto its primitive power, purity, and simplicity; nor do I reflect blare on them who walk conscientiously in such a church state and order as they approve of, or suppose it the best they can attain unto; only I think it lawful for all Christ's disciples at all times to yield obedience unto all his commands, and to abstain from being servants of men in what he hath not enjoined.

AN ANSWER TO DR STILLINGFLEET'S BOOK

OF THE UNREASONABLENESS OF SEPARATION; IN DEFENCE OF THE VINDICATION OF NONCONFORMISTS FROM THE GUILT OF SCHISM.

SECTION I.

THE preceding discourse was written, for the most part, before the publishing of the treatise of the Rev. Dr Stillingfleet, entitled "The Unreasonableness of Separation;" yet was it not so without a prospect, at least a probable conjecture, that something of the same kind and tendency with the Doctor's book would be published in defence of the cause which he had undertaken. And I was not without hopes that the whole of it might have been both finished end communicated unto public view before any thing farther were attempted against our cause, whereby many mistakes might have been prevented; for as I was willing, yea, very desirous, if it were the will of God, that I might see, before my departure out of this world, the cause of conformity, as things are now stated between us and the church of England, pleaded with judgment, moderation, and learning, with the best of those arguments whereby our principles or practices are opposed, so, considering on what hand that work was now like to fall, I thought, "*si Pergama dextra,*" etc.; and am of the same mind still. But my expectation being frustrate, of representing our whole cause truly stated for the prevention of mistakes, by the coming out of this book against all sorts of Nonconformists, I thought it convenient to publish this first part of what I had designed, and to annex unto it the ensuing "Defence of the Vindication of Nonconformists from the Charge of Schism:" for although I do know that there is nothing material in the whole book of the "Unreasonableness of Separation" but what is obviated or answered beforehand in the preceding discourse, so as that the principles and demonstrations of them contained therein may easily be applied unto all the reasonings, exceptions, and pleas in and of that book, to render them useless unto the end designed, which is to reinforce a charge of schism against us; yet I think it necessary to show how unsuccessful, from the disadvantage of his cause, the Doctor hath been in his laborious endeavour to stigmatize all protestant dissenters from the church of England with the odious name of *schismatics*. I have, therefore, altered nothing of what I had projected, either as to matter or method, in this first part of the discourse designed on the whole subject of church affairs; for as I have not found either cause or reason from any thing in the Doctor's book to make the least change in what I had written, so my principal design being the instruction and confirmation of them who have no other interest in these things but only to know and perform their own duty, I was not willing to give them the trouble of perpetual diversions from the matter in hand, which all controversial writings are subject unto. Wherefore, having premised some general considerations of things insisted on by the Doctor, of no great influence into the cause in hand, and vindicated one principle, a supposition whereof we rely upon, — namely, the declension of the churches in the ages after the apostles, especially after the end of the second century, from the primitive institution of their state, rule, and order, — in the preface, I shall now proceed to consider and examine distinctly what is opposed unto the defence of our innocency as unto the guilt of schism. But some things must be premised hereunto; as, —

 1. I shall not depart from the state of the question as laid down by ourselves on our part, as unto our judgment of parochial churches, and our refraining from communion with them. Great pains are taken to prove the several sorts of dissenters to be departed farther from the church of England than they will themselves allow, and on such principles as are disavowed by them; but no disputations can force our assent unto what we know to be contrary unto our principles and persuasions.

2. We do allow those parochial assemblies which have a settled, unblamable ministry among them to be true churches, so far as they can pretend themselves so to be; — churches whose original form is from occasional cohabitation within precincts limited by the law of the land; — churches without church-power to choose or ordain their officers, to provide for their own continuation, to admit or exclude members, or to reform at any time what is amiss among them; — churches which are in all things under the rule of those who are set over them by virtue of civil constitutions foreign unto them, not submitted willingly unto by them, and such, for the most part, as whose offices and power have not the least countenance given unto them from the Scripture or the practice of the primitive churches; such as are chancellors, commissaries, officials, and the like; — churches in which, for the most part, through a total neglect in evangelical discipline, there is a great degeneracy from the exercise of brotherly love and the holiness of Christian profession. Whatever can be ascribed unto such churches we willingly allow unto them.

3. We do and shall abide by this principle, that communion in faith and love, with the administration of the same sacraments, is sufficient to preserve all Christians from the guilt of schism, although they cannot communicate together in some rites and rules of worship and order. As we will not admit of any presumed notions of schism, and inferences from them, nor allow that any thing belongs thereunto which is not contrary to gospel love, rules, and precepts, in the observance of Christ's institutions; so we affirm, and shall maintain, that men abiding in the principles of communion mentioned, walking peaceably among themselves; refraining communion with others, peaceably, wherein they dissent from them; ready to join with other churches in the same confession of faith and in the defence of it, and to concur with them in promoting all the real ends of Christian religion; not judging the church-state of others so as to renounce all communion with them, as condemning them to be no churches, continuing in the occasional exercise of all duties of love towards them and their members, — are unduly charged with the guilt of schism, to the disadvantage of the common interest of the protestant religion amongst us.

4. Whereas there are two parts of the charge against us, — the one for refraining from total communion with parochial as-

semblies, which what it is, and wherein it doth consist, hath been before declared; the other for gathering ourselves into another church-order in particular congregations, — as the reasons and grounds of the things themselves are distinct, so must they have a distinct consideration, and be examined distinctly and apart.

These things being premised, I shall proceed to examine what the reverend Doctor hath farther offered against our former vindication of the Nonconformists from the charge of schism. And I desire the reader to take notice that we delight not in these contentions, that we desire nothing but mutual love and forbearance; but we are compelled, by all rules of Scripture and natural equity, to abide in this defence of ourselves. For whereas we are charged with a crime, and that aggravated as one of the most heinous that men can incur the guilt of in this world, and to justify men in severities against us; being not in the least convinced in our consciences of any accessions thereunto, or of any guilt on the account of it, I suppose the Doctor himself will not think it reasonable that we should altogether neglect the protection of our own innocency.

In the method whereinto he hath cast his discourse, he begins with the reinforcement of his charge against our refraining from total communion with parochial assemblies. If the reader will be pleased to take a review of what is said in the preceding discourse unto this head of our charge, in several chapters, he will easily perceive that either the reasonings of the Doctor reach not the cause in hand, or are insufficient to justify his intention; which I must say, though I am unwilling to repeat it, is by all ways and means to load us with the guilt and disreputation of schism.

That which I first meet withal directly unto this purpose is part ii. p. 157. The forbearance of communion with the church of England in its parochial assemblies (that is, in the way and manner before described) he opposeth with two arguments. The first respects those who allow occasional communion with parochial churches, but will not comply with them in that which is constant and absolute for he says, "If the first be lawful, the latter is necessary, from the commands we have to preserve the peace and unity of the church. And the not doing it," he says, "is one of the provoking sins of the Nonconformists." But whether it be a sin or no is *"sub judice;"* that it is provoking unto some is sufficiently evident. I shall not make this any part of my contest. Those who have so expressed their charity as to give countenance unto this pretended advantage will easily free themselves from the force of this inference; for it must be remembered that this constant, total communion doth not only include a conscientious observance of all things appointed to be done by the rules or canons in those assemblies, but a renunciation also of all other ways and means of edification by joint communion as unlawful and evil. And it will be hard to prove that, on a concession of the lawfulness of communion in some acts of divine worship, it will be necessary for men to oblige themselves unto total, constant communion, with a renunciation and condemnation of all other ways and means of joint edification. It may also be lawful to do a thing, with some respects and limitations, at some times, which it may not be lawful to do absolutely and always. It may be necessary, from outward circumstances, to do that sometimes which is lawful in itself, though not necessary from itself; it can never be necessary to do that which is unlawful. Of the first sort they esteem occasional communion, and the other of the latter.

Some time is spent in taking off an exception unto this inference from the practice of our Saviour, who had occasional communion with the Jews in the temple and synagogues; which he proves to have been constant and perpetual, and not occasional only, and that he prescribed the same practice unto his disciples. But I think this labour might have been spared: for there is nothing more clear and certain than that our Lord Jesus Christ did join with the Jews in the observance of God's institutions among them on the one hand; and, on the other, that he never joined with them in the observance of their own traditions and pharisaical impositions, but warned all his disciples to avoid them and refuse them; whose example we desire to follow: for concerning all such observances in the church he pronounced theft sentence, "Every plant which my heavenly Father hath not planted shall be rooted up."

But the Doctor proceeds unto a second argument, p. 163, to the same purpose, from, as he calls it, "the particular force of that text," Phil. iii. 16 "Whereto we have already attained, let us walk by the same rule, let us mind the same thing." This is the text which gave the first occasion unto this whole dispute. The Doctor's intention is so indefensible from this place, that I thought, however he might persist in the defence of the cause he had undertaken, he would have forborne from seeking countenance unto it from these words of the apostle. But it is fallen out otherwise; and I am here, in the first place, called unto an account for the exceptions I put in unto his application of these words of the apostle in my "Vindication of the Nonconformists."

I will spare the reader as much as is possible in the repetition of things formerly spoken, and the transcription of his words or my own, without prejudice unto the cause itself.

After a reflection of some *obscurity and intricacy* in my discourse, he repeats my sense of the words according unto his apprehension, under four heads, about which I shall not contend, seeing whether he hath apprehended my mind aright or no, or expressed the whole of what I declared, belongs not unto the merit of the cause in hand. Nor, indeed, do I yet know directly what he judgeth this text doth prove, or what it is that he infers from it; though I know well enough what it is designed to give countenance unto, and what is the application that is made of it. And, therefore, he issues his whole dispute about it in this inquiry, *how far the apostle's rule hath an influence on this case*. But whosoever shall come unto a sedate consideration of this text and context, without prejudice, without preconceived opinions, without interest in parties or causes, will judge it to be a matter of art to apply them unto the present controversy, as unto the imposition of an arbitrary rule of walking in churches on all that are presumed to belong unto them.

But to clear these things, the Doctor proposeth three things to be debated:— "1. Whether the apostle speaks of different opinions or different practices. 2. Whether the rule he gives be mutual forbearance. 3. How far the apostle's rule hath an influence into this cause."

The first two of these belong not at all unto the present argument, and the last is but faintly proposed and pursued, though it be the foundation of his whole fabric. The reader, if he will put himself to so much trouble as to compare my former discourse with what is here offered in answer or opposition unto it, will easily see that nothing is pleaded that may abate the force of what was insisted on; for indeed the discourse of these things consists for the most part in diversions from the argument in hand, whereby an appearance is made of various arguings, and the proof of sundry things which belong not unto the case in hand.

Without any long deductions, artificial insinuations, or diverting reasonings, without wresting the text or context, these things are plain and evident in them:—

1. *A supposition of differences* among believers in and about opinions and practices relating unto religion and the worship of God. So is [it] at present between us and those of the church of England by whom we are opposed.

2. In this state, whilst these differences do continue, there is *one common rule*, according unto which those who so dissent among themselves are to walk in the things wherein they are agreed. Such is *the rule of faith and love*; which we all assent unto and are agreed in.

3. This rule cannot consist in a *precise determination* of the things in difference, with an authoritative prescription of *uniformity* in opinions and practice, because it is directed unto upon a supposition of the continuation of those differences between believers.

4. That during the continuation of these differences, or different apprehensions and practices, whilst on all hands they use the means of coming unto the knowledge of the truth in all things, *they should walk in love, mutually forbearing one another* in those things wherein they differed.

Until it be manifested that these things are not the design of the context, and to contain [not] the sense of the words, they are not only *useless* unto the Doctor's design, but *opposite* unto it, and destructive of it. But nothing is here attempted unto that purpose.

To draw any argument from these words applicable unto his design, t must be proved, —

1. That *besides the rule of faith, love, and worship* given by divine institution, and obligatory unto all the disciples of Christ or all churches, in all times and ages, the apostles gave a rule concerning outward rites, ceremonies, modes of worship, feasts, and fastings, ecclesiastical government, liturgies, and the like, unto which all believers ought to conform, on the penalty of being esteemed schismatics, and dealt withal accordingly; for this only is that wherein we are concerned.

2. That because the apostles made such a rule (which we know not what it is, or what is become of it), *the guides of the*

church (and that in such a church-state as the apostles knew nothing of) *have power to frame such a rule* as that described, and to impose the observation of it on all believers, on the penalties before mentioned.

It is manifest that no advantage unto the cause of imposition and uniformity, as it is stated at present, can be taken from these words of the apostle unless these two things be contained in them; but that either of them is so our author doth not say, nor go about, to prove, in his large discourse on this place. I might therefore forbear any farther examination of it without the least disadvantage unto our cause; but, that I may not seem to waive the consideration of any thing that is pretended material, I shall inquire into the particulars of it.

He proceeds, therefore, to answer *his own queries*; which he judged conducing unto his purpose. The first of them is, "*Whether the apostle speaks of different principles or of different practices.*" And I find nothing in the discourse ensuing that hath the least respect unto this inquiry, until towards the close of it, where he grants that different apprehensions are intended, such as were accompanied with different practices; but, in order hereunto, he gives us a large account of the scope of the place and the design of the apostle in it. The substance of it is: That the apostle treats concerning Judaical seducers; that the things in difference were the different apprehensions of men about the law, its ceremonies and worship, with the continuation of them, and the different practices that ensued thereon.

Be it so; what is our or his concernment herein? For it is most certain the apostle designed not the imposition of these things on the churches of the Gentiles, nor did urge them unto a uniformity in them, but declared their liberty from any obligation unto them, and advised them to "stand fast in that liberty," whatever others did practice themselves or endeavour to impose on them. What this conduceth unto his purpose I cannot understand.

But on the occasion of that expression, being "otherwise minded," he demands, "What sense can Dr Owen here put upon the being 'otherwise minded?' otherwise than what? — 'As many as be perfect be thus minded,' to pursue your main end; but if any be 'otherwise minded. Did any think they ought not to mind chiefly their great end? — that is incredible. Therefore the apostle must be understood of somewhat about which there were then very different apprehensions; and that, it is certain, there were about the law among Christian churches."

Neither do I well understand these things, or what is intended in them; for, —

1. I never gave occasion to him or any else to think that I would affix such a sense unto the apostle's words, as if they gave an allowance to men to be otherwise minded as unto the pursuit of their main end, of living to God in faith and love, with mutual peace among themselves.

2. What, then, do I intend by being otherwise minded? Even the same that he doth, and nothing else, — namely, different apprehensions about some things in religion, and particularly those concerning the law and its ceremonies; for, —

3. Let it be supposed that the apostle in particular intends dissensions about the law and the observance of its institutions, yet he doth not determine the case from the especial circumstances of that difference, so adjudging the truth unto one of the parties at variance, but from a general rule how the disciples of Christ ought to deport themselves towards one another during the continuation of such differences But, —

4. The truth is, the apostle hath dismissed the case proposed in the beginning of the chapter, verses 1–3, etc.; and upon the occasion of his expression of his own voluntary relinquishment and renunciation of all the privileges which the Jews boasted in, and of his attainments thereon in the mysteries of the gospel, verses 12–14, he gives a general direction for the walking of all Christians, in the several degrees and measures of their attainments in the same kind. And herein he supposeth two things: (1.) That there were things, — all the fundamental doctrines of the gospel, concerning the person, offices, and grace of Christ, — which they had all in common attained unto: "Whereto we have already attained," — we, all of us in general. (2.) That in some things there were different apprehensions and practices amongst them, which hindered not their agreement in what they had attained: "If any one be 'otherwise minded,'" — one than another. "We that are perfect and those which are weak, 'let us walk by the same rule.'"

Wherefore, although I cannot discern how any thing in this discourse hath the least influence into the case in hand, yet to give a little more light unto the context, and to evidence its unserviceableness unto the Doctor's intention, I shall give a brief account of the Judaical teachers of those days.

The Jews were by this time distributed into three sorts:—

1. Such as, being *obdurate* in their unbelief and rejection of the person of Christ, opposed, persecuted, and blasphemed the gospel in all places. Thus was it with the generality of the nation. And the teachers of this sort advanced the excellency, necessity, and usefulness of the law in contradiction unto Christ and the gospel. These the apostle describes, 1 Thess. ii. 14, 15: "The Jews, who both killed the Lord Jesus, and their own prophets, and have persecuted us; and they please not God, and are contrary to all men: forbidding us to speak to the Gentiles that they might be saved, to fill up their sins alway: for the wrath is come upon them to the uttermost."

2. Such as *professing faith in Christ Jesus* and obedience unto the gospel, yet were of the mind that the whole law of Moses was not only to be continued and observed among the Jews, but also that it was to be imposed on the Gentiles who were converted unto the faith. They thought the gospel did not erect a new church-state, with a new kind of worship, but only was a peculiar way of proselyting men into Judaism; against which the apostle disputes in his Epistle into the Hebrews, especially in the seventh and eighth chapters. The teachers of this sort greatly troubled the churches, even after the declaration of the mind of the Holy Ghost in these things by the apostles, Acts xv. Those who continued obstinate in this persuasion became afterward to be Ebionites and Nazarenes, as they were called, wholly forsaking the Christian church of the Gentiles. These were generally of the sect of the Pharisees, and seem to be the least sort of the three; for, —

3. There were others who, acquiescing in the liberty of the Gentiles declared by the apostles, Acts xv., yet judged themselves and all other circumcised Jews obliged unto the observation of the law and its institutions. These legal observances were of two sorts:—

(1.) Such as were confined and limited unto the temple, and unto the land of Canaan; and, —

(2.) Such as might be observed anywhere among the nations. They acted accordingly. Those who lived at Jerusalem adhered unto the temple worship; the whole church there did so. Their judgment in these things is declared, Acts xxi. 20, 21,

"Thou seest, brother, how many thousands of Jews there are which believe; and they are all zealous of the law: and they are informed of thee, that thou teachest all the Jews which are among the Gentiles to forsake Moses, saying that they ought not to circumcise their children, neither to walk after the customs." They were not at all offended with Paul that he did not impose the law on the Gentiles, verse 25, but only that, as they had been informed, he taught the Jews to forsake the law, and to reject all the institutions of it. This they thought unlawful for them. And this they spoke principally with respect unto the temple-service, as appears by the advice given unto Paul on this occasion, verses 23, 24. Those who lived amongst the Gentiles knew that there was no obligation on them unto the sacrifices and especial duties of the temple, but continued only in the observance of such rites and institutions about meats, washings, days, new-moons, sabbaths, and the like, which the Gentiles were freed from.

Hence there were two sorts of churches in those days (if not three) in separation, more or less, from the apostate church of the unbelieving Jews, which yet was not finally taken away:—

1. The church of Jerusalem and those churches of Judea which were of the same mind and communion with them. These continued in the observance of all the law and of the services of the temple, being allowed them by the apostles.

2. Those of the Jews who lived in the *nations*, and observed all the rites of the law which were not confined unto the land of Canaan. And, —

3. The churches of the Gentiles, which observed none of these things, forbearing only their liberty in one or two instances, not to give the others offence. Some differences and disputes happened sometimes about these things and the practice of them; whereon Peter himself fell into a mistake, Gal. ii. 14. And there seems to have been great disputes about them at Rome, Rom. xiv. Yea, it is judged that, according unto their different apprehensions of these things, there were two churches at Rome, one of the Circumcision, the other of the Gentiles, walking in distinct communion each by themselves However, the different rule of this kind that was between the churches of Jerusalem and Antioch is sufficiently declared, Acts xv.; the one church continued "zealous of the law," chap. xxi. 20, and the other "rejoiced for the consolation" of being delivered from it,

chap. xv. 31. Yet was there no schism between these churches, but a constant communion in faith and love. Such differences in opinions and practices were not yet formed into an interest, obliging men to condemn them as schismatics who differ from them; for, not to speak of what orders and rules for decency particular churches may make by common consent among themselves, to make the observation of arbitrary institutions, not prescribed in the Scripture, upon many churches, to be the rule of communion in them and between them, which whosoever observe not are to be esteemed guilty of schism (which Victor, bishop of Rome, first attempted), is contrary to the rules of the Scripture, the principles of Christian faith, love, and liberty, to the example of the apostles, hath no countenance given unto it in the primitive churches, and will certainly make our differences endless.

I judge that in the beginning of the chapter the apostle intends those of the first sort; and that as well because he calls them "dogs" and the "concision," — which answers unto the account he gives of them, 1 Thess. ii. 14, 15, — as also because he speaks of them as those who advanced the pretended privileges of Judaism absolutely against Christ the gospel, and the righteousness of God revealed therein. Hereon, in opposition unto them, he declares that they had nothing to boast of but what he himself had a right unto as well as they, and which he had voluntarily relinquished and renounced for Christ and the gospel; whereon he testifies what he had attained. If any one do judge that he intends those of the second sort, I will not contend about it, because of the severity of expression which he useth concerning them, Gal. v. 12. But discharging the consideration of them, the direction in this place concerns those of the third sort only, answering unto that which was prescribed and followed by the apostles in all places, — namely, that there should be mutual forbearance, in some difference of practice, between them and the Gentile believers.

His second inquiry, p. 168, is, "Whether the rule which the apostle lays down be only a rule of mutual forbearance." I do not find that I said anywhere that it was only a rule of mutual forbearance, but that the words of the apostle do enjoin a mutual forbearance among those who are differently minded, p. 26. And I must here say (which I desire to do without offence), that there is no need of any farther answer unto that part of the Doctor's discourse, but a transcription of that which he pretends to oppose; for what is spoken unto that end consists in a perpetual diversion from the argument in hand.

I did not before precisely determine what was the rule which the apostle doth intend; I only proved sufficiently that it was not such a rule as is pleaded for by the Doctor. But the meaning of the phrase and expression is plain enough, Τῷ αὐτῷ στοιχεῖν κανόνι. It is directly used once more by the apostle, Gal. vi. 16, Ὅσοι τῷ κανόνι τούτῳ στοιχήσουσιν· — "As many as walk according to this rule." And what rule is that? — namely, what, as unto the substance of it, he lays down in the words foregoing: Verses 14–16, "God forbid that I should glory, save in the cross of our Lord Jesus Christ. For in Christ Jesus neither circumcision availeth any thing, nor uncircumcision, but a new creature. And as many as walk according to this rule;" that is, the rule of faith in Christ alone for justification and sanctification, without trusting unto or resting on any of those things which were in difference among them. The places, in scope, design, and manner of expression, are parallel; for this is plainly that which he pleads for in this context, — namely, that justification and sanctification are to be obtained alone through Christ, and faith in him, by the gospel, without the least aid and assistance from the things that were in difference among them. Wherefore, not farther to contend in so plain a matter, the rule here intended by the apostle is no Book of Canons, but the analogy of faith, or the rule of faith in Christ as declared in the gospel, in opposition unto all other ways and means of justification, sanctification, and salvation; which we ought to walk in a compliance withal, and that with love and forbearance towards them that in things not corruptive or destructive of this rule do differ from us.

But saith our author, "The sense, according to Dr Owen, is this, that those who are agreed in the substantials of religion should go on and do their duty, without regarding lesser differences." Abate that expression of, "Without regarding lesser differences," which is not mine, and supply in the room of it, "Mutually forbearing each other in lesser differences." And be it so that it is my sense; at first view it looks as like the sense of the apostle as any man need desire. But saith the Doctor, "This sense is uncertain; because it sets no bounds to differences, and supposeth the continuance of such differences among them, which he designed to prevent by persuading them so often in this epistle to be of 'one mind.' Besides, the differences then on foot were none of the smaller differences of opinions, but that which they differed about was urged on the one hand as necessary to salvation, and opposed on the other as pernicious and destructive unto it." And again, p. 169, "Let Dr Owen name any other smaller differences of opinions which might be an occasion of the apostle's giving such a rule of mutual forbearance."

I answer briefly, — 1. The sense is very *certain*; because it gives the *due bounds* unto the differences supposed, — namely, such as concern not *the substantials of religion*.

2. It doth *suppose the continuance* of these differences, because the apostle doth suppose the same: "If in any thing ye be otherwise minded;" which hinders no kind of endeavours to compose or remove them.

3. The differences intended were not those between them who *imposed the observation of the law on the Gentiles as necessary unto salvation*, and those by whom they were opposed; for the apostle gives no such rule as this in that case.

4. I do expressly assign those *lesser differences*, which the direction here is applicable unto, — namely, those between the blind sort of Jews mentioned before and the Gentile believers; which the apostle states and applies the same rule unto, Rom. xiv. What remains in answer unto this second inquiry doth proceed on mistaken suppositions, and concerns not the case under consideration.

Page 170, he proceeds unto his last inquiry, which, indeed, is alone pertinent unto his purpose, — namely, "How this rule hath an influence on our case."

What *this rule is*, concerning which this inquiry is made, he doth not declare. Either the precise signification of the rule in this place, or the direction given with respect unto that rule, may be intended; that is, the general rule of our walking in our profession of the gospel, or the especial rule given by the apostle with respect thereunto in the case under consideration, may be so intended. If by the rule in the first sense, he understands a rule, canon, or command, establishing a church-state, with rites and modes of worship, with ceremonies, orders, and government, nowhere appointed in the Scripture or of divine revelation, it is openly evident that there was no such rule then, that no such is here intended but that only whereunto the grace of the gospel in mercy and peace is annexed, as Gal. vi. 16; which is not such a rule. If he intend by it a direction, that where there are different apprehensions in matters of less importance, not breaking in on the analogy of faith, accompanied with different practices, so far as they are necessary from those different apprehensions, the major part of those among whom the differences are should compel the minor to forbear their practice according unto their apprehension and comply with them in all things, on all sorts of penalties if they refuse so to do, — it will be hard to find such a direction in these words. Yet this must be the rule and this the direction that can give any countenance unto the Doctor's cause. But if by *this rule*, the analogy of faith as before described be intended, and the direction be to walk according to it, with mutual forbearance and love as unto things of lesser moment, then this rule hath little advantageous influence into it

1. But then saith the Doctor, "So far as men agree they are bound to join together, as to opinion or communion." I grant it (though it be not proved from this place), where such a communion is required of them regularly and in a way of duty. And, —

2. Saith he, "That the best Christians are bound to unite with others, though of lower attainments, and to keep within the same rule." No doubt; howbeit the apostle speaks of no such things in this place, but only that we should all "walk by the same rule," in what we have "already attained." Yea, but, —

3. "This rule takes in all such orders which are lawful and judged necessary to hold the members of a Christian society together." What rule doth this? Who shall appoint the orders intended? Who shall judge of their necessity? Are they of the institution of Christ or his apostles? Are they determined to be necessary in the Scripture, the rule of faith? If so, we are agreed. But if by these "orders" he intends such as men do or may at any time, under pretence of church authority, invent and impose as necessary, making alterations in the original state and rule of the church, as also in its worship and discipline, it will be strange to me if he can find them out either in the rule h re mentioned or the direction given with reference unto it, seeing such a practice seems to be plainly condemned in the words themselves. And it is known that this pretended power of rule or canon making for the unity of the church was that which at length ruined all churches in their state, order, and worship, if

such a ruin be acknowledged to have befallen them in the Roman apostasy.

He therefore objects out of my discourse, p. 171, "Let the apostle's rule be produced, with any probability of proof to be his, and we are all ready to subscribe and conform unto it." To which he replies, This is the apostle's rule, to go as far as they can, and if they can go no farther, to sit down quietly and wait for farther instruction, and not to break the peace of the church upon present dissatisfaction, nor to gather new churches out of others, upon supposition of higher attainments."

Ans. 1. Upon a supposition that those who make and impose these new, *unscriptural orders* are *the church*, and that as the church they have authority so to make and impose them, if this be not the rule of the apostle, I believe some men judge it ought so to have been. But, —

2. The apostle's rule is not that *we should go as far as we can*, as though there were any thing of dispute and difficulty in the matter; but that *"whereto* we have already attained," we should "walk by the same rule."

3. He doth not intimate any thing about *breaking the peace of the church*, but only what would do so, by an imposition on one another in differences of lesser moment, whilst the general rule of faith and love is attended unto.

4. "To be quiet, and wait for farther instruction," is the direction given unto both parties, whilst the differences did continue between them, and that in opposition unto mutual impositions.

5. A church that is really so, or so esteemed, may break the peace with its own members and others as well as they with it; and where the fault is must be determined by the causes of what is done.

6. For what is added about "gathering of churches," it shall be considered in its proper place. But as unto the application of these things unto the present case, there lies in the bottom of them such an unproved presumption of their being *the church*, — that is, according unto divine institution, for in their being so in any other sense we are not concerned, — of their church power and authority by whom such orders and rules are made, as we can by no means admit of.

I can more warrantably give this as the apostle's rule than that of our author: "What you have attained unto in the knowledge of the doctrine and mysteries of the gospel, walk together in holy communion of faith and love; but take heed that you multiply not new causes of divisions and differences, by inventing and imposing new orders in divine worship or the rule of the church, casting them out who agree with you in all things of divine revelation and institution."

He adds from my words, "If the rule reach our case, it must be such as requires such things to be observed as were never divinely appointed, as national churches, ceremonies, and modes of worship." To which he replies, "And so this rule doth, in order unto peace, require the observation of such things; which, although they be not particularly commanded of God, yet are enjoined by lawful authority, provided that they be not unlawful in themselves, nor repugnant unto the word of God."

Ans. 1. Let the reader, if he please, consult the place whence these words are taken in my discourse, and he will find this evasion obviated.

2. What is intended by *"This rule?"* Is it the rule given by the apostle? Who that reads the words can possibly pretend unto any such conception of their meaning? If he understand a rule of his own, I know not what it may or may not include.

3. I deny, and shall for ever deny, that the rule here intended by the apostle doth give the least countenance unto the invention and imposition of things not divinely instituted, not prescribed, not commanded in the word, on the pretence that those who so invent and impose them judge them lawful, and that they have authority so to do.

He objects again unto himself out of my discourse, that "The apostles never gave any such rules themselves about outward modes of worship, with ceremonies, feasts, fasts, liturgies," etc. Whereunto he replies, "What then?" I say then, —

1. It had been happy for Christians and Christian religion if those who pretended to be their successors had followed their example, and made *no such rules* at all; that they would not have thought themselves wiser than they, or more careful for the good of the church, or better acquainted with the mind of Christ in these things than they were; for that multiplication of rules, laws, canons, about the things mentioned, and others of an alike nature, which the apostles, never gave any example of or encouragement unto, which afterward ensued, hath been a principal means of altering the state of the church from its

original institution, of corrupting its worship, and administering occasion unto scandal and endless strifes.

2. If the *apostles gave no such rules themselves*, it may be concluded safely that it was because in their judgment no *such rule was to be given*. Other reason hereof cannot be assigned; for if it might have been done according to the mind of Christ, and by virtue of the commission which they had from him, innumerable evils might have been prevented by the doing it. They foresaw what differences would arise in the church, what divisions the darkness and corrupt lusts of men would cast them into, about such things as these, and probably knew much whereunto the mystery of iniquity tended; yet would they not appoint any arbitrary rules about things not ordained by our Lord Jesus Christ, which might have given some bounds unto the inclinations of men in making and multiplying rules of their own unto the ruin of the church.

3. Then, I say, we beg the pardon of all who concern themselves herein, that we scruple the complying with such rules in religion and the worship of God as the apostles thought not meet to appoint or ordain.

But he adds, "It is sufficient that they gave this general rule, that all lawful things are to be done for the church's peace."

Ans. What is to be done for the church's peace we shall afterward consider. "To be done," is intended of acts of religion in the worship of God. I say, then, the apostles never gave any such rule as that pretended. The rule they gave was, that all things which Christ hath commanded were to be done and observed; and for the doing of any thing else they gave no rule. Especially, they gave not such a large rule as this, that might serve the turn and interest of the worst of men in imposing on the church whatever they esteemed lawful, as (not by virtue of any rule of the apostles, but in an open rejection of all they gave) it afterward fell out in the church. This is a rule which would do the work to the purpose of all that have the reputation of governors in the church, be it the pope or who it will: for they are themselves the sole judges of what is lawful; the people, as it is pretended, understand nothing of these things. Whatever, therefore, they have a mind to introduce into the worship of God, and to impose on the practice of men therein, is to be done by virtue of this apostolical rule for the "church's peace," provided they judge it "lawful;" and surely no pope was ever yet so stark mad as to impose things in religion which he himself judged unlawful. Besides, things may be lawful in themselves, that is, morally, which yet it is not lawful to introduce into the worship of God, because not expedient nor for edification; yea, things may be lawful to be done sometimes, on some occasions, in the worship of God, which yet it would be unlawful to impose by virtue of a general binding rule for all times and seasons. Instances may be multiplied in each kind. Therefore, I say, the apostles never gave this rule; they opened no such door unto arbitrary imposition; they laid no such yoke on the necks of the disciples, which might prove heavier, and did so, than that of the Jewish ceremonies which they had taken away, — namely, that they were to do and observe all that should by their rulers be imposed on them as lawful in their judgment. This sovereignty over their consciences was reserved by the apostles unto the authority of Christ alone, and their obedience was required by them only unto his commands. This is that which, I see, some would be at: — To presume themselves to be the church, at least the only rulers and governors of it; to assume to themselves alone the judgment of what is lawful and what is unlawful to be observed in the worship of God; to avow a power to impose what they please on all churches, pretended to be under their command, so that they judge it lawful, be it never so useless or trifling, if it hath no other end but to be an instance of their authority; and then assert that all Christian people must, without farther examination, submit quietly unto this state of things and comply with it, unless they will be esteemed damned schismatics. But it is too late to advance such principles a second time.

He adds from my paper, or as my sense, "The apostles gave rules inconsistent with any determining rule, — namely, of mutual forbearance," Rom. xiv. "But then," saith he, "the meaning must be, that whatever differences happen among Christians, there must be no determination either way. But this is directly contrary to the decree of the apostles at Jerusalem, upon the difference that happened in the Christian churches." But they are not my words which he reports. I said not that "the apostles gave rules inconsistent with any determining rule," but with such a rule, and the imposition of the things contained in it on the practice of men, in things not determined (that is, whilst differences about them do continue), as he contends for. And, —

1. Notwithstanding this rule of forbearance given by the apostle expressly, Rom. xiv., yet as unto the right and truth in the things wherein men are at difference, *every private believer is to determine of them, so* far as he is able, in his own mind; "every man is to be fully persuaded in his own mind" in such things, so far as his own practice is concerned.

2. The church wherein such differences do fall out may *doctrinally determine* of the truth in them, as it is the pillar and ground of truth, supposing them to be of such weight as that the edification of the church is concerned in them; for otherwise there is no need of any such determination, but every one may be left unto his own liberty. There are differences at this day in the church of England in doctrine and practice, some of them, in my judgment, of more importance than those between the same church and us; yet it doth not think it necessary to make any determination of them, no, not doctrinally.

3. If the church wherein such differences fall out be not able in and of itself to make a doctrinal determination of such differences, they may and ought to crave the counsel and advice of other churches with whom they walk in communion in faith and love. And so it was in the ease whereof an account is given us, Acts xv. The determination or decree there made, concerning the necessary observance of the Jewish rites by the Gentiles converted unto the faith, by the apostles, elders, and brethren, under the guidance of the Holy Ghost, as his mind was revealed in the Scripture, gives not the least countenance unto the making and imposing such a rule on all churches and their members as is contended for.

For, — (1.) It was only a *doctrinal determination*, without imposition on the practice of any. (2.) It was a *determination against impositions directly*. And whereas it is said that it was a determination contrary to the judgment of the imposers, which shows that the rule of forbearance, where conscience is alleged both ways, is no standing rule, — I grant that it was contrary to the judgment of the imposers, but imposed nothing on them, nor was their practice concerned in that erroneous judgment. They were not required to do any thing contrary to their own judgment, and the not doing whereof did reflect on their own consciences. Wherefore, the whole rule given by the apostles, and the whole determination made, is, that no impositions be made in the consciences or practice of the disciples of Christ, in things relating to his worship, but what were necessary by virtue of divine institution. They added hereunto, that the Gentiles enjoying this liberty ought to use it without offence, and were at liberty, by virtue of it, to forbear such things as wherein they had, or thought they had, a natural liberty, in case they gave offence by the use of them. And the apostles, who knew the state of things in the minds of the Jews, and all other circumstances, give an instance in the things which at that season were to be so forborne. And whereas this determination was not absolute and obligatory on the whole case unto all churches, — namely, whether the Mosaical law were to be observed among Christians, — but some churches were left unto their own judgment and practice, who esteemed it to be still in force, as the churches of the Jews; and others left unto their own liberty and practice also, who judged it not to oblige them; both sides or parties being bound to continue communion among them in faith and love; there is herein a perpetual establishment of the rule of mutual forbearance in such cases, nothing being condemned but impositions on one another, nothing commended but an abstinence from the use of liberty in the case of scandal or offence. I had therefore reason to say that the false apostles were the only imposers, — that is, of things not necessary by virtue of any divine institution And if the author insinuate that the true apostles were such imposers also, because of the determination they made of this difference, he will fail in his proof of it. It is true, they imposed on or charged the consciences of men with the observance of all the institutions and commands of Christ, but of other things none at all.

The last thing which he endeavours an answer unto on this occasion lies in these words: "The Jewish Christians were left unto their own liberty, provided they did not impose on others; and the dissenters at this day desire no more than the Gentile church did, — namely, not to be imposed on to observe those things which they are not satisfied it is the mind of Christ should be imposed on them." So is my sense, in the places referred unto, reported. Nor shall I contend about it, so as that the last clause be changed; for my words are not, "They are not satisfied it is the mind of Christ that they should be reposed on them," but, "They were not satisfied it is the mind of Christ they should observe." This respects the things themselves, the other only their imposition. And one reason against the imposition opposed is, that the things themselves imposed are such as the Lord Christ would not have us observe, because not appointed by himself.

But hereunto he answers two things: —

1. "That it was agreed by all the governors of the Christian church that the Jewish Christians should be left unto their own liberty, out of respect unto the law of Moses, and out of regard unto the peace of the Christian church, which otherwise might have been extremely hazarded." But, —

(1.) The *governors* of the Christian church which made the determination insisted on were the apostles themselves.

(2.) There was no such determination made, that *the Jews should be left unto their own liberty in this matter*, but there was only a connivance at their inclination to bear their old yoke for a season; the determination was only on the other hand, that no imposition of it should be made on the Gentiles.

(3.) The determination itself was no act of *church government or power*, but a *doctrinal declaration* of the mind of the Holy Ghost.

(4.) It is well that *church-governors* once judged that impositions in things not necessary were to be forborne, for the sake of the peace of the church; others, I hope, may in due time be of the same mind.

2. He says, "The false apostles imposing on the Gentile Christians had two circumstances in it, which extremely alter their case from that of our dissenters;" for, —

(1.) "They were none of their lawful governors, but went about as seducers, drawing away the disciples of the apostles from them." It seems, then, —

[1.] That those who are lawful governors, or pretend themselves so to be, may impose what they please without control, as they did in the Papacy and the councils of it. But, —

[2.] Their imposition was merely doctrinal, wherein there was no pretence of any act of government or governing power; which made it less grievous than that which the dissenters have suffered under. Were things no otherwise imposed on us, we should bear them more easily.

(2.) Saith he, "They imposed the Jewish rites as necessary to salvation, and not merely as indifferent things." And the truth is, so long as they judged them so to be, they are more to be excused in their doctrinal impositions of them than others are who by an act of government, fortified with I know not how many penalties, do impose things which themselves esteem indifferent, and those on whom they are imposed do judge to be unlawful.

Whereas he adds, "That he hath considered all things that are material in my discourse, which seem to take off the force of the argument drawn from this text," I am not of his mind; nor I believe will any indifferent person be so, who shall compare what I wrote therein with his exceptions against it; though I acknowledge it is no easy thing to discover wherein the force of the pretended argument doth lie That we must walk according unto the same rule in what we have attained; that wherein we differ we must wait on God for teaching and instruction; that the apostles, elders, and brethren at Jerusalem determined from the Scriptures, or the mind of the Holy Ghost therein, that the Jewish ceremonies should not be imposed on the Gentile churches and believers; and that thereon those churches continued in communion with each other who did and did not observe those ceremonies, — are the only principles which, in truth, the Doctor hath to proceed upon. To infer from these principles and propositions that there is a national church of divine institution (for what is not so hath no church-power properly so called, the nature of its power being determined by the authority of its institution or erection); that this church hath power in its governors and rulers to invent new orders, ceremonies, and rites of worship, new canons for the observation of sundry things in the rule of the church and worship of God, which have no spring nor cause but their own invention and prescription, and is authorized to impose the observation of them on all particular churches and believers who never gave their consent unto their invention or prescription; and hereon to declare them all to be wicked schismatics who yield not full obedience unto them in these things, — it requires a great deal of art and skill in the managers of the argument.

SECTION II.

PART ii., sect. xxi., p. 176, our author proceeds to renew his charge of schism, or sinful separation, against those "who though they agree with us," saith he, "in the substantials of religion, yet deny any communion with our church to be lawful." But apprehending that the state of the question here insinuated will not be admitted, and that it would be difficult to find them out who deny any communion with the church of England to be lawful, he adds, that he doth not speak of "any improper acts of communion, which Dr Owen calls communion in faith and love, which they allow to the church of England." But why the acts hereof are called "Improper acts of communion." I know not. Add unto faith and love the administration of the same sacraments, with common advice in things of common concernment, and it is *all the communion* that the true churches of Christ have among themselves in the whole world; yea, this church-communion is such as that, —

1. Where *it is not*, there is no evangelical communion at all. Whatever acts of worship or church-order men may agree in the practice of, if the foundation of that agreement be not laid in a joint communion in faith and love, they are neither accepted with God nor profitable unto the souls of men; for, —

2. These are the things, — namely, faith and love, — which enliven all joint duties of church order and worship, are the life and soul of it; and how they should be only improperly that which they alone make other things to he properly, I cannot understand.

3. Where there is no defect in these things, — namely, in faith and love, — the charge of schism on dissenting in things of lesser moment is altogether unreasonable. It is to he desired that an overweening of our differences make us not overlook the things wherein we are agreed. This is one of the greatest evils that attend this controversy. Men are forced by their interest to lay more weight on a few outward rites and ceremonies, which the world and the church might well have spared, had they not come into the minds of some men none know how, than upon the *most important graces and duties* of the gospel. Hence, communion in faith and love is scarce esteemed worth taking up in the streets, in comparison of uniformity in rites and ceremonies! Let men be as void of, and remote from, true gospel faith and love as is imaginable, yet if they comply quietly with, and have a little zeal for, those outward things, they are to be approved of as very orderly members of the church! And whatever evidences, on the other hand, any can or do give of their communion in faith and love with all that are of that communion, yet if they cannot in conscience comply in the observance of those outward things mentioned, they are to be judged schismatics and

breakers of the church's unity, whereas no part of the church's unity doth, or ever did, consist in them.

In his procedure hereon, our author seems to embrace occasions of contending, seeking for advantages therein in things not belonging unto the merit of the cause; which I thought was beneath him. From my concession, that some at least of our parochial churches are true churches, he asks, "In what sense? Are they churches rightly constituted, with whom they may join in communion as members?" I think it is somewhat too late now, after all this dispute about the reasons of refraining from their communion, and his severe charge of schism upon us for our so doing, to make this inquiry Wherefore he answers himself. "No; but his meaning is, saith he, 'that they are not guilty of any such heinous errors in doctrine, or idolatrous practice in worship, as should utterly deprive them of the being and nature of churches;'" — which I suppose are my words But then comes in the advantage. "Doth," saith he, "this kindness belong only unto some of our parochial churches? I had thought that every parochial church was true or false according unto its frame or constitution; which, among us, supposeth the owning the doctrine and worship established in the church of England." I answer briefly, It is true, every church is true or false according unto its original frame and constitution. This frame and constitution of churches, if it proceed from, and depend upon, the institution of Christ, is true and approvable; if it depend only on a national establishment of doctrine and worship, I know not well what to say unto it. But let any of these parochial churches be so constituted as to answer the legal establishment in the land, yet if the generality of their members are openly wicked in their lives, and they have no lawful or sufficient ministry, we cannot acknowledge them for true churches. Some other things of the like nature do ensue, but I shall not insist on them.

He gathers up, in the next place, the titles of the causes alleged for our refraining communion with those parochial assemblies; which he calls our separation from them. And hereon he inquires, "Whether these reasons be a ground for a separation from a church wherein it is confessed there are no heinous errors in doctrine, or idolatrous practice in worship;" that is, as he before cited my words, "as should utterly deprive them of the being and nature of churches." And if they be not, then saith he, "Such a separation may be a formal schism, because they set up other churches of their own."

The rule before laid down, "That all things lawful are to be done for the church's peace," taking in the supposition on which it proceeds, is as sufficient to establish church tyranny as any principle made use of by the church of Rome, notwithstanding its plausible appearance. And that here insinuated of the unlawfulness of separation from any church in the world (for that which hath pernicious errors in doctrine and idolatry in worship, destroying its being, is no church at all), is as good security unto churches in an obstinate refusal of reformation, when the souls of the people are ruined amongst them for the want of it, as they need desire. And I confess I suspect such principles as are evidently suited unto the security of the corrupt interests of any sort of men.

I say, therefore, — 1. That though a church, or that which pretends itself on any grounds so to be, do not profess any heinous error in doctrine, nor be guilty of idolatrous practice in worship, destroying its nature and being, yet there may be sufficient reasons to refrain from its communion in church order and worship, and to join in or with other churches for edification; that is, that where such a church is not capable of reformation, or is obstinate in a resolution not to reform itself, under the utmost necessity thereof, it is lawful for all or any of its, members to reform themselves, according to the mind of Christ and commands of the gospel.

2. That where men are no otherwise members of any church but by an inevitable necessity and outward penal laws, preventing their own choice and any act of obedience unto Christ in their joining with such churches, the case is different from theirs whose relation unto any church is founded in their own voluntary choice, as submitting themselves unto the laws, institution, and rule of Christ in that church which we shall make use of afterward.

3. The Doctor might have done well to have stated the true nature of schism, and the formal reason of it, before he had charged a formal schism on supposition of some outward acts only.

4. What is our judgment concerning parochial assemblies, how far we separate from them or refrain communion with them, what are the reasons whereon we do so, hath been now

fully declared, and thereunto we must appeal on all occasions; for we cannot acquiesce in what is unduly imposed on us, either as unto principles or practice.

"To show," as he saith, "the insufficiency of our cause of separation, he will take this way, — namely, to show the great absurdities that follow on the allowance of them;" and adds, "These five especially I shall insist upon:— 1. That it weakens the cause of Reformation; 2. That it hinders all union between the protestant churches; 3. That it justifies the ancient schisms, which have been always condemned by the Christian church; 4. That it makes separation endless; 5. That it is contrary to the obligation that lies on all Christians to preserve the peace and unity of the church."

Now, as I shall consider what he offers on these several heads, and his application of it unto the case in hand, so I shall confirm the reasons already given of our separation (if it must be so called) from parochial assemblies, with these five considerations:— 1. That they strengthen the cause of Reformation; 2. That they open a way to union between all protestant churches; 3. That they give the just grounds of condemning the ancient schisms that ever any Christian church did justly condemn; 4. That they give due bounds unto separation; 5. That they absolutely comply with all the commands of the Scripture for the preservation of the peace and unity of the church.

I shall begin with the consideration of the absurdities charged by him on our principles and practice.

The FIRST of them is, "That it weakens the cause of the Reformation." This he proves by long quotations out of some French divines. We are not to expect that they should speak unto our cause, or make any determination in it, seeing to the principal of them it was unknown. "But they say that which is contrary unto our principles." So they may do, and yet this not weaken the cause of the Reformation; for it is known that they say somewhat also that is contrary to the principles of our episcopal brethren, for which one of them is sufficiently reviled, but yet the cause of Reformation is not weakened thereby.

The first testimony produced is that of Calvin. A large discourse he hath, Institut., lib. iv. cap. 1, against causeless separations from a true church; — and by whom are they not condemned? No determination of the case in hand can be thence derived; nor are the grounds of our refraining communion with parochial assemblies the same with those which he condemns as insufficient for a total separation; nor is the separation he opposed in those days, which was absolute and total, with a condemnation of the churches from which it was made, of the same nature with that wherewith we are charged, at least not with what we own and allow. He gives the notes of a true church to be, — the pure preaching of the word, and the administration of the sacraments according unto Christ's institution. Where these are he allows a true church to be, not only without diocesan episcopacy, but in a form and under a rule opposite unto it and inconsistent with it. And if he did at all speak to our case, as he doth not, nor unto any of the grounds of it, why should we be pressed with his authority on the one hand more than others from whom he differed also on the other? Besides, there is a great deal more belongs unto the pure preaching of the word and the administration of the sacraments according unto Christ's institution than some seem to apprehend. They may, they ought to be so explained, as that, from the consideration of them, we may justify our whole cause. Both these may be wanting in a church which is not guilty of such heinous errors in doctrine or idolatry in worship as should overthrow its being; and their want may be a just cause of refraining communion from church which yet we are not obliged to condemn as none at all.

Calvin expresseth his judgment, N. 12: "I would not give countenance unto errors, no, not to the least, so as to cherish them by flattery or connivance. But though I say that, the church is not to be forsaken for trifling differences, wherein the doctrine (of the gospel) is retained safe and sound, wherein the integrity of godliness doth abide, and the use of the sacraments appointed of the Lord is preserved;" — and we say the same.

And this very Calvin, who doth so severely condemn separation from a true church as by him stated, did himself quietly and peaceably withdraw and depart from the church of Geneva, when they refused to admit that discipline which he esteemed to be according to the mind of Christ. It is certain, therefore, that, by the separation which he condemns, he doth not intend the peaceable relinquishment of the communion of any church, as unto a constant participation of all ordinances in it, for want of due means of edification, much less that which hath so many other causes concurring therewith.

For the other learned men whom he quotes unto the same purpose, I see not any thing that gives the least countenance unto his assertion that our principles weaken the cause of the Reformation. It is true, they plead other causes of separation from the church of Rome than those insisted on by us with respect unto the church of England; and, indeed, they had been otherwise much to blame, having so many things as they had to plead of greater importance. Did we say that the reasons which we plead are all that can be pleaded to justify the separation of the Reformed churches from the church of Rome, it would weaken the cause of Reformation; for we should then deny that idolatry and fundamental errors in faith were any cause or ground of that separation. However, we know that the imposition of them on the faith and practice of all Christians is more pleaded in justification of a separation from them than the things themselves. But allowing those greater reasons to be pleaded against the Roman communion, as we do, it doth not in the least follow that our reasons for refraining communion with parochial assemblies do weaken the cause of the Reformation.

However, let me not be misinterpreted as unto that expression of "destroying our faith," — which the communion required with the church of England, as unto all the important articles of it, doth not do, — and I can subscribe unto the words of Daillè, as quoted by our author out of his Apology: "If," saith he, "the church of Rome hath not required any thing of us which destroys our faith, offends our consciences, and overthrows the service which we believe due to God, — if the differences have been small, and such as we might safely have yielded unto, — then he will grant their separation was rash and unjust, and they guilty of the schism."

He closeth his transcription of the words of sundry learned men who have justified the separation of the Reformed churches from the church of Rome, wherein we are not in the least concerned, with an inquiry, "What triumph would the church of Rome make over us, had we no other reasons to justify our separation from them but only those which (as is pretended) we plead in our cause?" I say, whereas we do plead, confirm, and justify all the reasons and causes pleaded for the separation of the Reformed churches from them, not opposing, not weakening any of them by any principle or practice of ours, but farther press the force of the same reasonings and causes in all instances whereunto they will extend, I see neither what cause the Papists have of triumph nor any thing that weakens the cause of the Reformation. He adds farther, "How should we be hissed and laughed at, all over the Christian world, if we had nothing to allege for our separation from the Roman church but such things as these!" I answer, that as the case stands, if we did allege no other reasons but those which we insist on for our refraining communion with our own parochial assemblies, we should deserve to be derided for relinquishing the plea of those other important reasons which the heresies, and idolatries, and tyranny of that church do render just and equal: but if we had no other causes of separation from the church of Rome but what we have for our separation from our parochial assemblies at home, as weak as our allegations are pretended to be, we should not be afraid to defend them against all the Papists in the world; and let the world act like itself in hissing.

Whereas, therefore, the cause of Reformation is not in any thing weakened by our principles, no argument, no reason solidly pleaded to justify the separation from the church of Rome being deserted by us, neither testimony, proof, nor evidence being produced to evince that it is weakened by us, I shall, in the second place, as was before proposed, prove that the whole cause of the Protestants' separation from the church of Rome is strengthened and confirmed by us:—

There were some general principles on which the Protestants proceeded in their separation from the church of Rome, and which they constantly pleaded in justification thereof.

1. The first was, that *the Scripture, the word of God, is a perfect rule of faith and religious worship*; so as that nothing ought to be admitted which is repugnant unto it in its general rule or especial prohibitions, nothing imposed that is not prescribed therein, but that every one is at liberty to refuse and reject any thing of that kind. This they all contended for, and confirmed their assertion by the express testimonies of the writers of the primitive churches. To prove this to have been their principle in their separation from the church of Rome were to light, as they say, a candle in the sun. It were easy to fill up a volume with testimonies of it. After a while this principle began to be weakened, when the interest of men made them except from this rule things of outward order, with some rites and ceremonies, the ordaining whereof they pleaded to be left unto churches as they

saw good. Hereby this principle, I say, was greatly weakened; for no certain bounds could ever be assigned unto those things that are exempted from the regulation of the Scripture. And the same plea might be managed for many of the popish orders and ceremonies that were rejected, as forcibly as for them that were retained. And whereas all the Reformed churches agreed to abide by this principle in matters of faith, there fell out an admirable harmony in their confessions thereof. But leaving the necessity of attending unto this rule in the matter of order, ceremonies, rites, and modes of worship, with the state of churches in their rule and polity, those differences and divisions ensued amongst them which continue unto this day. But this persuasion in some places made a farther progress, — namely, that it was lawful to impose on the consciences and practices of men such things in religious worship, provided that they concerned outward order, rites, rule, and ceremonies, as are nowhere prescribed in the Scripture, and that on severe penalties, ecclesiastical and civil. This almost utterly destroyed the great fundamental principle of the Reformation, whereon the first reformers justified their separation Yore the church of Rome; for whereas it is supposed the right of them who are to be the imposers to determine what doth belong unto the heads mentioned, they might under that pretence impose what they pleased, and refuse those whom they imposed them on the protection of the aforesaid principle, — namely, that nothing ought to be so imposed that is not prescribed in the Scripture. This hath proved the rise of all endless differences and schisms amongst us; nor will they be healed until all Christians are restored unto their liberty of being obliged, in the things of God, only unto the authority of the Scripture.

The words of Mr Chillingworth unto this purpose are emphatical; which I shall therefore transcribe, though that be a thing which I am very averse from:—

"Require," saith he, "of Christians only to believe Christ, and to call no man master but him only; let those leave claiming of infallibility who have no right unto it, and let them that in their words disclaim it, disclaim it likewise in their actions; in a word, take away tyranny, which is the devil's instrument to support errors, and superstitions, and impieties in the several parts of the world, which could not otherwise long withstand the power of truth, — I say, take away tyranny, and restore

Christians to their just and full liberty of captivating their understandings to the Scripture only, that universal liberty, thus moderated, may quickly reduce Christendom to truth and unity," part i., chap. 4, sect. 16.

This fundamental principle of the first Reformation we do not only firmly adhere unto, rejecting all those opinions and practices whereby its force is weakened and impaired, but also do willingly suffer the things that do befall us in giving our testimony thereunto. Neither will there ever be peace among the churches of Christ in this world until it be admitted in its whole latitude, especially in that part thereof wherein it excludes all impositions of things not prescribed in the Scripture; for there are but few persons who are capable of the subtlety of those reasonings, which are applied to weaken this principle in its whole extent. All men can easily see this, that *the sufficiency of the Scripture* in general, as unto all the ends of religion, is the only foundation they have to rest and build upon. They do see, actually, that where men go about to prescribe things to be observed in divine worship not appointed in the Scripture, no two churches have agreed therein, but endless contentions have ensued; that no man can give an instance in particular of any thing that is necessary unto the rule of the church, or the observance of the commands of Christ in the worship of God, that is not contained in the Scripture; and hereon are ready to resolve to call no man master but Christ, and to admit of nothing in religion but what is warranted by his word.

2. The second principle of the Reformation, whereon the reformers justified their separation from the church of Rome, was this: "That Christian people were not tied up unto blind obedience unto church-guides, but were not only at liberty, but also obliged to judge for themselves as unto all things that they were to believe and practice in religion and the worship of God." They knew that the whole fabric of the Papacy did stand on this basis or dunghill, that the mystery of iniquity was cemented by this device, — namely, that the *people were ignorant*, and to be kept in ignorance, being obliged in all things unto an implicit obedience unto their pretended guides. And that they might not be capable of nor fit for any other condition, they took from them the only means of their instruction unto their duty, and the knowledge of it; that is, the use of the holy Scripture. But the first reformers did not only vindicate their right unto

the use of the Scripture itself, but insisted on it as a principle of the Reformation (and without which they could never have carried on their work), that they were in all concernments of religion to judge for themselves. And multitudes of them quickly manifested how meet and worthy they were to have this right restored unto them, in laying down their lives for the truth, — suffering as martyrs under the power of their bishops.

This principle of the Reformation, in like manner, is in no small degree weakened by many, and so the cause of it. Dr Stillingfleet himself, pp. 127, 128, denies unto the people all liberty or ability to choose their own pastors, to judge what is meet for their own edification, what is heresy or a pernicious error, and what is not, or any thing of the like nature. This is almost the same with that of the Pharisees concerning them who admired and followed the doctrine of our Saviour, Ὁ ὄχλος οὗτος ὁ μὴ γινώσκων τὸν νόμον, John vii. 49; — "This rabble which knoweth not the law." Yet was it this people whom the apostles directed to choose out from among themselves persons meet for an ecclesiastical office, Acts vi.; the same people who joined with the apostles and elders in the consideration of the grand ease concerning the continuation of the legal ceremonies, and were associated with them in the determination of it, Acts xv.; the same to whom all the apostolical epistles, excepting some to particular persons, were written, and unto whom such directions were given, and duties enjoined on them, as suppose not only a liberty and ability to judge for themselves in all matters of faith and obedience, but also an especial interest in the order and discipline of the church; those who were to say unto Archippus, their bishop, "Take heed to the ministry which thou hast received in the Lord, that thou fulfil it," Col. iv. 17; unto whom of all sorts it is commanded that they should examine and try antichrists, spirits, and false teachers, — that is, all sorts of heretics, and heresies, and errors, 1 John ii., iii., etc.; that people who, even in following ages, adhered unto the faith and the orthodox profession of it when almost all their bishops were become Arian heretics, and kept their private conventicles in opposition unto them, at Constantinople, Antioch, Alexandria, and other places, and who were so many of them burnt here in England by their own bishops, on the judgment they made of errors and heresies. And if the present people with whom the Doctor is acquainted be altogether unmeet for the discharge of any of these duties, it is the fault of somebody else besides their own.

This principle of the Reformation, in vindication of the rights, liberties, and privileges of the Christian people, to judge and choose for themselves in matters of religion, to join freely in those church-duties which are required of them, without which the work of it had never been carried on, we do abide by and maintain. Yea, we meet with no opposition more fierce than upon the account of our asserting the liberties and rights of the people in reference unto church order and worship. But I shall not be afraid to say, that as the Reformation was begun and carried on on this principle, so when this people shall through an apprehension of their ignorance, weakness, and unmeetness to discern and judge in matters of religion for themselves and heir own duty, be kept and debarred from it; or when, through their own sloth, negligence, and viciousness, they shall be really incapable to manage their own interest in church-affairs, as being fit only to be governed, if not as brute creatures, yet as mute persons, and that these things are improved by the ambition of the clergy, engrossing all things in the church unto themselves, as they did in former ages, — if the old popedom do not return, a new one will be erected as bad as the other.

3. Another principle of the Reformation is, "That there was not any catholic, visible, organical, governing church, traduced by succession into that of Rome, whence all church power and order was to be derived." I will not say that this principle was absolutely received by all the first reformers here in England, yet it was by the generality of them in the other parts of the world; for as they constantly denied that there was any catholic church but that invisible of elect believers, allowing the external denomination of "the church" unto he diffused community of the baptized world, so believing and professing that the pope is antichrist, that Rome is mystical Babylon, the seat of the apostatized church of the Gentiles, devoted to destruction, they could acknowledge no such church-state in the Roman church, nor the derivation of any power and order from it. So far as there is a declension from this principle, so far the cause of the Reformation is weakened, and the principal reason of separation from the Roman church is rejected; as shall be farther manifested if occasion require it.

This principle we do firmly adhere unto; and not only so, but it is known that our fixed judgment concerning the divine institution, nature and order of evangelical churches, is such as is utterly exclusive of the Roman church, as a body organized in and under the pope and his hierarchy, from any pretence unto church state, order, or power. And it may be hence judged who do most weaken the cause of Reformation, we or some of them at least by whom we are opposed.

A SECOND absurdity that he chargeth on our way is, "That it would make union among the protestant churches impossible, supposing them to remain as they are," sect. xxiv., p. 186. To make good this charge he insists on two things:—

"1. That the Lutheran churches have the same and more ceremonies and unscriptural impositions than our church hath.

"2. That notwithstanding these things, yet many learned protestant divines have pleaded for union and communion with them; which upon our principles and suppositions they could not have done." But whether they plead for union and communion with them, by admitting into their churches, and submitting unto those ceremonies and unscriptural impositions, — which is alone unto the Doctor's purpose, — or whether they judge their members obliged to communicate in local communion with them under those impositions, he doth not declare. But whereas neither we nor our cause are in the least concerned in what the Doctor here insists upon, yet because the charge is no less than that our principles give disturbance unto the peace and union of all protestant churches, I shall briefly manifest that they are not only conducive thereunto, but such as without which that peace and union will never be attained:—

1. It is known unto all, that from the first beginning of the Reformation there were *differences* among the churches which departed from the communion of the church of Rome. And as this was looked on as the greatest impediment unto the progress of the Reformation, so it was not morally possible that in a work of that nature, begun and carried on by persons of all sorts, in many nations, of divers tongues and languages, none of them being divinely inspired, it should otherwise fall out. God, also, in his holy, wise providence, suffered it so to be, for causes known then to himself; but since, sundry of them have been made manifest in the event. For whereas there was an agreement in all fundamental articles of faith among them and all

necessary means of salvation, a farther agreement, considering our sloth, negligence, and proneness of men to abuse security and power, might have produced as evil effects as the differences have done; for those which have been on the one hand, and those which have been on the other, have been, and would have been, from the corrupt affections of the minds of men and their secular interests.

2. These differences were principally in or about *some doctrines of faith*, whereon some fiery spirits among them took occasion, mutually and unjustly enough, to charge each other with heresy; especially was this done among the Lutherans, whose writings are stuffed with that charge, and miserable attempts to make it good. There were also other differences among them, with respect unto church order, rites, ceremonies, and modes of worship. The church of England, as unto the government of the church and sundry other things, took a way by itself; which at present we do not consider.

3. Considering the *agreement* in all fundamental articles of faith between these churches thus at difference, and of what great use their union might be unto the protestant religion, both as unto its spiritual and political interest in this world, the effecting of such a union among them hath been attempted by many. Private persons, princes, colloquies or synods of some of the parties at variance, have sedulously engaged herein. I wish they had never missed it, in stating the nature of that union, which in this case is alone desirable and alone attainable, nor in the causes of that disadvantageous difference that was between them; for hence it is come to pass, that although some verbal compositions have sometimes by some been consented unto, yet all things continue practically amongst them as they were from the beginning. And there are yet persons who are managing proposals for such a union, with great projection in point of method for the compassing of it and stating of the principles of agreement; some whereof I have by me. But the present state of things in Europe, with the minds of potentates not concerned in these things, leave little encouragement for any such attempt, or expectation of any success.

4. After the trial and experience of a *hundred and fifty years*, it is altogether in vain to be expected that any farther reconciliation or union should be effected between these protestant churches by either party's relinquishment of the doctrines they

have so long taught, professed, and contended for, or of their practice in divine worship, which they have so long been accustomed unto. We may as well expect that a river should run backwards as expect any such things.

In this state of things, I say, the principles we proceed upon are the most useful unto the procuring of peace and union among these churches, in the state wherein they are, and without which it will never be effected. I shall, therefore, give an account of those of them which are of this nature and tendency:—

1. And the first is, *the absolute necessity of a general reformation in life and manners of all sorts of persons belonging unto these churches*. It is sufficiently known what a woful condition the profession even of the protestant religion is fallen unto. How little evidence is there left of the power of evangelical grace working in the hearts of men! What little diligence in the duties of holiness and righteousness! What a deluge of all sorts of vices hath overwhelmed the nations! And what indications there are of the displeasure of God against us on the account of these things! Who doth not almost tremble at them? Calvin, unto whom I was newly sent by our reverend author, in answer to them who pleaded for a separation from a true church because of the wickedness of many of its members, or any of them, adds unto it: "It is a most just offence, and unto which there is too much occasion given in this miserable age. Nor is it lawful to excuse our cursed sloth, which the Lord will not let go unpunished, as he begins already to chastise us with grievous stripes. Woe, therefore, unto us, who by our dissolute licentiousness in flagitious sins do cause that the weak consciences of men should be sounded for us!" And if it were so then, the matter is not much mended in the age wherein we live. The truth is, sin and impiety are come to that height and impudence, sensuality and oppression are so diffused among all sorts of persons, conformity unto the fashion of the world become so universal, and the evidences of God's displeasure, with the beginnings and entrances of his judgments, are so displayed, as that if the reformation pleaded for be not speedily endeavoured and vigorously pursued, it will be too late to talk of differences and union; destruction will swallow up all. Until this be agreed on, until it be attempted and effected in some good measure, all endeavours for farther union, whatever their appearing success should be (as probably it will be very small), will be of no use unto the honour of religion, the

glory of Christ, nor good of the souls of men. In the meantime, individual persons will do well to take care of themselves.

2. That all these *differing churches*, and whilst these differences do continue, be taught to prefer their general interest, in opposition unto the kingdom of Satan and Antichrist in the world, before the lesser things wherein they differ, and those occasional animosities that will ensue upon them. It hath been observed in many places that the nearer some men or churches come together in their profession, the more distant they are in their affections; as the Lutherans in many places do more hate the Calvinists than the Papists. I hope it is not so among us. This makes it evident that the want of necessary peace and union among churches cloth not proceed from the things themselves wherein they differ, but from the corrupt lusts and interests of the persons that differ. This evil can no otherwise be cured but by such a reformation as shall, in some measure, reduce primitive simplicity, integrity, and love, such as were among the churches of the converted Jews and Gentiles, when they walked according unto the same rule in what they had attained, forbearing one another in love as unto the things wherein they differed. Until this also be effected, all endeavours for farther union, whilst these differences continue (as they are like to do, unless the whole frame of things in Europe should be changed by some great revolution), will be fruitless and useless.

Were this conscientiously insisted on, out of a pure love unto Jesus Christ, with zeal for his glory, it would not only be of more use than innumerable wrangling disputes about the points in difference, but more than he exactest methods in contriving formularies of consent, or colloquies, or synodical conferences of the parties at variance, with all their solemnities, orders, limitations, precautions, concessions, and orations. Let men say what they will, it must be the revival, flourishing, and exercise of evangelical light, faith, and love that shall heal the differences and breaches that are among the churches of Christ; nor shall any thing else be honoured with any great influence into that work.

3. That all *communion of churches*, as such, consists in the communion of faith and love, in the administration of the same sacraments, and common advice in things of common concernment. All these may be observed when, for sundry reasons, the members of them cannot have local, presential communion

in some ordinances with each church distinctly. If this truth were well established and consented unto, men might be easily convinced that there is nothing wanting unto that evangelical union among churches which the gospel requires, but only their own humble, holy, peaceable, Christian walking in their several places and stations. But where men put their own interests and possession of present advantages, clothed under the pretence of things necessary thereunto, into *conditions of communion*, or divest it of that latitude wherein Christ hath left it, by new limitations of their own, it will never be attained on the true evangelical principles that it must proceed upon; for however any may be displeased with it, I must assert and maintain that there is nothing required by our Lord Jesus Christ unto this end of the communion of churches, nor to any other end of church order or worship whatever, but that only in whose observance and performance there is an actual exercise of evangelical grace in obedience unto him.

4. That all private members of these several churches which agree in the communion before mentioned be left unto their own *liberty* and consciences to communicate in any of these churches, either occasionally or in a fixed way and manner. Neither orders nor compulsory decrees will be useful in this matter, in comparison of their own declared liberty. And so it was among the primitive churches.

5. Where men are invincibly hindered from *total communion* with any church, by impositions which they cannot comply withal without sin; or, by continuing in it, are deprived of the due means of their edification, the churches whereunto they did belong refusing all reformation; it is lawful for them, in obedience unto the law of Christ, to reform themselves, and to make use of the means appointed by him for their edification, abiding constantly in the communion of all true churches before described. I confess this is that which we cannot digest, — namely, an imagination that the Lord Jesus Christ hath obliged his disciples, those that believe in him, to abide always in such societies as wherein not only things are imposed on their obedience and observance which he hath not commanded, but they are also forced to live in the neglect of expressed duties which he requireth of them, and the want of that means of their own edification which, without the restraint at present upon them, they might enjoy according into his mind and will. Believers

were not made for churches, nor for the advantage of them that rule in them; but churches were made for believers and their edification, nor are of any use farther than they tend thereunto.

These are the premises whereon we proceed in all that we do; and they are so far from being obstructive of the peace and union of the protestant churches, as that without them they will never be promoted nor attained. And I do beg of this worthy person that he would not despise these things, but know assuredly that nothing would be so effectual to procure the union he desireth as a universal reformation of all sorts of persons, according unto the rule and law of Christ; which, it may be, no man hath greater ability and opportunity in conjunction for than himself: for woe be unto us, if, whilst we contend about outward peace in smaller things, we neglect to make peace with God, and so expose ourselves and the whole nation unto his desolating judgments, which seem already to be impendent over us!

The THIRD absurdity which he chargeth on our practice is, "That it will justify the ancient schisms, which have been always condemned in the Christian church;" and in the management of this charge he proceedeth, if I mistake not, with more than ordinary vehemency and severity, though it be a matter wherein we are least of all concerned.

To make effectual this charge, he first affirms in general, "That, setting aside a few things, they pleaded the same reasons for their separation as I do for ours;" which how great a mistake it is shall be manifested immediately. Secondly, He gives instances in several schisms that were so condemned by the Christian church, and whose practice is justified by us.

In answer hereunto, I shall first premise some things in general, showing the insufficiency of this argument to prove against us the charge of schism, and then consider the instances produced by him. I say, —

1. In times of *decay*, the declining times of churches or states, it cannot be but that some will be uneasy in their minds, although they know not how to remedy what is amiss, nor, it may be, fix on the particulars which are the right and true causes of the state which they find troublesome unto them; and whilst it is so with them, it is not to be admired at that some persons do fall into irregular attempts for the redressing of what is amiss. The church, where the instances insisted on happened, was

falling into a mysterious decay from its original institution, order, and rule; which afterward increased more and more continually. But all being equally involved in the same declension, the remedies which they proposed who were uneasy, either in themselves or in the manner of their application, were worse than the disease; which yet lying uncured and continually increasing, proved in the issue the ruin of them all. But here lay the original of the differences and schisms which fell out in the third, fourth, and fifth centuries, that having all in some measure departed from the original institution, rule, and order of evangelical churches in sundry things, and cast themselves into new forms and orders, their differences and quarrels related all unto them, and could have had no such occasion had they kept themselves unto their primitive constitution. Wherefore, those schisms which were said to be made by them that continued sound in the faith, as those of the Audians and Meletians, as by some is pretended, and Johannites[17] at Constantinople, with sundry others, seeing they deserted not any order of divine institution, but another which the churches were insensibly fallen into, no judgment can be made, upon a mere separation, whether of the parties at difference were to blame. I am sure enough that sometimes neither of them could be excused. Whether the causes, reasons, ends, designs, and ways of the management of those differences that were between them, on which schisms in their present order did ensue, were just, regular, according to the mind of Christ, proceeding from faith and love, is that whose determination must fix aright the guilt of the divisions that were among them. And whereas we judge most of those who so separated from the church of old, as is here alleged, to have failed in these things, and therein to have contracted guilt unto themselves, as occasioning unwarrantable divisions and missing wholly the only way of cure for what was really blameworthy in others; yet, whereas we allow nothing to be schism properly but what is contrary to Christian love, and destructive of some institution of Christ, we are not much concerned who was in the right or wrong in those contests which fell out among the orthodox themselves, but only as they were carried on unto a total renunciation of all communion whatever but only that which was enclosed unto their own party.

---

17 An account of these schisms is given by Dr Owen afterwards. See page 413. — Ed.

2. To evidence that we give the *least countenance* unto the ancient schisms, or do contract the guilt with the authors of them, the thing aimed at, there are three things incumbent on him to prove:—

(1.) That our *parochial churches*, from whom we do refrain actual presential communion in all ordinances where it is required by law, which cannot be many and but one at one time, do succeed into the room of that church in a separation from which those schisms did consist; for we pass no judgment on any other church but what concerns ourselves as unto present duty, though that in a nation may be extended unto many or all of the same sort. But these schisms consisted in a professed separation from the whole catholic church, — that is, all Christians in the world who joined not with them in their opinions and practices, — and from the whole church-state then passant and allowed. But our author knows full well that there are others, who, long before our parochial churches, do lay claim unto the absolute enclosure of this church-state unto themselves, and thereon condemn both him and us, and all the Protestants in the world, of the same schism that those of old were guilty of; especially they make a continual clamour about the Novatians and Donatists. I know that he is able to dispossess the church of Rome from that usurpation of the state and rights of the ancient catholic church from whence those separations were made; and it hath been sufficiently done by others. But so soon as we have cast that out of possession, to bring in our parochial assemblies into the room of it, and to press the guilt of separation from them with the same reasons and arguments as we were all of us but newly pressed withal by the Romanists, — namely, that hereby we give countenance unto them, yea, do the same things with them who made schisms in separating from the catholic church of old, — is somewhat severe and unequal.

Wherefore, unless the church from which they separated, which was the whole catholic church in the world not agreeing and acting with them, and those parochial assemblies from whose communion we refrain, are the same and of the same consideration, nothing can be argued from those ancient schisms against us, nor is any countenance given by us unto them; for if it be asked of us, whether it be free or lawful for believers to join in society and full communion with other churches besides those that are of our way and especial communion, we freely answer that we no way doubt of it, nor do judge them for their so doing.

(2.) It must be proved, unto the end proposed, that the *occasions and reasons* of their separation of old were the same, or of the same nature only, with those which we plead for our refraining communion from parochial assemblies. Now, though the Doctor here makes a flourish with some expressions about zeal, discipline, purity of the church, edification (which he will not find in any of their pretences), yet in truth there is not one thing alleged wherein there is a coincidence between the occasions and reasons pleaded by them and ours.

It is known that the principal thing in general which we insist upon is, *the unwarrantable imposition of unscriptural terms and conditions of communion upon* us. Was there any such thing pleaded by them that made the schisms of old? Indeed, they were all of them imposers, and separated from the church because they would not submit unto their impositions. Some bishops, or some that would have been bishops but could not, entertaining some new conceit of their own, which they would have imposed on all others, being not submitted unto therein, were the causes of all those schisms which were justly esteemed criminal. So was it with the Novatians and Donatists in an especial manner. Even the great Tertullian (though no bishop) left the communion of the church on this ground; for because they would not admit of the strict observance of some austere severities, in fasting, abstinence from sundry meats, and watching, with the like, which he esteemed necessary, though no way warranted by Scripture rule or example, he utterly renounced their communion, and countenanced himself by adhering unto the dotages of Montanus. It is true, some of them contended for a severity of discipline in the church; but they did it not upon any pretence of the neglect of it in them unto whom the administration of it was committed, but for the want of establishing a false principle, rule, or erroneous doctrine which they advanced, — namely, that the most sincere penitents were never more to be admitted into ecclesiastical communion: whereby they did not establish but overthrow one of the principal ends of church discipline. They did not, therefore, press for the power or the use of the keys, as is pretended, but advanced a false doctrine, in prejudice both unto the power and use of them. They pretended, indeed, unto the purity of the church; not that there were none impure, wicked, and hypocritical among them, but that none might be admitted who had once fallen, though really made pure by sincere repentance. This was their zeal for purity: If a man were overtaken, if they could catch him in such a fault as, by the rules of the passant discipline, he was to be cast out of the church, there they had him safe for ever. No evidence of the most sincere repentance could prevail for a re-admission into the church. And because other churches would admit them, they renounced all communion with them, as no churches of Christ. Are these our principles? are these our practices? do we give any countenance unto them by any thing we say or do? I somewhat wonder that the Doctor, from some general expressions, and casting their pretences under new appearances, should seem to think that there is the least coincidence between what they insisted on and what we plead in our own defence He may see now more fully what are the reasons of our practice, and I hope thereon will be of another mind; not as unto our cause in general, which I am far enough from the expectation of, but as unto this invidious charge of giving countenance unto the schisms condemned of old in the church. And we shall see immediately what were the occasions of those schisms; which we are as remote from giving countenance unto as unto the principles and reasons which they pleaded in their own justification.

(3.) It ought, also, to be proved that the separation which is charged on us is of the same nature with that charged on them of old; for otherwise we cannot be said to give any countenance unto what they did: for it is known they so separated from all other churches in the world as to confine the church of Christ unto their own party, to condemn all others, and to deny salvation unto all that abode in their communion; which the Donatists did with the greatest fierceness. This was that which, if any thing, did truly and properly constitute them schismatics; as it doth those also who deny at this day church-state and salvation unto such churches as have not diocesan bishops. Now, there is no principle in the world that we do more abhor. We grant a church-state unto all, however it may be defective or corrupted, and a possibility of salvation unto all their members, which are not gathered in pernicious errors, overthrowing the foundation, nor idolatrous in their worship, and who have a lawful ministry, with sufficient means for their edification, though low in its measure and degrees. We judge none but with respect unto our own duty, as unto the impositions attempted to be laid on us, and the acts of communion required of us, which we cannot avoid; nor can any man else, let him pretend what he will to the contrary, avoid the making of a judgment for himself in these things, unless he be brutishly. These things are sufficient to evidence that there is not the least countenance given unto the ancient schisms by any principles of ours; yet I shall add some farther considerations, on the instances he gives unto the same purpose.

The first is that of the Novatians, whose pretences were the discipline and purity of the churches; wherein he says, "There was a concurrence of Dr Owen's pleas; zeal for reformation of discipline, the greater edification of the people, and the asserting of their right in choosing such a pastor as was likely to promote their edification." I am sorry that interest and party should sway with learned men to seek advantages unto their cause so unduly. The story, in short, is this:— Novatus, or Novatianus rather, being disappointed in his ambitious design to have been chosen bishop of the church of Rome, Cornelius being chosen by much the major part of the church, betook himself to indirect means to weaken and invalidate the election of Cornelius; and this he did by raising a new principle of false doctrine, whereunto he as falsely accommodated the matter of fact. The error he broached and promoted was, that "there was no place for repentance" (such as whereon they should be admitted into the church) "unto them who had fallen into sin after baptism;" nor, as some add, "any salvation to be obtained by them who had fallen in the time of persecution." This the ancient church looked on as a pestilent heresy; and as such was it condemned in a considerable council at Rome with Cornelius, Euseb., lib. vi. cap. 43; where also is reported the decree which they made in the case, wherein they call his opinion "cruel" or inhuman, and "contrary to brotherly love." As such it is strenuously confuted by Cyprian, Epist. li., ad Antonianum. But because the church would not submit unto this novel, false opinion of his, contrary to the Scripture and the discipline of the church, he and all his followers separated from all the churches in the world, and rebaptized all that were baptized in the orthodox churches, they denying unto them the means of salvation, Cyprian ad Jubaianum, Epist. lxxi, Euseb., lib. vii. cap. 8. That which was most probably false also in matter of fact when this foolish opinion,

— which Dionysius of Alexandria, in his epistle to Dionysius of Rome, calls "a most profane doctrine, reflecting unmerciful cruelty on our most gracious Lord Jesus Christ," Euseb. lib. vii. cap. 8, — was invented, to be subservient unto it, was, that many of those by whom Cornelius was chosen bishop were such as had denied the faith under the persecution of Decius the emperor. This also was false in matter of fact; for although that church continued in the ancient faith and practice of receiving penitents after their fall, yet there were no such number of them as to influence the election of Cornelius. So Cyprian testifieth: "*Factus est Cornelius episcopus, de Dei et Christi ejus judicio, de clericorum pœne omnium testimonio, de plebis suffragio,*" etc., Epist. li. On that false opinion and this frivolous pretence they continued their schism. Hence, afterward, when Constantine the emperor spake with Acesius the bishop of the Novatians at Constantinople, finding him sound in the faith of the Trinity, which was impugned by Arius, he asked him why then he did not communicate with the church; whereon he began to tell him a story of what had happened in the time of Decius the emperor, pleading nothing else for himself; the emperor replying only, "O Acesius, set up a ladder, and climb alone by thyself into heaven," left him, Socrat., lib. i. cap. 7.

This error endeavoured to be imposed on all churches, this false pretence in matter of fact, with the following pride in the condemnation of all other churches, denying unto them the lawful use of the sacraments, and rebaptizing them who were baptized in them, do, if we nay believe the Doctor herein, contain all my pleas for the forbearance of communion with parochial assemblies, and have countenance given unto them by our principles and practices!

Of the Meletians, whom he reckons up in the next place, no certain account can be given. Epiphanius reports Meletius himself to have been a good, honest, orthodox bishop, and in the difference between him and Peter, bishop of Alexandria, to have been more for truth, as the other was more for love and charity; and according unto him, it was Peter, and not Meletius, that began the schism, Hæres 68, N. 2, 3. But others give quite another account of him. Socrates affirms that in time of persecution he had sacrificed to idols; and was for that reason deposed from his episcopacy by Peter of Alexandria, lib. iii. cap. 6. Hence he was enraged against him, and filled all Thebais and Egypt with tumults against him, and the church of Alexandria, with intolerable arrogance, because he was convicted of sundry wickednesses by Peter, Theod. Hist., lib. i. cap. 8; and his followers quickly complied with the Arians for their advantage. The error he proceeded on, according to Epiphanius, was the same with that of Novatus; which how it could be if he himself had fallen in persecution and sacrificed, as Socrates relates, I cannot understand. This schism of bishop Meletius also it is thought meet to be judged that we should give countenance unto!

All things are in like manner uncertain concerning Audius and his followers, whom he mentions in the next place. The man is represented by Epiphanius to have been a good man, of a holy life, sound in the faith, full of zeal and love to the truth; but finding many things amiss in the church, among the clergy and people, he freely reproved them for covetousness, luxury, and disorders in ecclesiastical affairs. Hereon he stirred up the hatred of many against himself, as Chrysostom did for the same cause afterward at Constantinople. Hereupon he was vexed, persecuted, and greatly abused; all which he bare patiently, and continued in the discharge of his duty; as it fell out also with Chrysostom. Nevertheless, he abode firmly and tenaciously in the communion of the church, but was at length cast out, as far as it appears by him, for the honest discharge of his duty whereon he gathered a great party unto himself. But Theodoret and others affirm him to have been the author of the impious heresy of the Anthropomorphitæ, his principal followers being those monks of Egypt who afterward made such tumults in defence of that foolish imagination; and that this was the cause why he was cast out of the church, and set up a party of the same opinion with him, lib. iv. cap. 10. Yea, he also ascribes unto him some foolish opinions of the Manichees. What is our concernment in these things I cannot imagine.

Eustathius, the bishop of Sebaste in Armenia, and his followers, are also instanced in as *orthodox schismatics*; and as such were condemned in a council at Gangræ in Paphlagonia. But, indeed, before that council, Eustathius had been condemned by his own father, Eulanius, and other bishops, at Cæsarea in Cappadocia; and he was so for sundry foolish opinions and evil practices, whereby he deserved to be so dealt withal. It doth not unto me appear certainly whether he fell into those opinions before his rejection at Cæsarea, where he was principally if not only charged with his indecent and fantastical habit and garments. Wherefore, at the council of Gangræ he was not admitted to make any apology for himself, nor could be heard, because he had innovated many things after his deposition at Cæsarea; such as forbidding of marriage, shaving of women, denying the lawfulness of priests keeping their wives who were married before their ordination, getting away servants from their masters, and the like, Socrat. Hist., lib. ii. cap. 3. These were his pretences of sanctity and purity, as the Doctor acknowledgeth; and I appeal unto his ingenuity and candour whether any countenance be given unto such opinions and practices thereon by any thing we say or do.

This instance, and some others of an alike nature, the Doctor affirms that he produced in his sermon, but that "they were gently passed over by myself and Mr B." I confess I took no notice of them, because I was satisfied that the cause under consideration was no way concerned in them. And the Doctor might to as good purpose have instanced in forty other schisms, made for the most part by the ambition of bishops, in the churches of Alexandria, Antioch, Constantinople, Rome, and sundry other places; yea, in that made by Epiphanius himself at Constantinople, upon as weighty a cause as that of those who contended about and strove for and against the driving of sheep over the bridge, when there were none present.

The story of the Luciferians is not worth repeating. In short, Lucifer, the bishop of Caralli in Sardinia, being angry that Paulinus, whom he had ordained bishop at Antioch, was not received, fell into great dissension with Eusebius, bishop of Vercelli in Italy, who had been his companion in banishment, because he approved not what he had done at Antioch. And continuing to contend for his own bishop, it occasioned a great division among the people, whereon he went home to his own place, leaving behind him a few followers, who wrangled for a time about the ordination of bishops by Arians, by whose means Lucifer had been banished, and so after a while disappeared.

I had almost missed the instance of the Donatists, but the story of them is so well known that it will not bear the repetition; for although there be no mention of them in Socrates or Sozomen, or the History of Theodoret, yet all things that concerned them are so fully declared in the writings of Austin and Optatus against them, as there needs no other account of them.

And this instance of an heretical schism is that which the Papists vehemently urge against the church of England itself and all other Protestants. Here their weapon is borrowed for a little while to give a wound unto our cause, but in vain; yet I know full well that it is easier for some men, on their principles, to flourish with this weapon against us than to defend themselves against it in the hands of the Papists. In brief, these Donatists were upon the matter of the same opinion with the Novatians; and as these grounded their dissension on the receiving those into the church who had fallen and sacrificed under Decius, so did those on a pretence of severity against those who had been traditors under Maximinus. Upon this pretence, improved by many false allegations, Donatus, and those that followed him, rejected Cæcilianus, who was lawfully chosen and ordained bishop of Carthage, setting up one Majorinus in opposition unto him. Not succeeding herein on this foolish unproved pretence, that Cæcilianus had been ordained by a traditor, they rejected the communion of all the churches n the world, confined the whole church of Christ unto their own party, denied salvation unto any other, rebaptized all that came unto them from other churches, and, together with a great number of bishops that joined with them, fell into most extravagant exorbitances.

Upon the consideration of these schisms the Doctor concludes, "That, on these grounds, there hath scarce been any considerable schism in the Christian church but may be justified upon Dr Owen's reasons for separation from our church." Concerning which I must take the liberty to say, that I do not remember that ever I read, in any learned author, an inference made or conclusion asserted that had so little countenance given unto it by the premises whence it is inferred, as there is unto this by the instances before insisted on, whence it pretended to be educed.

All that is of argument in this story is this: That there were of old some bishops, with one or two who would have been bishops and could not, who, to exalt and countenance themselves against those who were preferred to bishoprics before them and above them, invented and maintained false doctrinal principles, the confession whereof they would have imposed on other churches; and because they were not admitted, they separated at once from all other churches in the world but their own, condemning them as no churches, as not having the sacraments or means of salvation; for which they were condemned as schismatics: therefore, those who own not subjection to diocesan bishops by virtue of any institution or command of Christ, who refrain communion from parochial assemblies, because they cannot, without sin to themselves, comply with all things imposed on them in the worship of God and ecclesiastical rule, without judging their state, or the salvation of their members, are, in like manner as they, guilty of schism.

But we have fixed grounds whereon to try, examine, judge, and condemn all schisms that are justly so called, — all such as those before mentioned. If separations arise and proceed from principles of false doctrine and errors, like those of the Novatians and Donatists; if they are occasioned by ambition and desire of pre-eminence, like those that fell out among the bishops of those days, when their parishes and claims were not regulated by the civil power as now they are; if they do so from a desire to impose principles and practices not warranted in the Scripture on others, as it was with Tertullian; if for slight reasons they rend and destroy that church state and order which themselves approve of, as it was with all the ancient schismatics who were bishops, or would fain have been; if those that lake them or follow in them deny salvation unto all that join not with them, and condemn all other churches as being without God's covenant and the sacraments, as did the Donatists and those do who deny these things unto all churches who have not diocesan bishops; if there be not a sufficient justifiable cause pleaded for it, that those who make such a separation cannot abide in the communion which they forsake without wounding their own consciences, and do give evidences of their abiding in the exercise of love towards all the true disciples of Christ, — we are satisfied that we have a rule infallibly directing us to make a judgment concerning it.

Our author adds, [in the FOURTH place,] sect. xxvi. p. 197, "Another argument against this course of separation is, that these grounds will make separation endless; which is to suppose all the exhortations of the Scripture to peace and unity among Christians useless." But why so? Is there nothing in the authority of Christ and the sense of the account which is to be given unto him, nothing in the rule of the word, nothing in the work of the ministry and exercise of gospel discipline, to keel professed disciples of Christ unto their duty, and within the bounds of order divinely prescribed unto them, unless they are fettered and staked down with human laws and constitutions? Herein I confess I differ, and shall do so whilst I am in this world, from our reverend author and others. To say, as he doth (upon a supposition of the taking away of human impositions, laws, and canons), that "there are no bounds set unto separation but what the fancies of men will dictate unto them," is dishonourable unto the gospel, and somewhat more. To suppose that the authority of Christ, the rule of the word, and the work of the ministry, are not sufficient to prescribe bounds unto separation, efficaciously affecting the consciences of believers, or that any other bounds can be assigned as obligatory unto their consciences, is what cannot be admitted. The Lord Christ hath commanded love and union among his disciples; he hath ordained order and communion in his churches; he hath given unto them and limited their power; he hath prescribed rules whereby they and all their members ought to walk; he hath forbidden all schisms and divisions; he hath appointed and limited all necessary separations, and hath truly given all the bounds unto it that the consciences of men are or can be affected withal. But then it is said, "If this be all, separation will be endless." If such a separation be intended as is an unlawful schism, I say, it may be it will; even as persecution and other evils, sins and wickednesses, will be, notwithstanding his severe prohibition of them. What he hath done is the only means to preserve, his own disciples from all sinful separation, and is sufficient thereunto. Herein lieth the original mistake in this matter, — we have lost the apprehension that the authority of Christ, in the rule of his word and works of his Spirit, is every way sufficient for the guiding, governing, and preserving of his disciples, in the church-order by him prescribed, and the observance of the duties by him commanded. It hath been greatly lost in the world for many ages; and, therefore, instead of faithful ministerial endeavours to enforce a sense of it on the consciences of all Christians, they have been let loose from it, through a confidence in other devices to keep them unto their duty and order. And if these devices, be they ecclesiastical canons or civil penalties, be not enforced on them all, the world is made to believe that they are left unto the dictates of their own fancies and imaginations; as if they had no concern in Christ or his authority in this matter. But, for my part, I shall never desire nor endeavour to keep any from schism or separation, but by the ways and means of Christ's appointment, and by a sense of his authority on their own consciences.

The remainder of his discourse on this head consists in a lepid dramatical oration, framed and feigned for one of his opposers, wherein he makes him undertake the patronage of schism before Cyprian and Austin. The learned person intended is very well able to defend and vindicate himself; which I suppose also he will do. In the meantime, I cannot but say two things: —

1. That the *imposition* on him of extenuating the guilt of any real schism is hat which none of his words do give the least countenance unto.

2. That he Doctor's attempt, in his feigned oration, to accommodate his principles or ours unto the case of the Donatists, for their justification (the weakness whereof is evident to every one who knows any thing of the case of the Donatists), is such an instance of the power of interest, a design to maintain a cause causelessly undertaken, by all manner of artifices and pretences, prevailing in the minds of men otherwise wise and sober, as is to be lamented.

We come at length, in the FIFTH place, sect. xxviii., p. 209, unto that which is indeed of more importance duly to be considered than all that went before; for, as our author observes, it is that "wherein the consciences of men are concerned." This argument, therefore, he takes from the obligation which lies upon all Christians to preserve the peace and unity of the church. For the confirmation of this argument, and the application of it unto the case of them who refrain from total communion with our parochial assemblies, — which alone is the case in hand, — he lays down sundry suppositions, which I shall consider in their order, although they may be all granted without any disadvantage unto our cause. But they will be so the better when they are rightly stated:— His first supposition is, "That Christians are under the strictest obligations to preserve the peace and unity of the church." This being the foundation of all that follows, it must be rightly stated; and to that end three things may be inquired into:— 1. What is *that church* whose peace and unity we are obliged to preserve; for there are those who lay the firmest claim unto the name, power, and privileges of the church, with whom we are obliged to have neither peace nor unity in the worship of God. 2. What is *that peace and unity* which we are so obliged to preserve. 3. By what means they are to be preserved.

1. (1.) We are obliged to "follow peace with all men," to "seek peace and pursue it," and "if it be possible, to live peaceably with all men."

(2.) There is a peculiar obligation upon us to seek the peace and prosperity of the *whole visible church of Christ* on earth, and therein, as we have opportunity, to do good unto the whole household of faith. And, considering what differences, what divisions, what exasperations there are among professors of the name of Christ all the world over, to abide steadfast in seeking the good of them all, and doing good unto them as we have opportunity, is as evident an indication of gospel love as any thing else whatever can be.

(3.) As unto *particular churches*, there is an especial obligation upon us to preserve their peace and unity, from our own voluntary consent to walk in them, in obedience unto the commands of Christ. Where this is not, we are left unto the general obligation of seeking the peace of all men, and of the whole professing church in an especial manner, but have no other peculiar obligation thereunto: for being cast into churches of this or that form, merely by human constitution and laws, or by inveterate traditions, lays no new obligation upon any to seek their peace and unity; but whilst they abide in them, they are left unto the influence of other general commands, which are to be applied unto their present circumstances. For into what state or condition soever Christians are cast, they are obliged to live peaceably whilst they abide in it.

2. It may be inquired, what is that peace and unity of the church that we are bound to preserve. There may be an agreement, with some kind of peace and unity, in evil. They are highly pretended unto in the church of Rome; but they are so in idolatry, superstition, and heresy. There may be peace and unity in any false and heretical church, — the unity of Simeon and Levi, brethren in evil. But the peace and unity which we are obliged to observe in particular churches is the consent and agreement of the church in general, and all the members of it, walking under the conduct of this guide in a due observation of all the institutions and commands of Christ, performing towards the whole and each other the mutual duties required by him, from a principle of faith and love. This, and this alone, is that unity and

peace which we are peculiarly obliged to preserve in particular churches; what is more than this relates unto the general commands of love, unity, and peace, before mentioned.

3. Wherefore this states the means whereby we are to preserve this peace and unity: for we are not to endeavour it, — (1.) By a *neglect* or omission of the observance of any of the commands of Christ; nor, (2.) By *doing or practising* any thing in divine worship which he hath not appointed; nor, (3.) By *partaking* in other men's sins, through a neglect of our own duty; nor, (4.) By *foregoing* the means of our own edification, which he commands us to make use of; — for these things have no tendency to the preservation of that peace. And his third supposition is, "That nothing can discharge a Christian from the obligation to communion with his fellow-members, but what is allowed by Christ or his apostles as a sufficient reason of it." It is fully agreed unto, where a man is a member of any church of divine institution by his own consent and virtual consideration, nothing can discharge him from communion with that church but what is allowed by Christ as a sufficient reason for it.

But a little farther inquiry may be made into these things. It was before asserted that all things lawful were to be done for the preservation of the peace of the church. Here it is pleaded that there are many obligations on us to preserve its peace and unity. I desire to know unto whom these rules are obligatory, — who they are that ought to yield obedience unto them. If it be said that these rules are not prescribed unto the rulers and guides of the church, but unto them only who are under their conduct, I desire a proof of it, for at the first view it is very absurd; for as the preservation of the peace and unity of the church is properly incumbent on them who are the rulers of it, and it is continually pleaded by them that so it doth, so all the rules given for that end do or should, principally and in the first place, affect them and their consciences. And these are the rules of their duty herein which are laid down by the Doctor. I desire therefore to know, that since there are such obligations on us to preserve the peace and unity of the church, that for that end we must do what we lawfully may, whether the same rule doth not oblige us to forbear the doing of what we may lawfully forbear, with respect unto the same end. Nay, this obligation of forbearing what we may do, and yet may forbear to do without sin, for the peace and unity of the church, — especially when any would be offended with our doing that which we may lawfully forbear to do, — is exemplified in the Scripture, confirmed by commands and instances, is more highly rational, and less exposed unto danger in practice, than the other of doing what we can.

Now, things that are not necessary in themselves, nor necessary to be observed by a just scandal and offence in case of their omission, are things that may be lawfully forborne. Suppose, now, the rules insisted on to be given principally and in the first place unto the rulers of the church, I desire to know whether they are not obliged by them, for the preservation of the peace and unity of the church, to forbear the imposition of such things on the practice of the whole church in the worship of God as, being no way necessary in themselves, nor such whose omission or the omission of whose imposition, can give scandal or offence unto any. If they are obliged by them so to do, it will be evident where the blame of the division amongst us must lie. To say they are not obliged hereunto by virtue of these rules, is to say that although the preservation of the peace and unity of the church be incumbent on them in a particular manner, — and the chief of them can assign no other end of the office they lay claim unto but only its expediency, or, as is pretended, its necessity unto the preservation of the peace and unity of the church, — yet they are not, by virtue of any divine rules, obliged thereunto. But it seems to me somewhat unequal, that in this contest about the preservation of the peace of the church, we should be bound by rules to do all that we can, whatever it be, and those who differ from us be left absolutely at their liberty, so as not to be obliged to forbear what they may lawfully so do. But to proceed.

Upon these suppositions, and in the confirmation of them, the Doctor produceth a passage out of Irenæus, whose impartial consideration he chargeth on us with great solemnity, "As we love our own souls." Now, although that passage in that great and holy person be not new unto me, having not only read it many a time in his book, but frequently met with it urged by Papists against all Protestants, yet, upon the Doctor's intimation, I have given it again the consideration required. The words as they lie in the author are to this purpose: —

"We shall also judge them who make schisms, being vain, '*qui sunt immanes*,' or '*inanes*,' not having the love of God, rather considering their own profit than the unity of the church, — who, for small or any causes, rend and divide the glorious body of Christ, and as much as in them lies destroy it, speaking peace but designing war, straining at a gnat and swallowing a camel; for there can be no rebuke of things by them, to equal the mischief of schism," lib. iv. cap. 62.

I know not why he should give us such a severe charge for the impartial consideration of these words, — that as we love our souls, we should impartially and without prejudice consider them. We hope that, out of love to the truth, the glory of Christ, and care of our own souls, we do so consider, and have long since so considered, whatever belongs unto the cause wherein we engaged, and the oppositions that are made unto it; nor will we be offended with any that shall yet call on us to persist and proceed in the same way: but why such a charge should be laid on us with respect unto these words of Irenæus, I know not; for although we greatly value the words and judgment of that holy person, that great defender of the mystery and truth of the gospel and of the liberty of the churches from unwarrantable impositions yet it is the word of Christ and his apostles alone whereby we must be regulated and determined in these things, if we love our own souls.

Besides, what are we concerned in them? Is every separation from a church a schism? Our author shows the contrary immediately. Is refraining communion in a church-state not of divine institution, and in things not prescribed by the Lord Christ in the worship of God, [yet] holding communion in faith and love with all the true churches of Christ in the world, *a damnable schism*, or any schism at all? Hath the reverend author in his whole book once attempted to prove it to be so, though this be the whole of the matter in difference between us? Is our forbearance of communion in parochial assemblies, upon the reasons before pleaded, especially that of human impositions, of the same nature with the schism from the whole catholic church, without pretence of any such impositions? Doth he judge us to be such as have no love unto God, such as prefer our own profit before the unity of the church? I heartily wish and pray that he may never have a share in that profit and advantage which we have made unto ourselves by our principles and practice. Poverty, distress, ruin to our families, dangers, imprisonments, revilings, with contemptuous reproaches, comprise the profit we have made unto ourselves. Is our refraining communion in some outward order, modes, and rites, of men's institution, — our want of conscientious submission unto the courts of chancellors, commissaries, officials, etc., — a rending and destroying of the glorious body of Christ? Is it cemented, united, and compacted or "fitly framed together" by these things? They formerly pretended to be his coat; and must they now be esteemed to be his glorious body, when they no way belong unto the one or the other? Is the application of these things unto us an effect of that love, charity, and forbearance which are the only preventive means of schism, and whereof if men are void it is all one upon the matter whether they are schismatics or no, for they will be so when it is for their advantage? Wherefore, we are not concerned in these things. Let whosoever will declare and vehemently assert us to be guilty of schism, which they cannot prove, we can cheerfully subscribe unto these words of Irenæus.

It may not be impertinent on this occasion to desire of some others that, as they love their own souls, and have compassion for the souls of other men, they would seriously consider what state and condition things are come unto in the church of England; — how much ignorance, profaneness, sensuality, do spread themselves over the nation; what neglect of the most important duties of the gospel, yea, what scoffing at the power of religion, doth abound amongst us; what an utter decay and loss there is of all the primitive discipline of the church what multitudes are in the way of eternal ruin, for want of due instruction and example from them who should lead them; how great necessity there is of a universal reformation, and how securely negligent of it all sorts of persons are; what have been the pernicious effects of imposing things unnecessary and unscriptural on the consciences and practices of men in the worship of God, whereby the church hath been deprived of the labour of so many faithful ministers, who might have at least assisted in preventing that decay of religion, which every day increaseth among us; how easy a thing it were for them to restore evangelical peace and unity amongst all Protestants, without the loss of their ministry, without the diminution of their dignity, without deprivation of any part of their revenues, without the neglect of any duty, without doing any thing against their light and consciences, with respect unto any divine obligation; — and thereon set themselves seriously to endeavour the remedy of these and other evils of the like nature, under a sense of that great account which they must shortly give before the judgment-seat of Jesus Christ.

He proceeds to consider the cases wherein the Scripture allows of separation; which he affirms to be three: —

The first is, in case of *idolatrous worship*. This, none can question, they do not see, from whom yet we all separate as from idolaters.

The second is, in case of *false doctrine being imposed instead of true*; which he confirms with sundry instances. But there is a little difficulty in this case; for, —

1. It is uncertain when a doctrine may be said to be *imposed*. Is it when it is taught and preached by the guides and governors of the church, or any of them, without control? If so, then is such preaching a sufficient cause of separation, and will justify them who do at present separate from any church whose ministers preach false doctrine. How false doctrine can be otherwise imposed I know not, unless it be by exacting an express confession of it as truth.

2. What false doctrine it is, which is of this importance as to justify separation, is not easily determinable.

3. If the guides and governors of the church do teach this false doctrine, who shall judge of it, and determine it so to be, and that ultimately, so as to separate from a church thereon? Shall the people do it themselves? are they meet, are they competent for it? are they to make such a judgment on the doctrine of their guides? do they know what is heresy? have they read Epiphanius or Binius? How comes this allowance to be made unto them, which elsewhere is denied?

The third is, *in case men make things indifferent necessary to salvation, and divide the church on that account*. But, —

1. I know not which is to precede or go before, their division of the church or the just separation, nor how they are to be distinguished; but it was necessary to be so expressed.

2. There are two things in such an imposition, — first, The practice of things imposed; secondly, The judgment of them that impose them. The former alone belongs unto them who are imposed on; and they may submit unto it without a compliance with the doctrine, as many did in the apostles' days. For the judgment of the imposers, it was their own error and concernment only.

3. Why is not the imposing of things indifferent, so as to make the observation of them necessary unto men's temporal salvation in this world, so as that the refusal of it shall really affect the refusers with trouble and ruin, as just a cause of separation as the imposing of them as necessary unto eternal salvation, which shall never affect them?

4. This making things indifferent necessary unto salvation, and as such imposing of them on others, is a thing impossible, that never was nor ever can be; for it is the judgment of the imposers that is spoken of, and to judge things indifferent in themselves to be in themselves necessary to salvation is a contradiction. If only the judgment of the imposers, that such things are not indifferent, but necessary to salvation, be intended, and otherwise the things themselves may lawfully be imposed, I know not how this differs from the imposition of indifferent things under any other pretence.

In his following discourse concerning miscarriages in churches, where no separation is enjoined, we are not at all concerned, and therefore shall not observe the mistakes in it, which are not a few.

But may there not be other causes of peaceable withdrawing from the communion of a church besides those here enumerated?

1. Suppose a church should impose the observation of *Judaical ceremonies*, and make their observation necessary, though not to salvation, yet unto the order and decency of divine worship, it may declare them to be in themselves indifferent, but yet make them necessary to be observed.

Or, —

2. Suppose a church should be so *degenerated* in the life and conversation of all its members, that, being immersed in various sins, they should have only a form of godliness, but deny the power of it; the rule of the apostle being to avoid and turn away from them.

3. Suppose a church be fallen *into such decays in faith*, love, and fruits of charity, as that the Lord Jesus Christ by his word declares his disapprobation of it; and in that state refuses to reform itself, and persecutes them who would reform themselves. Or, —

4. Suppose the ministry of any church be such as is insufficient and unable to dispense the word and sacraments unto

edification, so as theft the whole church may perish as unto any relief by or from the administration of the ordinances of the gospel. I say, in these and such other cases, a peaceable withdrawing from the communion of such churches is warrantable by the rule of the Scripture.

Section III.

The third part of the Doctor's discourse he designs to examine the pleas, as he speaks, for *separation*; and these he refers to four heads whereof the first respects the constitution of the church. And those which relate hereunto are four also:— 1. That parochial churches are not of Christ's institution; 2. That diocesan churches are unlawful; 3. That our national church hath no foundation; 4. That the people are deprived of their right in the choice of their pastors.

The first of these, — namely, that our parochial churches are not of Christ's institution, — he begins withal, and therein I am alone called to an account. I wonder the Doctor should thus state *the question* between us. The meaning of this assertion, that our parochial churches are not of Christ's institution, must be either they are not so because they are parochial, or at least in that they are parochial. But is this my judgment? have I said any thing to this purpose? Yea, he knows full well that in my judgment there are no churches directly of divine institution but those that are parochial or particular churches. We are not, therefore, to expect much in the ensuing disputation, when the state of the question is so mistaken at the entrance.

If he say or intend that there are many things in their parochial churches observed, practised, and imposed on all their members, in and about the worship of God, which are not of divine institution, we grant it to be our judgment, and part of our plea in this case. But this is not at all spoken unto.

Wherefore, the greatest part of the ensuing discourse on this head is spent in perpetual diversions from the state of the case under consideration, with an attempt to take advantage for some reflections, or an appearance of success, from some passages and expressions belonging nothing at all unto the merit of the cause; — a course which I thought so learned a person would not have taken in a case wherein conscience is so nearly concerned.

Some mistakes occurring in it have been already rectified, as that wherein he supposeth that my judgment is for the democratical government of the church; as also what he allegeth in the denial of the gradual declension of the primitive churches from their first original institution, hath been examined.

I shall, therefore, plainly and directly propose the things which I assert and maintain in this part of the controversy, and then consider what occurs in opposition unto them, or otherwise seems to be of any force towards the end in general of charging us with schism; and they are these that follow:—

1. *Particular churches or congregations, with their order and rule, are of divine institution, and are sufficient unto all the ends of evangelical churches.* I take *churches* and *congregations* in the same sense and notion as the church of England doth, defining the church by a *congregation of believers*; otherwise there may be occasional congregations that are not stated churches.

2. Unto these churches there is committed by Christ himself all the ordinary power and privileges that belong unto any church under the gospel; and of them is required the observance of all church duties, which it is their sin to omit.

3. There is *no church of any other form, kind, nature, or constitution that is of divine institution*. Things may be variously ordered in and amongst Christians, or their societies may be cast or disposed of into such respective relations to and dependence on one another, in compliance with the political state, and other circumstances of time and places, as may be thought to tend unto their advantage. That which we affirm is, that no alteration of their state from the nature and kind of particular churches is of *divine institution*.

4. *Such churches whose frame, constitution, and power are destructive of the order, liberty, power, privileges, and duties of particular churches, are so far contrary unto divine institution, and not to be complied withal.*

Hereon we affirm, that whereas we are excluded from total communion in our parochial assemblies, by the imposition of things unto us unlawful and sinful as indispensable conditions of their communion, and cannot comply with them in their rule and worship on the reasons before alleged, it is part of the duty we owe to Jesus Christ to gather ourselves into particular churches or congregations for the celebration of divine worship, and the observation, doing, or performance of all his commands. These are the things which in this case we adhere unto, and which must all of them be overthrown before any colour can be given unto any charge of schism against us; and what is spoken unto this purpose in the Doctor's discourse we shall now consider. Only, I desire the reader to remember that all these principles or assertions are fully confirmed in the preceding discourse.

That which first occurs in the treatise under consideration unto the point in hand is the exception put in unto a passage in my former discourse, which is as follows:—

"We do not say that because communion in ordinances should be only in such churches as Christ hath instituted, that therefore it is lawful and necessary to separate from parochial churches; but if it be on other grounds necessary so to separate or withhold communion from them, it is the duty of them that do so to join themselves in or unto some other particular congregation."

I have not observed any occasion wherein the Doctor is more vehement in his rhetoric than he is on that of this passage, which yet appears to me to be good sense and innocent.

1. Hereunto he says, p. 221, —

"That this is either not to the business, or it is a plain giving up of the cause of Independency." If he judge that it is "not to the business," I cannot help it, and he might, as I suppose, have done well to have taken no notice of it, as I have dealt with many passages in his discourse; but if it be "a giving up of the cause of Independency," I say, whatever that be, let whoso will take it, and dispose of it as it seems good unto them. But in proof hereof he says, —

"Wherefore did the dissenting brethren so much insist upon their separate congregations, when not one of the things now particularly alleged against our church was required of them?"

I answer, —

(1.) If any did in those times plead for separate congregations, let them answer for themselves; I was none of them. They did, indeed, plead for distinct congregations, exempt in some few things from a penal rule then endeavoured by some to be imposed on all. But there was no such difference nor restraint of communion between any of them as is at present between us and parochial churches.

(2.) It is very possible that there may be other reasons of forbearing a conjunction in some acts of church-rule, which was all that was pleaded for by the dissenting brethren, than those which are alleged against total communion with parochial churches, in worship, order, and discipline.

2. He adds, secondly, "But if he insists on those things common to our church with other reformed churches, then they are such things as he supposes contrary to the first institution of churches," etc.

I fear I do not well understand what this means, nor what it tends unto; but according as I apprehend the sense of it, I say, —

(1.) I insist principally on such things as are *not common unto them with other reformed churches*, but such as are peculiar unto the church of England. These vary the terms and practices of our communion between them and it.

(2.) The things we except against in parochial churches are not contrary to their first institution as parochial, — which, as hath been proved, is the only kind of churches that is of divine institution, — but are contrary unto what is instituted to be done and observed in such churches: which one observation makes void all that he would infer from the present suppositions; as, —

3. He inquireth hereon, "What difference there is between separating from our churches because communion in ordinances is only to be enjoyed in such churches as Christ hath instituted, and separating from them because they have things repugnant unto the first institution of churches."

The Doctor, I fear, would call this sophistry in another, or at least complain theft it is somewhat oddly and faintly expressed. But we shall consider it as it is:—

(1.) Separation from parochial churches, because communion in ordinances is only to be enjoyed in such churches as Christ hath instituted, is denied by us; it is so in the assertion opposed by him, and I do not know whether it be laid down by him as that which we affirm or which we deny.

(2.) There is great ambiguity in the latter clause, of "Separating from them because they have things repugnant unto the first institution of churches:" for it is one thing to separate from a church because it is not of divine institution, — that is, not of that kind of churches which are divinely instituted, — and another to do so because of things practised and imposed in it contrary to divine institution; which is the case in hand.

4. But he after saith, "Is not this the primary reason of separation, Because Christ hath appointed unalterable rules for the government of his church, which are not to be observed in parochial churches?"

I answer, No, it is not so; for there may be an omission, at least for a season, in some churches, of some rules that Christ hath appointed in the government of his church (and we judge his rules as unto right unalterable), which may not be a just cause of separation. So the church of the Jews continued a long time in the omission of the observance of the feast of tabernacles. But the principal reason of the separation we defend is the practising and imposing of sundry things in the worship of the church not of divine institution, yea, in our judgment contrary thereunto, and the framing of a rule of government of men's devising, to be laid on all the members of them; this is the primary cause pleaded herein.

But because the Doctor proposeth a case on those suppositions, whereon he seems to lay great weight, — though, indeed, however it be determined, it conduceth nothing unto his end, but argues only some keenness of spirit against them whom he opposeth, — I shall at large transcribe the whole of it:—

"Let us, then," saith he, "(1.) suppose that Christ hath, by unalterable rules, appointed that a church shall consist only of such a number of men as may meet in one congregation so qualified; and that those, by entering into covenant with each other" (whereof we shall treat hereafter), "become a church and choose their officers, who are to teach, and admonish, and administer sacraments, and to exercise discipline, by the consent of the congregation. And let us (2.) suppose such a church not yet gathered, but there lies fit matter for it dispersed up and down in several parishes. (3.) Let us suppose Dr Owen about to gather such a church. (4.) Let us suppose not one thing peculiar to our church required of these members, neither the aërial sign of the cross, nor kneeling at the communion, etc. I desire to know whether Dr Owen be not bound by this unalterable rule to draw these members from communion with parochial churches, on purpose that they might form a congregational church according to Christ's institution? Either, then, he must quit these unalterable rules and institutions of Christ" (which he will never do whilst he lives), "or he must acknowledge, that setting up a congregational church is the primary ground of this separation from our parochial churches," etc.

The whole design hereof is to prove that we do not withhold communion from their parochial assemblies because of the things that are practised and imposed in them in the worship of God and church-rule, but because of a necessity apprehended of setting up congregational churches. I answer, —

1. We know it is otherwise, and that we plead the true reason, and that which our consciences are regulated by, in refraining from their communion; and it is in vain for him or any man else to endeavour so to bird-lime our understandings by a multiplicity of questions, as to make us think we do not judge what we do judge, or do not do what we know ourselves well enough to do. If we cannot answer sophisms against motion, we can yet rise up and walk.

2. These things are consistent, and are not capable of being opposed one to the other, — namely, that we refrain communion on the reasons alleged, and thereon judge it necessary to erect congregational churches; which we should have no occasion to do were not we excluded from communion in parochial assemblies, as we are.

3. The case being put unto me, I answer plainly unto the Doctor's last supposition, whereon the whole depends, that if those things which we except against as being unduly practised and imposed in parochial assemblies were removed and taken away, I would hold communion with them, all the communion that any one is obliged to hold with any church, and would in nothing separate from them. This spoils the whole case. But then he will say, I am no Independent. I cannot help that; he may judge as he sees cause, for I am *"nullius addictus jurare in verba magistri,"* designing to be the disciple of Christ alone.

4. But ye suppose that in such churches, all the things excepted against being removed, there is yet a defect in some unalterable rule that concern the government of the churches, that they answer not in all things the strictness laid down in the Doctor's first supposition (although it is certain that if not all of them absolutely, yet the most of them, and of the most importance, would be found virtually in parochial assemblies upon the removal of the things excepted against), the inquiry is, what I would do then, or whether I would not set up a congregational

church gathered out of other churches. I answer, I tell you plainly what I would do.

(1.) If I were joined unto any such church as wherein there were a defect in any of the rules appointed by Christ for its order and government, I would endeavour peaceably, according as the duties of my state and calling did require, to introduce the practice and observance of them.

(2.) In case I could not prevail therein, I would consider whether the want of the things supposed were such as to put me on the practice of any thing unlawful, or cut me short of the necessary means of edification; and if I found they do not so do, I would never for such defects separate or withdraw communion from such a church. But, —

5. Suppose that from these defects should arise not only a real obstruction unto edification, but also a necessity of practising some things unlawful to be observed, wherein no forbearance could be allowed, I would not condemn such a church, I would not separate from it, would not withdraw from acts of communion with it which were lawful, but I would peaceably join in fixed personal communion with such a church as is free from such defects; and if this cannot be done without the gathering of a new church, I see neither schism nor separation in so doing.

Wherefore, notwithstanding all the Doctor's questions, and his case founded on as many suppositions as he was pleased to make, it abides firm and unshaken, that the ground and reason of our refraining communion from parochial assemblies is the practice and imposition of things not lawful for us to observe in them. And it is unduly affirmed, p. 223, that upon my grounds, "Separation is necessary, not from the particular conditions of communion with them, but because parochial churches are not formed after the congregational way;" for what form of churches they have, be it what it will, it is after the congregational way. And it is more unduly affirmed, and contrary unto the rules of Christian charity, that this plea of ours is "a necessary piece of art to keep fair with the presbyterian party;" for as we design to "keep fair," as it is called, with no parties, but only so far as truth and Christian love require, — and so we design it with all parties whatsoever, — so the plea hath been always insisted on by us, and was the cause of nonconformity in multitudes of our persuasion, before they had any opportunity to gather any congregational churches according to the rule of the gospel. Such things will never help nor adorn any cause in the issue.

But he presseth the due consideration of this art (that, as I suppose, they may avoid the snare of it) on the Presbyterians, by minding them what was done in former times, "in the debate of the dissenting brethren, and the setting up of congregational churches in those days." For saith he, "Have those of the congregational way since altered their judgment? Hath Dr Owen yielded, that in case some terms of communion in our church were not insisted on, they would give over separation? Were not their churches first gathered out of presbyterian congregations; and if Presbytery had been settled upon the king's restoration, would they not have continued in their separation?"

Ans. 1. There is no difference, that I know of, between Presbyterians and those whom he calls Independents, about particular churches; far the Presbyterians allow them to be of divine institution, grant them *the exercise of discipline* by their own eldership, in all ordinary cases, and none to be exercised in them without them or their own consent, as also their right unto the choice of their own officers: so that there could be no separation between them on that account.

2. When they begin in good earnest to reform themselves, and to take away the unsufferable conditions of communion excepted against, they may k now more of my judgment, if I am alive (which I do not believe I shall be), as unto separation; though I have spoken unto it plainly enough already.

3. It can not be said that the churches of the Independents were gathered out of presbyterian churches, for the presbyterian government was never here established; and each party took liberty to reform themselves acceding to their principles, wherein there was some difference.

4. Had he presbyterian government been settled at the king's restoration by the encouragement and protection of the practice of it, without a rigorous imposition of every thing supposed by any to belong thereunto, or a mixture of human constitutions, if there had any appearance of a schism or separation continued between the parties, I do judge they would have been both to blame: for as it cannot be expected that all churches, and all persons in them, should agree in all principles and practices belonging unto church-order, — nor was it so in the days of the apostles, nor ever since among any true churches of Christ, —

so all the fundamental principles of church-communion would have been so fixed and agreed upon between them, and all offences in worship so removed, as that it would have been a matter of no great art absolutely to unite them, or to maintain a firm communion among them; no more than in the days of the apostles and the primitive times, in reference to the differences that were among churches in those days, for they allowed distinct communion upon distinct apprehensions of things belonging unto church order or worship, all keeping the unity of the Spirit in the bond of peace. If it shall be asked, then, Why did they not formerly agree in the assembly? I answer, (1.) I was none of them, and cannot tell; (2.) They did agree, in my judgment, well enough, if they could have thought so; and farther I am not concerned in the difference.

It is therefore notorious, that occasion is given unto our refraining free communion with parochial churches by the unwarrantable imposition of things not lawful for us to observe, both in church order and worship; nor is it candid in any to deny it, though they are otherwise minded as unto the things themselves.

His second exception is unto a saying which I quoted out of Justice Hobart's Reports, who saith, "We know well that the primitive church in its greatest purity was but voluntary congregations of believers, submitting themselves to the apostles and other pastors; to whom they did minister of their temporals as God did move them." Hereunto, with a reflection on a dead man, I know not why, he replies, that this is "not to the purpose, or rather, quite overthrows my hypothesis." But why so? He will prove it with two arguments:—

The first is this: "Those voluntary congregations over which the apostles were set were no limited congregations of any one particular church; but those congregations over which the apostles were set are those of which Justice Hobart speaks: and therefore it is plain he spake of all the churches which were under the care of the apostles, which he calls 'voluntary congregations.'"

Ans. 1. Whereas this argument seems to be cast into the form of a syllogism, I could easily manifest how asyllogistical it is, did I delight to contend with him or any else. But, —

2. The conclusion which he infers is directly what I plead for, — namely, that all the churches under the care of the apostles were voluntary congregations.

3. There is a fallacy in that expression, "No limited congregations of any one particular church." No such thing is pretended; but particular churches are congregations. Such were all the churches over which the apostles were set; and therefore Justice Hobart speaks of them all. This, then, is that which he seems to oppose, — namely, that all the churches under the care of the apostles were particular voluntary congregations, as Justice Hobart alarms; and this is that which in the close, he seems to grant!

His second argument, which is no less ambiguous, no less a rope of sand, than the former, is this: "Those voluntary congregations over whom the apostles appointed pastors, after their decease were no particular congregations in one city. But those of whom Justice Hobart speaks were such, for he saith they first submitted unto the apostles and afterward to other pastors." What then? Why, "Justice Hobart could not be such a stranger to antiquity as to believe that the Christians in the age after the apostles amounted but to one congregation in a city."

Ans. 1. What this is designed to prove or disprove, or how it doth either of them, I do not understand; but I deny the proposition. The voluntary congregations over whom the apostles appointed pastors were all of them particular congregations, either in one city or more cities, for that is nothing unto our purpose.

2. Not to engage Justice Hobart or his honour, I do confess myself such a stranger unto antiquity (if that may be esteemed the reason of it) as not to believe that the Christians in the age afar the apostles amounted to any more than one church or congregation in a city, and shall acknowledge myself beholden to this reverend author if he will give me one undoubted instance where they so did. Only, let the reader observe that I intend not occasional meetings of any of the church with or without their elders, which were frequent. They met in those days in fields, in mountains, in dens and caves of the earth, in burying-places, in houses hired or borrowed, in upper rooms or cellars; whereof a large story might easily be given if it were to our present purpose. Dionysius of Alexandria sums them up briefly: Χωρίον, ἀγρὸς, ἐρημία, ναῦς, πανδοχεῖον, δεσμωτήριον· — "A field, a desert, a ship, an inn, a prison, were places of our meetings," Euseb., lib. 7 cap. 22. But I speak of stated churches, with their worship, power, order, and rule. But whether there were more

such churches in any one city is a matter of fact that shall be immediately inquired into. All that I here assert and confirm from the words of Justice Hobart is, that the churches in the days of the apostles were particular voluntary congregations; and the Doctor will find it a difficult task to prove that this overthrows my hypothesis.

Our author in the next place opposeth what I affirmed of the gradual deviation of the churches after the apostles from the rule of their first institution, which hath been already accounted for.

Sect. iv. p. 224. Upon an occasional expression of mine about the church of Carthage in Cyprian's time, he gives us a large account of the state of the church of Carthage at that time, wherein we are not much concerned. My words are, Vindic.[18] p. 41, "Though many alterations were before that time introduced into the order and rule of the churches, yet it appears that when Cyprian was bishop of the church of Carthage, the whole community of the members of that church did meet together to determine of things that were of their common interest, according unto what was judged to be their right and liberty n those days."

I thought no man who is so conversant in the writings of Cyprian as our author apparently is could have denied the truth hereof, nor do I say it is so done by him; only, he takes occasion from hence to discourse at large concerning the state of the church at Carthage in those days, in opposition to Mr Cotton, who affirms that there was found in that church the "express and lively lineaments of the very body of congregational discipline." Herein I am not concerned, who do grant that at that time there were many alterations introduced into the order and rule of the church. But that the people did meet together unto the determination of things of their common interest, such as were the choice of their officers, and the readmission of them into the fellowship of the church who had fallen through infirmity in time of persecution, or public offences and divisions, is so evident in the writings of Cyprian, — wherein he ascribes unto them the right of choosing worthy and of rejecting unworthy officers, and tells them that n such cases he will do nothing without their consent, — that it cannot be gainsaid. But here-

---

18 See his "Brief Vindication of the Nonconformists," etc. vol. xii. of his works.

on he asketh, where I had any reason to appeal to St Cyprian for the democratical government of the church; which, indeed, I did not do, nor any thing which looked like unto it. And he adds, that they have this advantage from the appeal, that we do not suppose any deviation then from the primitive institution; whereas my words are positive, that before that time there were many alterations introduced into the rule and order of the church. Such things will partiality in a cause, and aiming at success in disputation, produce.

Mr Cotton affirms that the lineaments of the congregational discipline are found in that church, that there is [not?] therein a just representation of an episcopal church; that is, I presume, diocesan, because that alone is unto his purpose. It is not lawful to make any church after the time of the apostles the rule of all church state and order, nor yet to be absolutely determined in these things by the authority of any man not divinely inspired; and yet I cannot but wish that all the three parties dissenting about church order, rule, and worship would attempt an agreement between themselves upon the representation made of the state of the church of Carthage in the days of Cyprian (which all of them lay some claim unto), although it will be an abridgment of some of their pretensions. It might bring them all nearer together, and, it may be, all of them in some things nearer to the truth; for it is certain, —

1. That the church of Carthage was at that time a particular church. There was no more church but one in that city. Many occasional meetings and assemblies in several places for divine exercises and worship there were; but stated churches, with officers of their own, members peculiarly belonging unto them, discipline among them, such as our reverend author doth afterward affirm and describe our parochial churches to be, there were none, nor is it pretended that there were.

2. That in this one church there were many *presbyters or elders*, who ruled the whole body or community of it by common advice and counsel. Whether they were all of them such as laboured in the word and doctrine, with the administration of the sacraments, or attended unto rule only, it doth not appear; but that they were many, and such as did not stand in any peculiar relation unto any part of the people, but concurred in common to promote the edification of the whole body, as occasion and

opportunity did require, is evident in the account given of them by Cyprian himself.

3. That among those elders, in that *one church*, there was one peculiarly called the *bishop*, who did constantly *preside* amongst them in all church-affairs, and without whom ordinarily nothing was done; as neither did he any thing without the advice of the elders and consent of the people. How far this may be allowed for order's sake is worth consideration; of divine institution it is not. But where there are many elders, who have equal interest in and right unto the rule of the whole church, and the administration of all ordinances, it is *necessary unto order* that one do preside in their meetings and consultations, whom custom gave some pre-eminence unto.

4. That *the people were ruled by their own consent*; and that in things of greatest importance, as the choice of their officers, the casting out and the receiving in of lapsed members, [they] had their suffrage in the determination of them.

5. That there was no *imposition* of liturgies, or ceremonies, or any human invention, in the worship of God, on the church or any members of it, the Scripture being the sole acknowledged rule in discipline and worship.

This was the state and order of the church of Carthage in those days; and although there were some alterations in it from the first divine institution of churches, yet I heartily wish that there were no more difference amongst us than what would remain upon a supposition of this state.

For what remains of the opposition made unto what I had asserted concerning congregational or particular churches, I may refer the Doctor and the reader unto what hath been farther pleaded concerning them in the preceding discourse; nor am I satisfied that he hath given any sufficient answer unto what was before alleged in the vindication, but hath passed by what was most pregnant with evidence unto he truth, and by a mistake of my mind or words diverts very much from the state of the question, which is no other but what I laid down before; yet I will consider what is material in the whole of his discourse on this subject.

Sect. v. p. 234. He says, I affirm that as to the "matter of fact concerning the institution of congregational churches, it seems evidently exemplified in the Scripture;" for which I refer the reader unto what is now again declared in the confirmation of it. And he adds, "The matter of fact is, that when churches grew too big for one single congregation in a city, then a new congregational church was set up under new officers, with a separate power of government;" — that is, in that city. But this is not at all the matter of fact. I do not say that there were originally more particular churches than one in one city; I do grant, in the words next quoted by him, that there is not express mention made that any such church did divide itself into more congregations, with new officers. But this is the matter of fact, that the apostles appointed only particular congregations; and that therefore they did not oblige the Christians about, in a province or diocese, to be of that church which was first erected in any town or city, but they founded new churches, with new officers of their own, in all places where there were a sufficient number of believers to make up such a church. And this I prove from the instance of the church of Jerusalem, which was first planted; but quickly after there were churches gathered and settled in Judea, Galilee, and Samaris. They planted churches κατὰ πόλεις καὶ χώρας, in the cities and villages, as Clemens speaks. "But what," saith he, "is this to the proof of the congregational way?" This it is, — namely, that the churches instituted by the apostles were all of them congregational, not diocesan, provincial, or national.- But saith he, "The thing I desired was, that when the Christians in one city multiplied into more congregations, they would prove that they did make new and distinct churches." He may desire it of them who grant that the Christians did multiply in one city into more congregations than one (which I deny) until the end of the second century, although they might and did occasionally meet, especially in times of persecution, in distinct assemblies. Neither will their multiplication into more congregations, without distinct officers, at all help the cause he pleadeth for; for his diocesan church consisteth of many distinct churches, with their distinct officers, order, and power, as he afterward describes our parishes to do under one bishop. Yet such is his apprehension of the justice of his cause, that what hath been pleaded twenty times against it, — namely, that speaking of one city, the Scripture still calls it the church of that place, but speaking of a province, as Judea, Galilee, Samaria, Galatia, Macedonia, it speaks of the *churches* of them; which evidently proves that it knows nothing of a diocesan, provincial, or national church, — he produceth in the justification of it, because he saith, that "it is evident, then, that there was but one church in one city," which was never denied, There were, indeed, then many bishops in one church, Phil. i. 1; Acts xx. 28. And afterward, when one church had one bishop only, yet there were two bishops in one city, which requires two churches, as Epiphanius affirms: Οὐ γὰρ πότε ἡ Ἀλεξάνδρεια δύο ἐπισκόπους ἔσχεν ὡς αἱ ἄλλαι πόλεις, Hæres. lxviii. s. 6; — "For Alexandria never had two bishops, as other cities had." Whether he intend two bishops in one church, or two churches in one city, all is one to our purpose.

But the Doctor, I presume, makes this observation rather artificially, to prevent an objection against his main hypothesis, than with any design o strengthen it thereby; for he cannot but know how frequently it is pleaded in opposition unto any national church-state, as unto its mention in the Scripture; for he that shall speak of the churches in Essex, Suffolk, Hertfordshire, and so of other counties, without the least intimation of any general church unto which they should belong, would be judged to speak rather the independent than the episcopal dialect.

But, saith he, p. 236, "I cannot but wonder what Dr Owen means, when, after he hath produced the evidence of distinct churches in the same province, he calls this plain Scripture evidence and practice for the erecting particular, distinct congregations; — who denies that," (I say, then, it is incumbent on him to prove, if he do any thing in this cause, that they erected churches of another sort, kind, and order also.) "But, saith he, "I see nothing like a proof of distinct churches in the same city; which was the thing to be proved, but because it could not be proved was prudently let alone."

But this was not the thing to be proved, nor did I propose it to confirmation nor assert it, but have proved the contrary unto the end of the second century. This only I assert, that every church in one city was only one church; and nothing is offered by the Doctor to the contrary, yea, he affirms the same.

But, saith he, sect. vi. p. 237, "Dr Owen saith, that the Christians of one city might not exceed the bounds of a particular church or congregation, no, although they had a multiplication of bishops or elders in them, and occasional distinct assemblies for some acts of divine worship. But then," saith he, "the notion of a church is not limited in the Scripture to a single congregation? Why so? "For," saith he, "if occasional assemblies be allowed for some acts of worship, why not for others," I say, Because they belong unto the whole church, or are acts of communion in the whole church assembled, and so cannot be observed in occasional meetings: "Do this," saith the apostle, "when you come together into one place." "And if," saith he, "the number of elders be unlimited, then every one of those may attend the occasional, distinct assemblies for worship, and yet altogether make up the body of one church." And so, say I, they may, and yet be one church still, joining together in all acts of communion that are proper and peculiar unto the church; for as the meetings intended were occasional, so also was the attendance of the elders unto them, as they found occasion, for the education of the whole church.

It may be the Doctor is not so well acquainted with the principles and practice of the congregational way, and therefore thinks that these things are contrary unto them. But those of that way do maintain that there ought to be in every particular congregation, unto the completeness of it, *many elders or overseers*; that the number of them ought to be increased as the increase of the church makes it necessary for their edification; that the members of such a church may and ought to meet occasionally in distinct assemblies, especially in 'the time of persecution, for prayer, preaching of the word, and mutual exhortation: so when Peter was in prison after the death of James, many met together in the house of Mary to pray, Acts xii. 12; which was not a meeting of the whole church. And that there were such private meetings of the members of the same church in times of persecution among the primitive churches may be proved by a multiplication of instances; but still they continued one church, and joined together in all acts of church-communion properly so called, especially if it were possible every Lord's day, as Justin Martyr declares that the church did in his time; "for all the Christians," saith he, then, "in the city and villages about," gathered together "in one place," for the ends mentioned. But still these distinct occasional assemblies did not constitute any *distinct societies or corporations,* as the distinct, companies do in a city. "But," saith he, "grant one single bishop over all these elders, and they make up' that representation of a church which we have from the best and purest antiquity." I say we would quickly grant it could, we see any warrant for it, or if he could prove that so it was from the beginning. However, this is no part of our present contest, — namely, whether, somewhile after the days of the apostles, in churches that were greatly increased and many elders in them, there was not one chosen (as at Alexandria) by those elders themselves to preside among them, who, in a peculiar manner, was called a bishop. But, if I mistake not, that alone which would advantage his cause is to prove that there were in one city, or anywhere else, many, not occasional assemblies of Christians or church-members, but many stated, fixed churches, with officers of their own, peculiarly related unto them, intrusted with church power and privileges, at least as much as he afterward pleads to be in our parochial churches, all under the government of one single bishop, making up a new church-state beyond that of particular congregations, by their relation unto him as their common pastor. This, I take it, is that which should have been proved.

All the difficulty wherewith our assertion is accompanied ariseth from the multiplication of believers and the increase of churches, in the apostles' time or presently after; for this seems to be so great as that those in one city could not continue in one church, notwithstanding the advantages of occasional assemblies. The church of Jerusalem had five thousand in it at the same time. The word grew and prevailed at Ephesus and other places. Whereto I shall briefly answer, as hastening unto a close of this unpleasing labour. I say, therefore, —

1. Whatever difficulty may seem to be in this matter, yet in point of fact so it was; there was no church before the end of the second century of any other species, nature, or kind, but a *particular congregational church* only, as hath been proved before. Let any one instance be produced of a church of one denomination, national, provincial, or diocesan, or of any other kind than that which is congregational, and I will give over this contest. But when a matter of fact is certain, it is too late to inquire how it might be. And on this occasion I shall add, that if in that space of time, — namely, before the end of the second century, — any proof or undoubted testimony can be produced of the imposition of the necessary use of liturgies, or of stated ceremonies of [or?] the practice of church-discipline, consistent with that now in use in the church of England, it will go a great way in the determination of the whole controversy between us.

2. The *admirable prevalency of the gospel* in those days consisted principally in its spreading itself all the world over, and

planting seminaries for farther conversions in all nations. It did, indeed, prevail more some cities and towns than in others, — in some places many were converted, in others the tender of it was utterly rejected; howbeit it prevailed not unto the gathering of such great numbers into any church solely as might destroy or be inconsistent with its congregational institution. For not all, not, it may be, half, not sometimes a third part of them who made some profession of the truth, and attended unto the preaching of the word, and many of whom underwent martyrdom, were admitted as complete members of the church, unto all the parts of its communion. Hence there were many who upon a general account were esteemed Christians, and that justly, where the churches were but small.

3. It doth not appear that in the next age after the apostles the churches were anywhere so increased in number as to bear the least proportion with the inhabitants of the cities and towns wherein they were. The church of Smyrna, in the days of Polycarpus, may justly be esteemed one of the greatest in those days, both from the eminency of the place and person, who was justly accounted the great instructor of all Asia, as they called him when he was carried unto the stake. But this church giveth such an account of itself, in its epistle unto the churches of Pontus about the martyrdom of Polycarpus, as manifests the church there to have been a very small number in comparison of the multitude of the other inhabitants, so as that it was scarcely known who or what they were, Euseb. lib. iv. cap. 15. So in the excellent epistle of the churches of Vienne and Lyons unto the churches of Asia and Phrygia, concerning the persecutions that befell them, as they declare themselves to have been particular churches only, so they make it evident that they bore in number no proportion unto the inhabitants of the places where they were, who could scarce discover them by the most diligent search, Euseb. lib. v. cap. 1.

4. As for the church of Jerusalem in particular, notwithstanding the great number of its original converts, — who probably were many of them strangers occasionally present at the feast of Pentecost, and there instructed in the knowledge of the truth, that they might, in the several countries whither they immediately returned, be instruments of the propagation of the gospel, — it is certain that many years after it consisted of no greater multitude than could come together in one place

to the management of church-affairs, Acts xv. 4, 22. Nor is it likely that Pella, an obscure place, whose name probably had never been known but on this occasion, was like to receive any great multitudes; nor doth Epiphanius say, as our author pretends, that they spread themselves from thence to Cœlo-syria, and Decapolis, and Basanitis, for he affirms expressly that all the disciples which went from Jerusalem dwelt at Pella. Only he says, that from thence the sect of the Nazarenes took its original, which spread itself (afterward) in Cœlo-syria, Decapolis, and Basanitis: Ἐκεῖθεν γὰρ, ἡ ἀρχὴ γέγονε (speaking of that sect) μετὰ τὴν ἀπὸ τῶν Ἱεροσολύμων μετάστασιν, πάντων τῶν μαθητῶν ἐν Πέλλῃ οἰκηκότων, — "they dwelled all at Pella."

Sect. vii. p. 239. He quotes another saying of mine, — namely, that I "cannot discern the least necessity of any positive rule or direction in this matter, seeing the nature of the thing and the duty of man do indispensably require it." And hereon he attempts to make advantage, in opposition unto another saying, as he supposeth, of mine, — namely, "that the institution of churches, and the rules for their disposal and government throughout the world are the same, stated and unalterable;" from whence he makes many inferences to countenance him in his charge of schism. But why should we contend fruitlessly about these things? Had he been pleased to read a little farther on the same page, he would have seen that I affirm the institution itself to be a plain command, which, considering the nature of the duties required of men in church-relation, is sufficient to oblige them thereunto, without any new revelation unto that purpose which renders all his queries, exceptions, and inferences of no use. For I do not speak in that place of the *original institution of churches*, whose laws and rules are universal and unalterable, but our *actual gathering* into particular churches; for which I say the necessity of duty is our warrant, and the institution itself a command. No great advantage will be made any way of such attempts.

The like I must say of his following discourse, p. 241, concerning churches in private families, wherewith I am dismissed. I do grant that a church may be *in a family*; there was so in the family of Abraham before the law. And if a family do consist of such numbers as may constitute a church meet for the duties required of it, and the privileges intrusted with it, — if it hath persons in it furnished with gifts and graces fit for the ministerial office, and they be lawfully called and set apart thereunto, — I see no reason why they should not be a church although they should be all in the same family. But what is this to the imprisoning of all religious worship in private families, that never were churches, nor can so be, with the admission of some others which our author would justify from this concession, I know not. But it is easy to see what our condition should always be if some men's power did answer their desires.

But the will of God be done!

I shall not farther concern myself to consider things charged but not proved, repeated but not confirmed, depending on a misunderstanding or misapprehension of words wherein the merit of the cause is not concerned.

That which I first undertook, was a vindication of the nonconformists from the charge of the guilt of schism. And this I engaged in for no other reason but to remove, as far as in me lay, the obstruction that seemed to be cast by the Doctor's sermon unto the uniting of all Protestants in the same common interest against Popery; for although the design might be good, as I hope it was, and he might judge well of the seasonableness of what he proposed unto its end, yet we found it (it may be from the circumstances of it, as unto time and place) to be of a contrary tendency, to the raising of new disputes, creating of new jealousies, and weakening the hands of multitudes who were ready and willing to join entirely in opposition unto Popery, and [in] the defence of the protestant religion. For if a party of soldiers (as the Doctor more than once alludes unto that sort of men) should be drawing up in a field with others, to oppose a common enemy, [and if] some persons of great authority and command in the army should go unto them, and declare that they were not to be trusted, that they themselves were traitors and enemies, fit to be destroyed when the common enemy was despatched or reconciled; it would certainly abate of their courage and resolution, in what they were undertaking with no less hazard, than any others in the army.

I have here again unto the same end vindicated the principles of the former vindication, with what brevity I could; for the truth is, I meet with nothing material in the Doctor's large discourse, as unto what he chargeth on those of the congregational persuasion, but what is obviated in the foregoing treatise. And if any thing of the same nature be farther offered in opposition unto the same principles, it shall (if God give life and strength) be considered in and with the second part of it, concerning the matter, form, rule, polity, offices, officers, and order of evangelical churches, which is designed; and it is designed not for strife and contention with any, — which, if it be possible, and as far as in me lieth, I shall always avoid, — but for the edification of them by whom it is desired.

www.ingramcontent.com/pod-product-compliance
Lightning Source LLC
Chambersburg PA
CBHW031057080526
44587CB00011B/717